ORGANIZING UNIONS

ORGANIZING UNIONS

MARY CORNISH AND LYNN SPINK

WITH THE ASSISTANCE OF
SUSAN URSEL, HARRIET SIMAND &
LAURELL RITCHIE

SECOND
STORY
Press

CANADIAN CATALOGUING IN PUBLICATION DATA

Cornish, Mary F.
Organizing unions

Includes bibliographical references.
ISBN 0-929005-55-4

1. Trade unions - Ontario - Organizing. I. Spink, Lynn. II. Title.

HD6490.072C35 1994   331.87'09713   C94-930078-0

Edited by Beth McAuley
Cover photograph and photographs on pages 12, 40, 72, 88, 150,
180, 192, 244, 268, and 280 by Vincenzo Pietropaolo
Photograph on page 132 by Lisa Sakulensky

Printed and bound in Canada

Second Story Press gratefully acknowledges the assistance of the
Ontario Arts Council and the Canada Council

Published by

SECOND STORY PRESS
760 Bathurst Street
Toronto, Ontario
M5S 2R6

Quick Reference Guide

> **As a worker in Canada you have a legal right to join a union. It is against the law for an employer to discipline or dismiss someone for joining a union.**

Are you beginning a campaign for a union?

Chapter Five — The Campaign for a Union

Do you have a problem at work and are you wondering how a union could help you?

Chapter One — Unions Make Good Sense

Do you want to know more about unions?

Chapter Two — Unions: Fact and Fiction

Do you want guidance in choosing the best union for your workplace?

Chapter Four — Choosing a Union

Are you worried about what your employer might do if you unionize?

Chapter Six — The Campaign: Management Reactions

Are you a union representative preparing for a hearing at the Labour Board?

Chapter Twelve — The Hearing Process

Is your group ready to negotiate your first contract?

Chapter Sixteen — Negotiating Your First Contract

CONTENTS

♦

INTRODUCTION AND
ACKNOWLEDGEMENTS

ORGANIZING UNIONS is designed to be a resource book, a primer, for employees who are thinking about organizing a union, and a practical handbook, a tool, for those who have decided they want to organize.

The genuine fear of very real penalties prevents many workers from taking the steps towards organizing. If they can be guaranteed that management won't know and can't get even if they join a union, then thousands more say they'd join.[1] We hope our book will help these workers to organize with more safety, supported by a good strategy and with an understanding of the law and what lies ahead.

Organizing Unions shows how to strengthen organizing drives by responding to the concerns of women, immigrant workers, people of colour, workers with disabilities, lesbians and gay men, and part-time and casual workers. Its inspiration comes from experiences and stories of people who've been a part of recent organizing campaigns, the people who know best what's what, what works, and what doesn't.

This book is based on the law in Ontario as of September 1993. Organizers from other jurisdictions in Canada will also find this book useful as much of the law is similar. To assist readers from other provinces with the similarities and differences, we have included a chart that compares key areas of Ontario's *Labour Relations Act* with other Canadian jurisdictions. (See Appendix H.)

This book does not deal with the construction industry which has a separate set of rules.[2]

Ontario's *Labour Relations Act* changed substantially as of January 1, 1993. We have used "*[New]*" or "1993 amendments" to note new rules or procedures. Unions, lawyers, and the Labour

Board use many words in a very specialized way. We have included a Glossary where words common to the world of labour relations are defined.

Whenever you see a small number in the text, it is an endnote. These endnotes are in a section at the back of the book that provides information about what is in the text, for example, the name of the case which deals with a point, and how it can be located. If the endnote just refers to "section 1," then it is a reference to section 1 of the *Labour Relations Act.*

Thank you to the many people who helped us with this book. They made a big difference and we're indebted to each of them. They include: Jane Adams, Pramila Aggarwal, Joe Aggimenti, Bonnie Alter, Jane Armstrong, Pat Armstrong, Rosemarie Barr, Andre Bekerman, Akua Benjamin, Penny Bertram, George Biggar, Pat Bird, Catherine Bowman, Mila Capati, Meerai Cho, Muriel Collins, Mary Cook, Jim Counahan, Rachel Cox, Sarah Cox, Stephanie Crawford, Jill Cunningham, Alex Dagg, Steven David, Karen Davies, Julie Davis, Ron Davis, Holly Du, Lynn Fairweather-Leinster, Gary Fane, Judy Fudge, Grace-Edward Galabuzzi, Linda Gallant, Shelly Gordon, Daina Green, Donna Gray, Helen Hang, Irene Harris, Guy Havell, Jim Hayes, Mary Hodder, Bill Howse, Daria Ivanochko, Brad James, Donna Johansen, Jamie Kass, John Lang, Christine Leonard, Barbara Linds, Carole MacDonald, Catherine Macleod, Georges Marceau, Graziano Marchese, D'Arcy Martin, Gina Martins, Hemi Mitic, Pat McDermott, Mike McHenry, Liz McIntyre, Maureen McPhee, Najja Modibo, Brendan Morgan, Monica Mulvihill, Winnie Ng, Denise Norman, Mary Ann O'Connor, Maureen O'Halloran, Helen O'Regan, Jim Pare, Brando Paris, Marion Perrin, Pat Phillips, Fernando Reis, Bill Reno, Wayne Roberts, Janis Sarra, Carrol Ann Sceviour, Chris Schenk, Ruth Scher, Brian Shell, Laura Sky, Danny Sun, The Three Guineas Foundation, Cisleta Thompson, Linda Torney, Sheila Trainor, Doreen Tripp, Bill Troupe, Josie Umengan, June Veecock, Fely Villasin, Julie White, and Marc Zwelling.

Beth McAuley was a superb and patient editor. Special thanks also go to the lawyers and staff at Cornish Advocates who devoted their time and expertise for over a year to the completing of this book, particularly Sue Guerriero, who was primarily responsible for typing the many drafts of the manuscripts and also Lucy Liegghio, Jayne Ivall, Boris Ulehla, Suzanne Lopez, Karen Sandercock, Sophia Ruddock, Karen Andrews, Sean Fitzpatrick, Margaret Keyes, and Roxann Kennedy, Danette Lelli, Heather Liddell, and Margo McLeod.

Mary Cornish and Lynn Spink
with the assistance of Susan Ursel,
Harriet Simand, and Laurell Ritchie
November 1993

♦

CHAPTER ONE

Unions Make
Good Sense

WITH A UNION, employees have basic protections, help in solving problems, and fair ways of dealing with change. A union contract gives you and your co-workers a clear set of rights that your employer must honour.

If you're just starting to think about organizing a union in your workplace, this chapter and the next may help answer some of your questions. If you've already made the choice and are eager to get started, you can turn directly to Chapter 4, "Choosing a Union."

This chapter is a quick introduction to the changing world of work and unions. Unions make sense for employees in a changing, shifting economy. Just as a union is good for workers when the economy is buoyant, so a union can make a difference during recessions and depressions.

Sections of this chapter cover:

- recent changes in jobs and work

- what a union can do if your employer's "restructuring"

- how a union can help employees who work part-time

- why clerical workers need unions and unions need them

- what unions can do about harassment

- how unions can improve quality of service and care

- unions and small workplaces

- the situation of homeworkers, domestic workers, and tele-workers
- enforcing employment laws
- organizing in the 1990s: making the connections
- whether it's hard to organize a union

RECENT CHANGES IN JOBS AND WORK

The first book on organizing in Ontario — *Getting Organized* — was written in the 1970s. Since then jobs have changed, and so has the law, the economy, and the workforce. Now unions are changing too.

In 1993, the unemployment rate was over 11 percent, 1.66 million were officially out of work, and a top official of the Bank of Canada defended high unemployment as natural and necessary.[1] Today multinational corporations can shift billions in investment across borders in an instant, and they control more wealth and jobs than governments do. They know that unemployment makes it harder to organize unions because without the prospect of alternatives people fear losing their jobs.

Technology has become part of our daily lives. It's one reason so many changes are taking place so quickly. In the 1970s we marvelled at the ease and speed of working on electric typewriters, the new office technology of the day. Part-time jobs were uncommon, except for students. The number of women working outside the home was accelerating. Employment equity was a phrase not yet invented.

Nearly half of the workers in Canada today are women. Overall, 38 percent of the men and women who work are covered by a union contract, but less than one out of every three women who work have the benefit of a union contract. More people with disabilities are working, though fewer than one in five has a job. By the year 2001, 62 percent of the workforce will be women, aboriginals, racial minorities, or workers with disabilities.[2]

The work people do is changing. Employers in industries such as fast food outlets demand versatility, they want interchangeable employees, programmed and ready to do every job in the organization. This approach keeps wages low.[3] Office employees are being assigned a greater variety of tasks ("multi-skilling"), without an increase in pay.

Employers are pushing workers for 60 seconds of work in every minute, an impossible demand to make of human beings.[4] Enthusiasts predict and plan for more "high value-added," "high-tech," and "knowledge-based" jobs, while others record the rapid increase in poorly-paid "bad" jobs. Men are taking low-paying jobs that once were filled by women.[5]

Employees face new problems, and for unions that want to organize the unorganized, there are new problems to solve.

> WE'VE GOT EVERYTHING. TQM. KAIZEN. JOB ROTATION. QUICK DIE CHANGE. JUST-IN-TIME. IT'S THE FLAVOUR OF THE MONTH.
>
> SURE PROFESSIONALS NEED A UNION. EMPLOYERS ARE INTERPRETING 'TOTAL QUALITY MANAGEMENT' AND 'CONTINUOUS QUALITY IMPROVEMENT' AS DOING MORE FOR LESS, WITH LITTLE OR NO CONCERN ABOUT THE IMPACT ON QUALITY OF SERVICE PROVIDED.
>
> JOB-SHARING? WE HAVE A WRITTEN AGREEMENT ABOUT HOW THE COLLECTIVE AGREEMENT IS GOING TO BE APPLIED. WE PROTECT THE FULL-TIME JOB. HAVE A POLICY ABOUT WHETHER THE OTHER PERSON HAS TO COVER IF THE JOB-SHARER IS SICK. FOR VACATIONS PEOPLE ARE TREATED LIKE PART-TIMERS, THINGS PEOPLE HAVEN'T REALLY THOUGHT ABOUT.

WHAT CAN A UNION DO IF YOUR EMPLOYER'S RESTRUCTURING?

Why do unions make sense when governments and business are shedding people and jobs? How can a union help employees in organizations that are cutting down and cutting back?

Having a union can bring some dignity, fairness, and even hope to a brutal management process that puts people out of work. Without a union to answer to, an employer can cut and slash without having to explain a thing. With a union, you know that the employer has to give an account of his plans, that he has to follow procedures and rules, and that he must justify what he's doing.

Often workers know the organizations they work for best, even better than employers do. Unions help make it possible to put forward proposals that can save both money and jobs. In corporations and work situations where this isn't possible, unions are moving beyond the bargaining table to work in coalitions, taking on a broader approach to defending workers' rights and community interests.

In Ontario, the law now requires regular meetings between management and union representatives in workplaces that are unionized. With a union, employees have an opportunity to get advance warning and information about the employers' plans for the future. It also means a chance to talk with others in similar circumstances, to get their advice, and to call on the experience and resources of larger organizations that can help prepare a creative response to an employer.

Unions can help employees look for and propose alternatives to a company's cutbacks and lay-offs. They might suggest different solutions — early retirements, transfers, job-sharing, a reduced workweek — depending on the circumstance and what the members decide they want. A union can identify potential job vacancies elsewhere in the organization for employees whose jobs are being eliminated. They can negotiate any necessary retraining, upgrading and adjustment programs so that their members can increase their skills for a tight job market.

Where lay-offs can't be stopped, having a union means employees have a structured process to handle these job losses and employees with the longest service have some protection. Having a union also means employees have a process for bringing people back to work if an organization later decides to increase jobs.

In workplaces where employers are eliminating jobs, employees who are left have heavier workloads. They have to do their usual work and also complete the tasks of jobs that have been cut. If you find you've got new duties and the same old pay, a union can help you get a review of those duties and the proper pay.

In organizations, such as large hospitals, that are restructuring through mergers, unions have ideas about how to protect services to the public as well as workers in those organizations. One idea is to protect hospital workers who lose their jobs by giving them first choice for new jobs in community agencies. Not only do workers benefit, but so does the public that receives experienced care from workers with decent pay and working conditions.[6] Union contracts could specify that employers have to hire from central registries of laid-off workers in the industry before hiring off the street.

Rather than announce job-cuts, some employers take steps to reduce jobs under the guise of employee participation programs such as total quality management, continuous quality improvement, quality circles, team management, and so on.[7] Unions differ about how to respond to these management techniques. Having a union means a chance to learn from workers who have dealt with similar situations. A union can negotiate with the employer so that workers who participate are guaranteed basic protections.

HOW A UNION CAN HELP EMPLOYEES WHO WORK PART-TIME

Unions make sense if you're a part-time worker. The 1993 law in Ontario makes it easier for part-time workers to organize.

Thirty-five and forty hour a week jobs are disappearing, and part-time jobs are at an all-time high. In Ontario, the number of part-time employees doubled between 1975 and 1993, from 430,000 to 861,000.[8] For employers, replacing full-time employees with part-time jobs is "a key cost-cutting strategy."[9] Almost one in three workers is employed part-time or part-year, and seven out of ten of those workers are women.

Of the women who were working in 1991, only 39 percent were in full-time full-year jobs. Almost 40 percent of the employed men did *not* have full-time year-round jobs.[10]

For some employers, converting full-time jobs to part-time work is the "just-in-time" people-version of the auto industry's "just-in-time" approach to low inventories and bringing in supplies only at the moment they're needed. The ads from one temporary employment agency neatly sum up how employers look at part-time and temporary workers. The ads feature silly green "Gumby" figures, tall ones, short ones, fat ones, and thin ones, smiling and stretching up and down a graph line. One ad asks, "Is your workforce as flexible as the economy?"[11] Employers may want a workforce of cheap, flexible Gumbys, but no worker aspires to fill that image. Unions can help humanize the working life of those who work in part-time jobs.

Only a few years ago many unions were reluctant to organize part-time employees. They opposed part-time work, believing that it would reduce the number of full-time jobs.[12] Unions were right about how part-time work would erode the number of full-time jobs.

Even today some full-time employees resent part-timers and don't want them to form unions. This is a narrow view. It isn't part-time workers who erode jobs. Part-time work is a money-saving strategy for employers. As long as part-time jobs mean cheap labour and a free hand for employers, employers will use part-time work to undercut the gains unions have made for full-time workers.

Part-time workers are vulnerable because most have little control over how many hours they work. Having a union can mean a guaranteed minimum number of hours of work, and the right to refuse to work inconvenient shifts without penalty.

Having a union means higher wages, better working conditions and benefits, and more predictable hours of work, whether you're working part-time by choice or because full-time work isn't available. Unions can push for reliable and dependable shifts and days of work so that part-timers can predict and plan their lives.

For those who want full-time work, having a union means fairer access to full-time jobs.

Having a union means being protected if you complain about unfair scheduling or work assignments. Unions bargain protections for part-timers so that employers can't overlook long-time employees and arbitrarily give the most hours and the best shifts to the most recently hired part-time employees.

Some unionized part-timers have drug and dental plans, paid sick days off, and shift bonuses and holiday pay.

In her book *Sisters and Solidarity*, Julie White reports that the sectors with the largest numbers of unorganized women workers — personnel and business services, trade, and education and health — are the ones with the highest proportion of jobs that aren't full-time jobs.[13] Women and men in those jobs need unions, and unions need the vitality new members from these industries can add to the labour movement.

> FOR THE OFFICE STAFF IT WASN'T ANTI-UNION FEELINGS. IT WAS THE CULTURE SHOCK, THE SEA CHANGE, OF THEM THINKING ABOUT A UNION FOR THEMSELVES. WE OVERCAME SOME OF THE FEAR BY GOING PUBLIC, GAVE THEM THEIR OWN LOGO, A SEPARATE IDENTITY.

CLERICAL WORKERS NEED UNIONS AND UNIONS NEED CLERICAL WORKERS

There are more secretaries in Canada than there are truck drivers or autoworkers.[14]

Fifty years ago clerical work was the leading occupation for women, and it still is. Ninety-eight percent of secretarial and clerk-typist jobs are held by women, and more women work in these jobs than in any other occupation.[15]

In 1993, in businesses such as insurance and banking the

majority of jobs were clerical jobs. You'll find clerical jobs everywhere — in the offices of manufacturing plants, hospitals, schools and universities, computer companies, law firms, department stores, and so on.

The mechanical side of clerical work has changed dramatically in just a few years. In 1972, an activist could write with assurance that office work was the work least likely to be affected by automation and technology.[16] By the late 1980s, copiers had already replaced carbon paper and erasers, and being monitored electronically was a fact of life for many clerical workers.[17] By 1990, the number of clerical workers was declining for the first time ever.

WHAT DIFFERENCE CAN A UNION MAKE TO A CLERICAL WORKER?

Clerical workers who belong to unions enjoy much better working conditions than their non-union counterparts, as well as higher wages and a fair measure of recognition for the value of the work they do.[18]

As well as better wages and the rights and benefits that other unionized workers have, a clerical worker with a union is more likely to have a job description, controls on any electronic monitoring of her work, fair access to promotions and transfers, a health and safety committee, regularly scheduled breaks from working at her computer screen, and the right to transfer to another work area without loss of pay when she's pregnant.

In spite of the advantages that having a union bring, the percentage of clerical workers who belong to unions is lower than the average.[19]

WHY HAVEN'T MORE CLERICAL WORKERS JOINED UNIONS?

Another way of looking at the problem is to ask, Why haven't unions organized more clerical workers?

In the early 1940s, industrial unions organized both office and factory workers in the same union, though plant workers dominated because of their greater numbers.[20] Over the years, labour boards have interpreted the difference in office and factory environments as fundamental, and have commonly insisted that people who work in the offices of factories be in a separate unit from the people who work on the shop floor. Unions focused on organizing factory workers, most of whom were men. These are the reasons why relatively few clerical workers in manufacturing firms have a union to represent them.

The 1993 law in Ontario says that, if they wish, an organized group of office employees can apply to be in the same union as plant workers and benefit from the advantages that working together bring. (See Chapter 8.) But still, clerical workers don't easily join unions. Why? Many clerical workers don't identify with the negative, adversarial image of unions that they see in the media. They're not comfortable with the language of battle and confrontation. There's a good reason for that discomfort. Most clerical employees get along just fine with their boss. They have to. Often they work right under his eye. It's part of many clerical jobs to be friendly, co-operative and understanding. In a non-union workplace, a secretary's or clerk's fate is often dependent on the fate or disposition of the person she works for.

Some clerical workers who deal with the public are in the front lines every day. They aren't there to fight battles, but rather to use their skills to defuse and mediate conflicts. In their pressure-cooker jobs they have to be tactful, helpful, and patient with any visitors or callers. Their responsibility is to avoid trouble, to smooth things over, to be a shield, a screen, a shock absorber. They're uncomfortable talking union if all that "union" means to them is conflict, trouble, an angry boss, and picket lines.

Being skeptical is part of the job for many clerical workers. Many have to screen callers, present a pleasant face to the rest of the organization and to the outside world, while at the same time watching for trouble. They see their supervisors at their worst, and know their weaknesses as well as their strengths. They know from experience that appearance and reality are often very different. Their role gives them a perspective, they know rhetoric for what it is, and they know that simple easy answers aren't sufficient ones.

If you're a clerical worker who is thinking about joining a union, you'll probably make the decision based on reason, not instinct. You'll need to know what a union can offer. You'll want facts and figures and proof that you and your co-workers will control the way the union relates to your employer.

WHAT CAN A UNION DO ABOUT SEXUAL AND RACIAL HARASSMENT?

Racism and sexism keep workers separate and unequal — only the employer benefits from these divisions. The work unions are doing to eliminate racism and sexism is an example of the co-operative, positive, productive side of the labour movement that builds unity in our communities.

SEXUAL HARASSMENT

Women who help organize unions say that sexual harassment is almost always an issue in workplaces where women want a union, but it's rarely mentioned until the women are confident they can trust the organizer to take the problem seriously.

"Sexual harassment in the Workplace: It has to STOP" is the theme of a 1993 union education project.[21] That project wouldn't have been possible in the 1970s when few union contracts outlined a method for union members to deal with sexual harassment. Then, as one union woman put it, if you'd gone to the microphone to speak about harassment at a union conference you would have been shouted down by the guys. Today, there are more women in unions, and more women in leadership positions in unions, and 43 percent of workers in unions in Canada have a contract that covers harassment.[22]

Unions that recognize that sexual harassment is a serious problem are fighting it in different ways: with workshops, education programs, policy statements, anti-harassment posters, videos and leaflets advising women of their rights. Some union leaders read their unions' anti-harassment and anti-discrimination statements aloud at the beginning of every meeting, as a reminder and a warning.

In cases where the harasser is also a union member, some

unions file a complaint against management, reflecting a Supreme Court decision that says it's up to the employer to keep a working environment that's free from harassment.[23] Other unions don't involve management in problems between workers, and have their own systems for handling complaints. The resolution of an harassment case can mean that the harasser must apologize, take special training, or it can suspend, transfer, or demote him.

If there's a sexual harassment problem where you work, then a union can help. A union representative can advise you on how to handle the problem before your union is in place, and once your union is in place you can negotiate a collective agreement that includes a process to deal with all harassment problems.

Sexual harassment is any unwanted attention of a sexual nature. It can be remarks about your appearance or your personal life, offensive written material, degrading pictures or graffiti, physical contact of any kind, or sexual demands. It can be any treatment that demeans you because you are a woman. Women in the workplace face sexual harassment most often from supervisors, but also from co-workers and from people they serve — customers, patients, clients.[24]

SEXUAL HARASSMENT IN THE WORKPLACE: It has to STOP.

RACIAL HARASSMENT

Many unions are now dealing with racial harassment problems in ways that parallel their response to sexual harassment problems.

They have taken the lead from their racial minority members, who have helped their unions identify how they are targeted for demeaning treatment in their workplaces, and how to fight that racism. Racial harassment can take many forms, for example, racist slurs or name-calling, extra supervision, harsh discipline, or failure to respect and accommodate cultural differences.

Unions have conducted poster campaigns to alert their members and employers that unions will not tolerate racism. Some unions have negotiated the right for union members to walk off the job if management and the union cannot resolve a harassment problem. Employees stay off work, with pay, until the case is resolved.

Sexism and racism still exist in union workplaces and within some unions, but union members are making progress on dealing with these behaviours. Many unions have tailored solutions to their particular circumstances, have taken the responsibility for educating members, and have extended their workplace campaigns against racial and sexual harassment into their communities by placing ads on buses and subways and in magazines. You may have seen union ads condemning domestic violence, or ads asserting zero tolerance for racism.

I'M TEACHING ANTI-RACISM WORKSHOPS. THE FIRST STEP IS EDUCATION. THE SECOND STEP IS EDUCATION TOO.

I REMEMBER TALKING TO MY MOTHER ABOUT RACISM IN OUR UNION. SHE SAID, DO YOU THINK TRADE UNIONS ARE CUT FROM A DIFFERENT CLOTH, WELL WE'RE NOT. WE'RE HUMAN, AND WHAT GOES ON INSIDE IS JUST A REFLECTION OF THE BIGGER PICTURE OUTSIDE. I WILL NOT LET WHAT I SEE AS A PROBLEM IN OUR MOVEMENT BEAT ME DOWN TO THE POINT WHERE I JUST GIVE UP.

OTHER KINDS OF DISCRIMINATION

Workers also may be singled out as being "different" by name calling and unfair treatment because of a difference such as ability, sexual orientation, religion, or homeland. This kind of harassment violates human rights' laws.

Unions deal with these kinds of discrimination by building on what they have learned about fighting racial and sexual harassment. Examples are union contracts that guarantee accessible workplaces and jobs for workers with disabilities, contracts that provide health benefits to employees' families, regardless of sexual orientation, and unions that act as advocates for members who cannot work on religious holidays.

HOW UNIONS CAN IMPROVE QUALITY OF SERVICE AND CARE

If you want to improve the quality of care and services you and your co-workers are able to give, then a union can help.

People who work directly with clients or with students, residents, patients, or children often worry that having a union will mean a deterioration in the quality of service they provide. The opposite is true. Unionized nursing homes, day-care centres, agencies, schools, and hospitals can provide better care, better service than their non-unionized counterparts.

Unionized workers are less likely to change jobs than workers without a union; they stay with the same employer for a longer period of time. This is important for human services where consistency of care is needed. Unionized workers are more likely to receive paid time-off if they're ill. Without that benefit, employees are more likely to go to work when they're sick because they can't afford not to, and therefore risk exposing co-workers, clients, kids, residents, and patients to contagious diseases.

Often unions act as advocates for the people they serve. Unionized day-care workers fight side by side with parents for better funding. Union members in nursing homes and homes for the aged don't fear losing their jobs if they document problems created by inadequate supplies, understaffing, or questionable work procedures, so that they can make the case for improvements.

Because people commonly associate unions with combatative and adversarial relations, it's understandable that workers whose job it is to serve and care for other human beings might assume that unions aren't relevant. After all, co-operation and harmonious social relationships are fundamental to their work. But nurses — 80 percent of whom are covered by a union contract — prove that unions, professional standards, and a focus on quality of service are not only compatible, but complementary.

UNIONS AND SMALL WORKPLACES

If you're working with fewer than 20 people, then your workplace is part of a major trend towards smaller companies. Although the giant firms (multinationals and transnationals) dictate the ebb and flow of the world's economy, they aren't the companies creating most of the new jobs. The majority of new jobs in Canada are in places with fewer than 20 employees, representing a major shift.[25] Small workplaces include retail shops, fast food outlets, attendant-care agencies, parts-assembly operations, cleaning companies, business service companies, and computer software firms.

Employees in small workplaces benefit from a union even when they don't have the kind of bargaining power large unions do. Forming a union becomes the basis for a relationship of respect on both sides. Forming a union is the easiest way to ensure that employers pay overtime, make unemployment insurance contributions, and follow the law on vacation and holiday pay. In a unionized workplace employees aren't on their own if the employer violates employment standards legislation.

Although it makes sense for employees in small workplaces to form unions, organizing small workplaces hasn't been a priority for many unions. There are many reasons for this.[26]

A small workplace doesn't necessarily mean that the employer is small. Take the banks for example, a branch may be small, but the corporation is very large and powerful. Even when employees in a few bank branches were successful in gaining union certification in the 1970s, the parent banks undermined the unions. Twenty years later there were only a handful of unionized bank employees left.[27]

Some unions will organize workplaces with less than 50 or even 25 employees only if the union already has local unions in that line of work. Most unions don't have enough staff to provide full services to a large number of small locals, and it can take as long to negotiate a collective agreement for 10 employees as it does for 100 or 500. Also, in most cases a bargaining unit representing only a few employees has less bargaining power than one with hundreds of members.

Another consideration is the fact that an employer or supervisor can easily discourage or intimidate employees when they're working at close quarters. But now in Ontario there's a speedy process to stop employers who interfere with workers who are organizing. The easiest way to organize, however, is to keep the campaign short and keep it secret. Chapter 5, "The Campaign for a Union," includes suggestions about doing this.

In spite of the difficulties, many employees in small workplaces are organizing. In Ontario in 1991-1992, the average size of bargaining units in the 660 applications that the Labour Board certified was 32 employees. Forty percent of the certificates the Board issued were to units of fewer than 10 employees![28]

Still, if your workplace has fewer than 20 employees, you may have to call several unions to find one that can help. If you can't find a union with the resources to help you organize, then you can form your own single union. We've outlined the steps to do this in Chapter 4, "Choosing a Union."

DOMESTIC WORKERS, HOMEWORKERS, AND TELEWORKERS

Domestic workers are covered by the labour relations law, but because the law also says there must be more than one employee to form a union, it's impossible for these employees when they work alone to form a union.[29]

WORKING IN THE SILENT WORLD

Homeworkers in the fashion industry are mainly immigrant women who sew at home for contractors. They work in isolation, and many care for their children at the same time. Often the contractor pays them less than the legal minimum wage. They don't get vacation pay, benefits, or overtime pay. They work when the contractor brings work, and must finish it to his deadline.

One union sponsored a survey of homeworkers in Toronto, and then helped form a Homeworkers' Association in 1992. The union assigned Holly, whose first language is Chinese, to help. The Association's members are all Chinese-speaking.

The law makes it difficult for homeworkers to organize. The labour movement wants the government to change the law. Until that happens, the Association is one way to bring people together. Holly helps the women plan social activities, such as family picnics, and educational programs on topics like training, health and safety, and the family. They spread the word by advertising in local Chinese newspapers.

Holly also helps women file complaints. When a contractor closed down and didn't pay three of the women for work they did, Holly helped the them apply to the Ontario government's Wage Protection Fund to get the back pay they're owed.

Lin is on the Board of the Association. Her contractor pays her a dollar a piece for blouses that she sees selling for $40 in stores in the mall. She is glad that the women are coming together. "If you work alone at home you don't know anything at all about the outside world, not even how to fill out forms. It's good to help people who work in the silent world, we who face the wall."

Employers in the garment industry and other light manufacturing businesses cut costs by replacing production in the factory
with contracts with homeworkers — women who work alone in
their own homes. This is not a new problem. One hundred years
ago Eaton's cut costs by contracting out sewing to homeworkers.[30]
Although homeworkers depend upon these employers for work,
employers insist that the women are not employees but are running
their own businesses.

The minimum standards legislation which covers homeworkers and domestic workers, almost all of whom are women, is
weak and very difficult for an individual to enforce. The Toronto-
based organization for domestic workers, INTERCEDE (International
Coalition to End Domestics' Exploitation), is lobbying for
improvements in the labour law and the employment standards
law. Advocates for homeworkers are doing the same. Community
organizations, unions, and activists have sponsored conferences and
prepared reports, recommending that the government make significant improvements in the law.

Homework is not limited to the garment industry. New technology is bringing deep, far-reaching changes to every workplace.[31]
Telework is the name given to office work done at home, or in
transit, using modems, computers, and fax machines. Contracting
out work to individuals in their homes is a cheap answer for
employers, who try to avoid paying overtime, workers' compensation, benefits, and holiday pay. For employees it can mean low
wages, having to pay for computer equipment, taking care of children at the same time, overwork, frustration, and isolation.

Two examples of homeworkers who *are* covered by a union
contract prove that unionizing has a lot to offer them. In both
cases the workers were unionized and working on the employer's
territory before they took on assignments to work at home. Unions
are responding to their employers' moves to sidestep existing union
contracts.

In one case, a unionized pizza company converted to a system
of having employees take telephone orders from their homes. The
workers voted to strike and eventually got a settlement where the
company must provide the workers with computer equipment, and

the union can use the computer system to communicate with its members.[32] The union members also have a grievance procedure, vacations, and medical and dental plans.

The second example is one union's response to the federal government's treasury board experiments with telework. The federal employees have a union that was in place before the treasury board began transferring work from government offices to employees working at computers at home. The union is closely monitoring the situation, and wants the rights of these union members clearly stated in the collective agreement. The union has developed a program to teach their members and other unionists about telework and how to deal with it.

The expansion of homeworkers, telework, and use of immigrant domestic workers shows it is important that unions organize in new ways. At the same time the labour movement is working with community organizations to see that the law is enforced and improved.

> WE NEED HELP FROM PEOPLE WHO ARE MORE INFORMED. WE WOULD LIKE TO BE INCLUDED IN THE LABOUR MOVEMENT. WE'D LIKE THEM TO SAY 'WHAT DO YOU NEED FROM US?' AND WE'D SAY 'WORKSHOPS,' 'THINK TANKS.' WE NEED A REAL EXCHANGE.

ENFORCING EMPLOYMENT LAWS

One of the biggest problems for employees who aren't unionized is employers who break the employment standards law and won't pay overtime, or holiday and vacation pay. Often workers are afraid to complain to anyone, for fear that their employer will penalize or even fire them.[33] Some unions are working to help non-unionized workers file complaints, and to protect them from reprisals.

For example, the council of unions in Victoria, British Columbia, sponsors a workers' advocacy program, where non-unionized workers can talk with an officer of the labour council who will file complaints on their behalf. The program is confidential, and neither the employer nor the employment standards branch of the government knows the name of the worker with the problem. When the employment standards branch gets the complaint, it investigates and audits the payroll records for all employees in the organization. If there's a problem, it's resolved for every employee, not just the one who complained.

A group of labour and community activists successfully lobbied the Ontario government to test a similar program in Toronto in 1993. Under the terms of the program, an employee from the Ministry of Labour works from the office of Toronto's Workers' Information and Action Centre, co-ordinating complaints and arranging for company audits.

"An injury to one is an injury to all" is a well-known union saying. These kinds of programs, where unions help unorganized workers get what's fairly and legally theirs, are another example of how unions look beyond the interests of their members to help others.

ORGANIZING IN THE 90s: MAKING THE CONNECTIONS

Not long ago unions used to give out leaflets at factory gates and then wait to hear from a "Norma Rae" (after the heroine of a movie about union organizing) from the plant who would call to find out about organizing a union. Today unions are reviving old ways and discussing new ways of connecting with unorganized workers.

WHERE ARE THE UNORGANIZED? WHO ARE THEY?

Just as jobs and work are changing, so is the composition of the labour movement. In 1975, about one in every four of the employees in the private sector belonged to unions.[34] The labour movement was dominated by men who worked in manufacturing and resource industries.

By 1992, the proportion of unionized private sector workers

was down to less than one in five, mainly because of the devastating loss of manufacturing jobs. Thirty years ago close to 80 percent of workers in the garment industry belonged to unions. Today only 20 percent do.[35] On the other hand, by 1992, 70 percent of the workers in the public sector — municipalities, hospitals, schools — were union members.[36] That's where the major growth in union members in Canada has been.

Julie White has done extensive research into the world of unions and women. She asks the question, "Where are the unorganized?" and analyzes the data to draw this conclusion: "If unions cannot organize in the private service sector, in small workplaces and among part-time workers, women and different ethnic groups, the decline in union membership will continue....There needs to be what has been called 'a fourth wave' of unionization, equivalent to the industrial organization of the 1930s, or the public sector unionization of the 1960s, but this time in the private service sector."[37]

BARGAINING STRUCTURES

Today there are lively discussions in the labour movement and among academics about systems that would extend the benefits of union wages and union membership to more workers.[38]

These approaches involve changing the law, and changing the structure of bargaining — top-down solutions for expanding the benefits of unionizing to more workers. "Broader-based bargaining," "sectoral bargaining," and "the decree system" are basically variations on a theme of unions bargaining with many employers in one industry or in one region at one time. Some labour analysts argue that legislating new systems of bargaining is a necessary response and a way to correct the rapid decline in unionized jobs and the overall decline in real wages.[39] Others in the labour movement oppose this approach, remembering that governments imposed broader bargaining in the construction industry as a tool to limit the power of construction unions.

Many think that unions must themselves re-organize in order to serve a broader group of members. Armine Yalnizyan draws lessons for food processing, auto parts, and data entry sectors in her study of the garment industry.[40] She argues that to survive, unions must consolidate in sectoral clusters within one national union. By pooling resources unions would be better equipped to serve their members; by working in sectoral groups unions would be better placed to make connections with unions in other countries. Others make a similar case for organizing white collar workers, proposing that unions must overcome their internal rivalries and perhaps create a single, co-ordinated campaign.[41]

Unions once represented employees in single industries and organized in limited areas. Now many are diversifying — organizing in an ever-wider range of sectors and industries. Some are merging together, or consolidating into larger organizations. Both approaches create tensions in the labour movement. Sometimes these frictions are creative, but often they may drain energy and resources. Both mirror what's going on in the corporate world, labour's own kind of "structural adjustment."

Judy Fudge documents ways in which employment law and labour relations are biased against women. She argues for more inclusive, broader bargaining structures. But first, she says, we need a broader kind of unionism as a force to prompt these changes in the law: "Union mergers, consolidated bargaining initiated by councils of unions which organize workers in specific sectors, associate-membership status for the households of trade union members, representation of unemployed workers, and community-based unions are possible avenues for addressing union fragmentation and rivalry."[42]

COMMUNITY-BASED ORGANIZING

"Community-based" organizing is a new phrase for ways of organizing that many used in the early days of the labour movement in Canada.

Rather than rely on legislation to extend the benefits of unionizing to new groups, this approach serves potential new union members in their own communities. Some unions have established centres or offices in neighbourhoods to provide services to individuals and community organizations, as well as services to union members. These unions provide meeting space for local groups and give advice on health and safety issues and other employees' rights under the law. Some help non-union workers with unemployment insurance and workers' compensation claims. They invite people from the local neighbourhood to union-sponsored events, and are working to revive the old community spirit of unions.

Some unions set up booths in shopping malls and at local fairs, taking the opportunity to talk with many people about organizing in an environment where they don't have to worry about being overheard "talking union."

Community-based organizing can also draw people from local unions and from local communities to help with union organizing campaigns. Unions train volunteers in the basics of an organizing campaign, building on the principle that unorganized workers will have more confidence in people who understand their culture and their job.

> THESE WOMEN WANTED A BOYCOTT, THEY'D HEARD
> ABOUT SOUTH AFRICA, THEY WANTED TO DO IT.
> BACK HOME THERE WERE BUNDES — STRIKES — THAT
> WOULD BRING THE WHOLE COUNTRY TO A HALT IN A DAY.
> ORGANIZERS HAVE TO LEARN ABOUT THE HISTORY OF THE
> PEOPLE THEY'RE ORGANIZING, SO THAT THEY CAN BRING
> IT BACK TO THEM, SO THAT THEY DON'T TAKE
> PEOPLE'S HISTORY AWAY FROM THEM.

SEPARATE ORGANIZING

Separate organizing describes an approach that women, workers of colour, workers with disabilities, and gay and lesbian union members have used within the labour movement. It's a method some want to adapt and use to make organizing more relevant for workers who feel left on the sidelines by unions as well as at work.

Linda Briskin describes "women's organizing" within unions,

and Ronnie Leah extends the discussion to record the experiences of black women union activists.[43] Briskin makes a distinction between women organizing separately as a goal (separatism) and union women organizing separately as a strategy towards strengthening the labour movement as a whole. She makes the case for separate organizing as part of an overall strategy where, within unions, women and workers of colour must balance the need for independence and recognition with the need for resources and relevance.

Briskin argues that organizing separately as a strategy will make unions more attractive to women, immigrants and people of colour, whose participation in turn will strengthen unions. The black women who Ronnie Leah interviewed agree that the strategy is essential if unions are to represent and to serve workers of colour.

ORGANIZING WOMEN

Unions need more women members, and women need unions. The section above on clerical workers examined some of the myths about clerical workers' reluctance to join unions. There are similar misunderstandings about retail employees. Patricia McDermott interviewed 50 Eaton's employees (44 were women) who joined a union in 1984, and then endured a long strike for a first contract.[44]

These workers' comments are instructive. When they first heard about the union, half were sure they wouldn't join. The women feared for their jobs and they assumed that unions were for male factory workers. McDermott's study proves that these obstacles, generally assumed to be insurmountable barriers, were in fact only temporary obstacles to organizing.[45] The women needed time to make up their minds, but once their decision was made, they didn't turn back.

Why did people join the union? The Eaton's employees' decision to join was influenced by friends and family members, especially family members who were union members. The women were impressed when a well-respected co-worker joined, and her support for the union made them more comfortable about joining. A large majority joined, not for better wages, but because of management's insensitive or arbitrary treatment of them or of a co-worker.

But first and foremost, the women joined because they were impressed with the female union organizers, who themselves had done retail work and who understood their problems.

McDermott concludes: "...(F)or women, possibly more than for men, joining a union is a social process in which the support of friends and family can be decisive.... The gender of the organizers and their familiarity with the employees' own work experience can also be critical."[46]

Pat Armstrong argues that while nurses have successfully adapted male models of professionalism and industrial unionism, these models aren't adequate today: "The different relations, the sense of vocation, and the questions of skill, discipline, evaluation, and decision-making that are increasing factors in women's service work cry out for new ways to represent and shape women's concerns."[47] She points towards new directions in how work is organized and in how workers organize in unions.

New Content and the Spirit of Unionism

For many the best part of the working day is the time spent with co-workers, especially during breaks.[48] The best of unionism builds on the social side of work, the spirit of community and common interest, people "in it together." In this approach, unions have a role beyond simply representing their members on wage issues. They offer a way of participating in everyday worklife and in the community beyond the workplace.

Some unions are bringing people together in ways that people had to use back in the days when unions were illegal, such as forming benefit societies. The Homeworkers' Association described on page 28 is one example of extending the heart of unionism to those who can't organize. Another example is where unions provide associate memberships that give workers access to insurance, help with workers' compensation, or give advice on health and safety matters, and so on.

In the early days of the labour movement, craft unions certified their members' competence in the field, such as bricklaying or carpentry. The union card became a "passport" to a job anywhere.

Education may again become the heart of unionism, and a way to reach unorganized workers. One idea is for union members to "sponsor" their non-unionized friends and neighbours as participants in workshops offered by their union. Unions also act as advocates for members who want to improve their professional qualifications. Some work with employers to arrange to hold community college courses at the workplace and help their members with the cost of books.[49]

Another way to bring benefits to more workers would be for several unions to co-ordinate a drive to organize all the retail outlets at one shopping mall at once.[50] Sales clerks would welcome the kind of security and benefits a union could bring. A good site for this is where the real estate investment is backed up by union pension funds. Union negotiators could work together to bring in a single benefit package for all union members in the mall and could bring in better scheduling of work hours. Union members could suggest ways to improve service to the public ("We're *organized* to serve you better"), and encourage family, friends, and neighbours to support the mall.

Unions could expand and extend the benefits of unionization to new groups by trying new ways of reaching part-time workers. Many part-time workers juggle two and three jobs and go without benefit plans or basic protections. Unions could feature "portable" union cards, and set up a system of co-ordinated benefits covering workers in several workplaces. This approach might be modelled after the Canada-Wide Industrial Pension Plan, where several employers and several unions benefit from centralizing the administration of the pension program.

COMMON VALUES

A union can be a guide in these difficult economic times. In the global marketplace, Shell Canada, already a profitable company, can announce that it's laying off employees and see its shares immediately increase in value on the stock market.[51] There, the market value overrides the human value that employees have.

Working together in a union, workers have strength in numbers that can't be measured in dollars. Belonging to a union can affirm our connections with one another as workers and as members of communities where co-operation, mutual respect, and fairness are principles worth practising, a counterweight to the power that employers hold over our lives.

Is It Hard to Organize a Union?

The basic steps in organizing a union aren't difficult. Four out of five groups that decide they want to organize a union get a union without difficulty. There are complications only when there's opposition to the idea.

There are detailed and formal steps to follow, but once the majority of people in a workplace decide they want a union, then getting a union certificate is a straightforward matter. The process involves hard work but usually it's not complex. Employees sign membership cards and make an application at the Labour Board. Most often the rest is done by telephone, by mail, and by fax.

How long does it take to decide to unionize? Sometimes a manager does something outrageously unfair and the majority of employees immediately decide to organize because it's the last straw.

More commonly, the process of arriving at a majority decision takes employees weeks or even months, especially in large workplaces. Workers need the opportunity to discuss the myths they've heard about unions, and they need clear information about what unions do. It's harder to find everyone in big organizations, and harder to communicate with each eligible employee. But it needn't take a long time. The information in the rest of this book will help speed up that process.

Chapter 6, "Management Reactions," explains how anti-union employers try to manipulate their employees away from thoughts of forming unions. Knowing your employer's strategies will help you make an informed decision. Chapter 4, "Choosing a Union," outlines questions you can ask union representatives to help you choose the right union, or, if you prefer, suggests ways to form your own union. ·

WE ONLY SPEND 20 PER CENT OF OUR TIME BARGAINING.
EIGHTY PER CENT OF THE WORK WE DO IS POLITICAL,
TRYING TO GET FUNDING, OPERATING GRANTS, GRANTS
FOR WAGE INCREASES, PAY EQUITY, SUBSIDIES.
IF WE DON'T GET THE FUNDING WE DON'T GET THE WAGES.

PEOPLE ARE FACING TAKEAWAYS. A NEW BOARD COMES
IN AND SAYS, WORKERS DON'T NEED THAT MUCH SICK
LEAVE, AND THEY TRY TO TAKE THOSE SICK DAYS AWAY.
WE TELL PEOPLE THERE'S A FUNDING CRISIS AND WE
CAN'T PROMISE YOU MORE WAGES RIGHT AWAY,
BUT WE CAN HELP YOU SECURE WHAT YOU HAVE.

I WORKED AS A CASUAL RN FOR YEARS, CAME IN
NIGHT AND DAY, NEVER SAID NO BECAUSE I WANTED
A FULL-TIME JOB. I ALWAYS GOT PASSED OVER.
WHEN I FINALLY GOT MAD ENOUGH TO COMPLAIN THE
DIRECTOR OF NURSING SAID SHE WANTED TO
KEEP RELIABLE PEOPLE LIKE ME ON-CALL.

♦

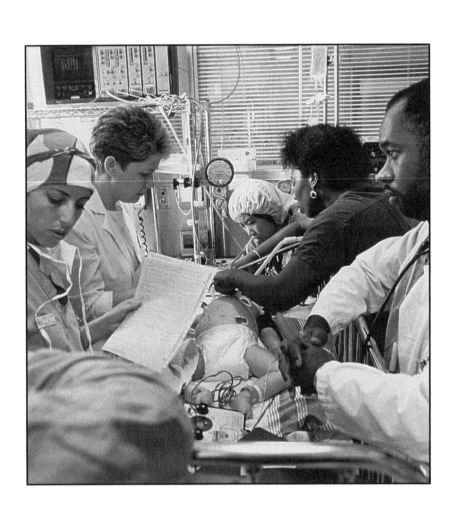

CHAPTER TWO

UNIONS:
FACT AND FICTION

THIS CHAPTER sorts out some of the facts from some of the common myths about unions. It covers:

- unions, business, and the media
- do unions make a difference?
- how unions work and what they do
- what people who are against unions say

UNIONS, BUSINESS, AND THE MEDIA

It's no wonder that for many people the word "union" brings to mind trouble and strife, strikes and picket lines. Newspapers, radio, and television report on labour conflicts, confrontations, demonstrations, and strikes as if being caught up in that turmoil is the essence of belonging to a union.[1] When union members watch the news about labour, they're more likely to feel a shock of disbelief than one of recognition.

Is it really true that we can't afford unions because they stifle productivity? Is it a fact that unions are out of touch, thrive only on conflict, and don't know what co-operation means?

These are myths. Anti-union messages are so much a part of our daily life that it's easy to assume that they're true. Corporations use myths like these to work against unions and to discourage employees from thinking about unionizing.

A union brings some balance into the relationship between employer and employees. Employees working together in a union are a challenge to employers' absolute authority and tight control.

Newspaper publishers, like many other large employers, don't like unions.[2] Editorial cartoonists depict "unions" by drawing an overfed, overlarge, white middle-aged man in overalls, with muscular hairy arms folded in defiance.[3] It's no wonder that faced with that picture many people can say without missing a beat, "Unions? Not for me."

We know that if employees have the facts, and answers to those tricky statements that critics of unions put forward, then organizing a union becomes a common sense, straightforward thing to do. This chapter looks at how unions can make a difference, at what they do and how they do it. It puts to rest five big myths that say unions are wrong for the times.

> WHY DO I WANT A UNION? I WANT THE BOSS TO
> FOLLOW THE EMPLOYMENT STANDARDS ACT.
> I WANT TO BE PAID WHEN I WORK OVERTIME.
>
> THERE'S NO REAL PROCESS WHEN THEY DISCIPLINE PEOPLE.
> THEY HAND OUT WARNINGS FOR DUMB LITTLE THINGS.
> MANAGEMENT'S THE LAWYER, THE JUDGE, THE ENQUIRY
> AND THE EXECUTION AT THE SAME TIME. THERE'S NOBODY
> ON THE OTHER SIDE TO SAY WAIT A MINUTE I DIDN'T DO
> THIS. NEXT THING YOU KNOW, BINGO! YOU'RE FIRED.
>
> THEY HAVE 'YOU ARE A PROFESSIONAL' DRUMMED INTO
> THEM IN THEIR EDUCATION AND TRAINING. 'YOU ARE
> INDEPENDENT, YOU CAN SPEAK ON YOUR OWN BEHALF.'
> THE REALITY IS THAT EVEN WHEN YOU'RE A SALARIED
> PROFESSIONAL, THERE IS NO AUTONOMY THERE,
> IN ANY SHAPE OR FORM.

WHY ORGANIZE?
DO UNIONS MAKE A DIFFERENCE?

The rights of an individual employee are limited. Without a union, your fate usually depends on such things as how well you're getting along with your boss. You're on your own if there's a problem. If your employer's breaking the employment standards law, such as not paying you for overtime, it's up to you alone to file a complaint. Without a union to back you up, the employer's word is often the last word.

In a union, employees' rights are written into a contract, called a collective agreement, which backs them up every day on the job. Belonging to a union gives employees the security of a legal contract, and as well can provide improvements in wages and benefits, offer new opportunities for training and education, and bring the excitement of being a part of a movement for change.

Most employees, except those in management, have the right to form unions. See page 66 for a summary of the jobs in which people aren't allowed to organize, or where the law imposes restrictions on organizing.

1. UNION MEMBERS HAVE MORE JOB PROTECTION
THAN NON-UNION EMPLOYEES.

Having a union means that fairness, not favouritism, rules the day. A union means management can't make up the rules as it goes along. Collective agreements set out rules for scheduling work, assigning overtime, and for transferring and promoting people. Many contracts outline the duties of each job, so that employees (and their supervisors) can be clear about what's expected from them.

A union also protects employees from harsh and hasty discipline or dismissal. They're not dependent on the goodwill of management nor are they left out in the cold if a friendly supervisor leaves.

If a unionized employee is fired or disciplined, she or he can file a formal complaint. This complaint is called a grievance. Every year hundreds of union workers who are unjustly fired get their jobs back because their unions defend them in grievance meetings and win. If the problem isn't solved at the grievance meetings, then a union can take it to arbitration, where an outside individual or board makes the final decision.

Unions are successful in getting jobs back, with full back pay, for almost one in five cases that go to arbitration. Another one in three workers get their jobs back, with a less harsh discipline. The arbitrator decides that the employer was right in less than half of the discharge cases.[4]

Unions also work to protect jobs in the event of lay-offs. In workplaces without a union the employer can pick and choose which employees to lay off. Unions can't guarantee every job if an employer is cutting back on jobs, but they can provide representation and a fair process. In some cases where an employer has announced lay-offs, unions have been able to prevent the lay-offs by bargaining leaves of absence and early retirement. In cases where lay-offs can't be prevented, the process in the collective agreement must be applied fairly.

Retraining and preventing job loss to new technologies are important union projects. Computers, robots, and other forms of technology often mean job losses and changes in job duties. Many union contracts state that the employer has to notify the union before they bring in new technology. Some outline rules for relocating or retraining workers whose jobs are lost or changed. Some unions belong to joint employer-union training boards. Securing retraining programs for their members is a priority for many unions.

> THERE'S A COMMON MISCONCEPTION ABOUT UNIONS —
> THAT THEY PROTECT INCOMPETENT PEOPLE. WE HAVE TO
> EXPLAIN, THESE PEOPLE HAVE A RIGHT TO REPRESENTA-
> TION. THERE ARE STANDARDS THEY HAVE TO MEET AND
> THERE ARE STANDARDS THAT MANAGEMENT HAS TO MEET.

2. UNION MEMBERS EARN MORE THAN NON-UNION EMPLOYEES IN THE SAME OCCUPATIONS.

Statistics Canada, an agency of the Canadian government and located in Ottawa, collects information to compare the wages of employees who have a union with the wages of employees in similar jobs in workplaces without a union.

Statistics Canada's surveys prove that people in union jobs earn more than people in non-union jobs.

In Canada, 29 percent of employed women work in data entry, bookkeeping, secretarial, and other clerical jobs.[5] The average weekly pay for a female clerical worker without a union in 1990 was $308. In contrast, a clerical worker with a union to represent her interests earned on average $418 a week.[6]

Women working in restaurants, hospitals, insurance, and other service organizations earned on average $207 weekly without a union and $332 with a union. Women in sales jobs earned $259 a week if they didn't belong to a union and $341 weekly if they had a union to represent them.

Men in service jobs averaged $247 weekly without a union and $564 with a union. In the transportation field, unionized men averaged $680 a week. The weekly wage for non-union jobs in transportation averaged $457.

Looking at the hourly wage in 1989, Statistics Canada found that a woman working full-time averaged $10.89 an hour if she didn't belong to a union and $13.98 if she did belong to a union. Being unionized means more pay for women, less difference in pay between men and women, and less difference in pay between the workers paid the most and those who are at the bottom of the wage scale.[7]

The biggest difference between union wages and non-union wages is for part-time workers. In 1990, the average hourly wage for those without a union was $8.87, compared with $14.47 an hour for part-timers with a union.[8]

Not getting paid for overtime is one of the most common complaints of non-union workers.[9] Union contracts mean that employees who work overtime get more pay, or they get time-off with pay for the extra work they do. Many union contracts outline a system for assigning overtime work so that it's done fairly.

While women in Canada still earn a lot less than men doing work of similar value, there's less difference between men's and women's wages in unionized workplaces.[10] Even in provinces and workplaces where pay equity is the law, women without unions to negotiate on their behalf do not appear to fare as well as unionized employees in similar jobs. Unions report that many unorganized nurses, office workers, library workers, and nursing assistants have decided to organize after hearing about pay equity settlements negotiated by unions.[11]

3. UNION MEMBERS HAVE GAINED MORE AND BETTER BENEFITS THAN NON-UNION EMPLOYEES.

Unions in Canada have negotiated a wide variety of benefits for their members. What is negotiated depends on the different priorities of their members and their negotiating power. Statistics show that a significant number of employees who are union members have benefits that non-union members do without.[12]

In addition to better maternity leave and shift bonuses, unions work on behalf of their members to negotiate paid sick leave, sick leave to care for family members who are ill, drug benefit plans, education leave, bereavement leave, job sharing, flexible work hours, dental plans, workplace child care, and vacation and holiday pay.

Severance pay is money over and above the notice pay employers must give when they let someone go. The law in some provinces provides severance pay as well as notice pay. However, when the workplace is unionized, employees are much more likely to be entitled to severance pay above minimum standards. Of the collective agreements that cover over 500 members, 45 percent have severance pay provisions that provide more than the law requires.[13]

Employees in Canada belong either to the Canada or to the Quebec Pension Plan and receive benefits when they retire. A union ensures that the employer makes the required deductions and contributions so that employees will have a pension when they retire. Most unions have negotiated additional retirement income for their members. In 1987, the average additional yearly pension was $9,110 for a man represented by a union and $5,372 for a woman with a union.[14]

4. UNION MEMBERS HAVE REPRESENTATIVES TO HELP THEM ENFORCE THEIR RIGHTS TO A HEALTHY AND SAFE WORKPLACE AND TO A WORKPLACE FREE OF DISCRIMINATION OR HARASSMENT.

Employees are covered by general legislation that deals with health and safety and some kinds of discrimination. If an employer is breaking or skirting the law, employees without a union are on their own. They can complain to a human rights commission or labour ministry, but many workers stay silent about problems because they have learned to expect their employers to get even if they complain.

In situations where people have filed complaints, the record of enforcement is poor.

Just because a government health and safety inspector doesn't find a problem, it doesn't mean that a workplace is safe. Every year hundreds of workers are killed, and more than half a million are injured on the job.[15] Employees without a union may be uneasy about speaking up in front of the supervisor when the inspector pays a visit. A worker who belongs to a union can point to dangerous chemicals or unsafe practices and know that the union will back them up if they're disciplined unfairly for speaking out.

Workplaces where there are unions are safer than non-union places. Under Ontario's health and safety laws employees have representatives on a committee with the employer, and employee representatives are trained to detect hazards. But without the backing a union gives, employee representatives have little real power. Health and safety representatives have the right to stop an unsafe production process. The law protects them. Employees can follow a process set out in the law, and refuse to do work they believe is

47

unsafe, without penalty.

Unions negotiate with employers to modify jobs and work-places to accommodate injured workers who need to return to work gradually. They act as advocates for permanently disabled workers, arranging for job transfers, retraining, and job modification.

Many people who don't belong to a union silently bear offen-sive remarks from supervisors for fear they'll lose their jobs. Strong racial and sexual harassment clauses in union contracts mean that unionized workers are more likely to be protected if they complain. They have a better chance of stopping harassers.

The anti-discrimination clauses in contracts go beyond govern-ment human rights laws. These clauses protect workers against discrimination on the ground of race, gender, disability, religion, party affiliation, sexual orientation, union activity, and family and marital relationship.

The leaders in the labour movement fight racism and discrimi-nation not only in the workplace but also within the union and in the broader community. A "zero tolerance for racism" campaign is a union benefit that can't be measured in dollars. The same is true for union public education programs to stop sexual harassment, harassment against lesbians and gay men, and violence against women.

> THE GREAT THING ABOUT WORKING IN THE UNION
> IS THAT NOBODY SAYS YOU CAN'T DO SOMETHING JUST
> BECAUSE YOU'RE DISABLED. NOBODY SAYS YOU CAN'T
> LEARN THAT. I NEVER BEFORE HAD A CHANCE
> TO FIND OUT WHAT I CAN DO!
>
> I THINK OF A UNION AS A FAMILY OF PEOPLE WHO
> LOOK OUT FOR EACH OTHER. THE MEMBERS MUST FEEL
> SUPPORTED. SO THAT A PERSON WHO'S JUST ARRIVED
> FROM SRI LANKA CAN GO TO THE FAMILY AND KNOW
> SHE OR HE'LL BE HEARD, UNDERSTOOD.
> THAT'S THE WAY IT SHOULD BE.

5. UNION MEMBERS HAVE AN OPPORTUNITY
TO LEARN MORE.

Some unions promote not only workplace training and development but also offer union education programs for their members. These programs are all voluntary, and some unions provide money for child care or on-site child care, to make it easier for parents to participate.

Adult basic education is a special service for members whose first language is English and who want to improve their literacy skills in English. There are also free courses in mathematics and computers. Unions also negotiate free English as a second language (ESL) classes held in garment factories, hospitals, homes for the aged, libraries, autoparts plants, and hotels. There are similar programs in French in French-speaking communities.

Local unions often hold evening and weekend workshops on the issues of health and safety, stopping sexual harassment, fighting racism, and women in non-traditional jobs. They also provide training for stewards and training in human rights leadership.

Unions also work with local community colleges to design and provide upgrading programs for union members who want certificates in specialized fields, such as nursing.

Some labour organizations offer union counsellor programs that train workers how to counsel co-workers about where to get help with problems such as housing, substance abuse, AIDS, stress, family violence, and financial difficulties.

The opportunity to do volunteer work on projects in the union can be an education in itself. Members can learn skills that will help them advance on the job. They can work and plan with the union finance committee, help organize a conference, or train to lead a workshop.

Many unions hold social activities that include the whole family. Some include family members in educational programs. Some unions hold week-long schools on special issues and train members to go back to their workplaces to lead workshops.

6. UNIONS WORK FOR CHANGE. IN UNIONS, WORKERS FIND STRENGTH IN NUMBERS.

Unions in Canada have worked for change for over 100 years. They've pressured governments for laws that benefit everyone, not just union members. Advances that we take for granted now, the minimum wage, the 40 hour work week, the Canada Pension Plan, and laws against child labour, were won by unions.

Unions believe in "solidarity," common causes, and working together so that each person in our society gets her or his fair share.

Unions raise millions of dollars every year for research into cancer and other diseases. They donate to arts foundations, women's shelters, unemployment help centres, labour education centres, food banks and charitable organizations .

And unions themselves are changing because there's been a big change in union membership. There are more women in unions now than ever before, and the number of union members who are workers of colour is rapidly increasing. They have lobbied and educated their fellow union members so that today strong anti-discrimination and sexual harassment clauses are becoming the rule rather than the exception in collective agreements. Unions have gone to court to establish the basic right to equal benefits for gay and lesbian union members. Affirmative action programs within the labour movement show progress too, and though progress is slow, it has been steady.[16] Many unions are taking the steps to bargain workplace employment equity programs, as well as to lobby governments for employment equity legislation.

The union demonstrations you see reported on television — those rallies against free trade, for employment equity, against cut backs in unemployment insurance, for better child care, against cuts in hospital services — those public demonstrations are only part of the picture. What you don't see is what happens behind the scenes: members doing solid research and drawing together the facts, educating themselves after work and in weekend workshops, voting on policies in general membership meetings, making links with other progressive groups, and preparing briefs to make the case to the politicians.

Unions help to keep our democracy working.

HOW DO UNIONS WORK?
WHAT DO UNIONS DO?

A union's main job is to represent the interests of the union members. This takes the pressure off individuals having to fend for themselves if there's a problem.

When a new group of employees join a union, the union's first task after they get certified is to bargain with the employer about what will be in the union's first collective agreement.

COLLECTIVE AGREEMENTS

A collective agreement is a written legal contract that lists the rules about pay, benefits, overtime, scheduling, promotions, pensions, health and safety, harassment, time-off, vacations, and how to handle complaints. It also states how long the agreement is for.[17]

In Canada employees aren't allowed to strike during the time covered by a collective agreement. Employers can't lock employees out of the workplace during that time either.[18]

By law, collective agreements cannot discriminate against individuals or particular groups of workers.

[New] They must also contain a clause that an employee can't be disciplined or discharged without just cause.[19]

CONSTITUTIONS

Unions are democratic organizations, but some have more respect for the role of their members than others. A union's constitution is a written document that tells you how the union works and can give you an idea of how democratic it is. A union's constitution lists the rules that the organization must follow.

A union's constitution should tell you:

• the rights of union members
• the structure of the union

- how the officers are elected
- the officers' job duties
- rules about negotiations with the employer
- rules about grievances
- rules about membership meetings
- rules about dues

A union constitution cannot discriminate and has to comply with human rights laws. There's a sample of a union constitution in Appendix B.

VOTING

Members of a union usually choose by a vote:

- the officers of their local union
- what they want to negotiate in the collective agreement
- whether to accept the proposed collective agreement
- whether to strike or settle
- delegates to regional or central meetings
- union policies

STEWARDS

There is usually one steward for each work area. Union members choose a co-worker to be a steward, who is their representative.

Stewards try to make sure that management follows the rules in the collective agreement. They listen to members' complaints, keep the union leadership informed about problems, distribute notices of meetings and other union activities, and meet together in a council of stewards to discuss problems and solutions. Stewards often handle the first steps of a union member's grievance.

GRIEVANCES

A grievance is how the union makes a complaint on behalf of the worker to the employer. The union uses a special form for grievances. (See boxed information.) The form describes the problem, shows what part of the collective agreement has been violated, and states the solution the member (the grievor) and the union want. Under the law, the union has a responsibility to be fair in representing its members.

GRIEVANCE FORM

UNION _Workers_   EMPLOYER _XYZ Inc._

DEPARTMENT _Machine Shop_

Nature of Grievance and Date of Occurrence .
I was disciplined without just cause, contrary to the collective agreement on May 5, 1993.

Settlement Requested _That I be given full redress._

Grievor's Signature _John Welder_
Union Steward's Signature _Marie Jones_
Date _May 6, 1993_

ARBITRATION

If the union and the employer can't agree on a solution, the union may take the grievance to arbitration.

An arbitration is a process where an arbitrator or arbitrators — either one or three outsiders who know labour relations laws and cases — hears what both sides have to say and then makes a decision. The employer doesn't have the final word. The arbitrator or, on rare occasions, a court does.

UNION DUES

Union members pay dues that come back to them in the form of union services. When the union requests it, the employer must deduct union dues from the regular pay cheque and send the money to the union. Dues pay for legal representation, educational programs, help with workers' compensation problems, strike benefits, the cost of offices and meeting halls, newsletters, and other resources, such as pay equity or health and safety expertise.

How much you pay depends on the union. On average, union dues are about two hours' pay per month for full-time workers. The amount is set by a vote of union members or their delegates and usually can only be changed by having another vote.

Each year when you fill out your income tax return, you deduct the amount you've paid in union dues from your income. That means you pay less income tax.

BEFORE THE UNION, I'D NEVER BEEN INVOLVED IN AN ORGANIZATION AT A LEVEL WHERE I HAD TO KNOW ABOUT RULES OF PROCEDURE, AND BASIC IDEAS OF DEMOCRACY, AND THE WAYS YOU SET UP A MEETING, THE WAYS YOU CAN DO IT AND BE DEMOCRATIC AND WAYS THAT ARE NOT, WAYS YOU CAN BE INCLUSIVE, AND WAYS THAT ARE NOT. THERE'S A PROCESS THERE THAT MOST PEOPLE DON'T HAVE MUCH EXPERIENCE WITH.

I DIDN'T HAVE ENOUGH CONFIDENCE IN MYSELF TO RUN FOR OFFICE, BUT THEN A MEMBER SAID TO ME YOU'VE GOT TO RUN. IT WAS EXCITING, IT WAS SCARY. I RAN ON ACCOUNTABILITY AND RESPONSIBILITY, EVEN THOUGH I WAS A PART OF THE BOARD I FELT WE WEREN'T BEING RESPONSIBLE TO OUR MEMBERS. NOW I'M PRESIDENT. IT'S TOUGH.

WHAT PEOPLE AGAINST UNIONS SAY — FIVE BIG MYTHS

When the government in Ontario wanted to amend the *Labour Relations Act* in 1991 to make unions stronger, employers fought hard to stop the changes.[20] They formed new organizations (All Business Coalition, More Jobs Coalition, Project Economic Growth) and used existing umbrella organizations (Ontario Chamber of Commerce, Canadian Manufacturers' Association, Ontario Business Council, Metro Toronto Board of Trade, Ontario Construction Association) to lobby members of parliament to defeat the new legislation. They raised money for a full-scale anti-union advertising campaign. The Woodstock District Chamber of Commerce ran an ad in the local paper warning, "STOP. Danger Ahead. Ontario NDP's Labour Laws. What's Dead in Moscow Still Lurks in Canada (Ontario)." Other ads threatened job loss, loss of investment, and loss of democratic rights.[21]

Business groups brought their arguments against unions to the government hearings on the changes, where a representative of the construction industry set the tone when he said, "It is battle and could very well escalate into full-scale war."[22] They used the same arguments that employers have used for decades. Here are some of those arguments, with some responses.

MYTH 1: UNIONS MEAN STRIKES.

That's not true. Unions normally negotiate a collective agreement without having to resort to a strike. Also, the law forbids many unions, such as those representing workers in nursing homes, from striking. When there's a dispute in these workplaces the employer and union must use an arbitration process to settle their differences.

The law is very restrictive about when a union can strike, and how that strike can legally occur. Unions are not allowed to strike (nor is the employer permitted to refuse to let union members work) during the time covered by the union contract. When the contract expires, usually after a one or two year term, the union must follow legal steps, with set time periods and consultation with government officials, before it can strike. The right to strike is essential to a strong labour movement, but it is defined very narrowly in Canada.[23]

It's the right to strike that gives many unions their bargaining power. In Canada, well over 90 percent of negotiations between employers and unions are settled without a strike. For example, in Ontario in 1992, 97 percent of negotiations were settled without a strike or a lockout.[24] You don't often read about these agreements, or see the settlement announced on the news.[25]

Not every strike is about pay. Sometimes workers strike about other important things like health and safety, or issues like the size of classrooms or unfair treatment.

Unions don't strike in a vacuum. There are at least two sides to every strike, one of which can be an aggressive or unyielding employer. When the crunch comes, it is the union members themselves who decide, usually by a secret ballot vote, on whether or not they're willing to strike. Going on strike is a last resort.

In Ontario, the law guarantees that a newly formed union won't have to strike to get its first collective agreement. If the union and your employer can't agree, the union can apply to have the Labour Board or an arbitrator set the terms in the agreement.[26] (On the other hand, if the new union members follow a set process and vote to go on strike, they can take that route too. It's up to the members and no one else.)

MYTH 2: UNIONS HURT PRODUCTIVITY.

That's not true. Recent academic studies show that unionized companies have higher rates of productivity than non-union firms.[27] One recent study concludes that the way a company handles conflict affects productivity, not whether or not its workers are represented by a union.[28] An agreement that a union negotiates with a company about work rules can mean a more stable production process because conflicts are worked through during the bargaining process.

Economists have argued with one another about the relation

between unions and productivity for decades. A lot depends on how you choose to measure productivity per worker, but on the whole a unionized workplace is a more productive and efficient workplace.[29] Even company executives say that the single most important reason for poor productivity is management not doing its job.[30] The presence of a union forces inefficient organizations to become more productive.

If management and the union have a good working relationship, then productivity is higher than in most non-union environments. If the relations are hostile, then productivity is lower than in the average non-union place.[31]

Unions increase overall efficiency because there's less turnover in unionized workplaces, workers stay longer and employers spend less time hiring and training new employees.[32]

Some employers whose employees are unionized even admit that unions mean better managers too! It's easier to be a bad manager when your employees dare not complain.

MYTH 3: UNIONS ARE RIGID. THEY DON'T LIKE CHANGE.

That's not true. Again, we only hear about problems and inflexibility in the news. The media rarely report on success stories.

Employers talk about "partnerships" in the workplace, but don't want a real partnership, where the relationship is between equals. Having a union gives employees more power to respond creatively to new demands for co-operation and participation. Employers who have brought in new forms of work organization do better when there's a union in place. A study of the U.S. machinery and metalworking industries shows that in non-union companies, employee participation programs don't improve productivity, but programs in unionized workplaces do.[33]

Unions are more likely to get information from management about changes, and have the resources to evaluate proposals. Employees are more likely to co-operate in something new when they know they have the protection of a union. When participation is imposed on employees without a union, the outcome is less likely to be genuine.

It's unionized grocery stores that have led the retail sector in bringing in new technologies.[34] An academic study in the United States concluded that unionization doesn't get in the way of technological change, that unions commonly have accepted change, and encouraged modernization.[35] Where new technology has meant the loss of jobs, unions have fought vigorously to protect their members and for training programs.

Inside unions, thousands of people volunteer their time and work co-operatively to reach decisions. They're used to arguments, and to finding practical solutions. They hold meetings, elect representatives, vote on policies, and work democratically for change. When it comes to bargaining with their employers, unions are experienced in the practical give and take that's required to reach an agreement.

Unions have led the way for change over the years. For example, they helped bring in the introduction of workers' compensation in 1915, the minimum wage (1920), old age pensions (1927), unemployment insurance (1935), medicare (1966), health and safety protections (1972), and laws on human rights (1962).

Unions know about change. They probably have more experience managing change and working for change than any other organization in the country.

MYTH 4: WE CAN'T AFFORD UNIONS IN TOUGH TIMES.

This myth says that unions keep investment away and make it difficult for business to trade and compete. That's not true. Unions are a vital part of an efficient and healthy economy. Businesses everywhere are suffering today, whether they include unions or not. When the economy in Europe was thriving a decade ago, the majority of workers in countries like France, Germany, and Sweden belonged to unions.

It's a mistake to accept competitiveness as the central measure of our society's worth. Think of how unproductive our economy is when unemployment is high and people's skills and energies are wasted.

What really affects companies in Canada that produce for

export is not unions, but rather the Free Trade Agreement, the value of the Canadian dollar, Canadian interest rates compared with those in the United States, and unfair trading practices.

In the months following the hearings on the bill to reform the *Labour Relations Act* in Ontario, 13 companies announced plans to make new investments of more than 1.6 billion dollars there.[36] The prospect of more unions didn't get in their way.

When times are tough employees need the assurance of representation and fair process that unions bring. Corporations use tough times as an excuse to push down wages, weaken unions, and dilute programs such as unemployment insurance, social housing, and medicare.

MYTH 5: BIG UNION BOSSES ONLY WANT YOUR MONEY.

People who talk about unions like this have been watching too many anti-union American movies.[37] The statement's a myth on three counts. Unions aren't that big, unions aren't run by bosses, and unions aren't in it for the money!

Unions in Canada are democratic organizations. They aren't controlled by union bosses but, rather, are led by elected officials who must work with an elected executive board. This board and its officers are responsible to the members of the union. If the members aren't satisfied with their leaders, they choose different ones at election time.

Unions collect dues so that they can pay for services for their members. Any union member may ask for and get an audited financial statement from the union as required by section 87 of the *Labour Relations Act*. By law, union finances are public and their accounts must be audited. Under the *Corporations and Labour Unions Returns Act,* unions in Canada have to file reports of their finances to the government in Ottawa every year. The salaries of union officers are listed in most union constitutions.

Compared with businesses, unions have relatively little wealth. The head offices of all of the 494 unions in Canada put together, including buildings, bank accounts, investments and strike funds, are worth 1.1 billion dollars. A medium-sized company like

Maclean Hunter (which publishes the weekly *Maclean's* magazine) alone controls more wealth than that. If you look at the 1990 list of the top corporations in Canada, every one of the first 147 has more Canadian assets than all of the unions in Canada combined. Bell Canada has 10 times as much wealth as all of the union head offices and all of the local unions in Canada combined.[38] Figures from the Business Council on National Issues, the special interest group of 160 of Canada's largest corporations, show that its members control over one trillion dollars in assets.

The strength of the labour movement is people, not money.

◆

CHAPTER THREE

LAWS AND
LEGAL ADVICE

THERE ARE LABOUR LAWS that provide protection to workers in the workplace and to workers who are organizing a union. There are also laws that provide further protections and rights for workers once they are organized. As a result of their resources and strength, unions are often better able to use these laws for the advantage of workers than individual workers.

This book focuses on Ontario laws. Appendix H very briefly sets out some of the key differences in organizing laws from province to province. While other provincial laws are often similar, you need to check the actual law in your own province if you are not from Ontario.

Having a general knowledge of workplace laws and of the resources available will help you understand the legal aspects of the campaign and will help you evaluate any legal assistance you are given. Employees who are assisted by unions are often best able to use these laws to the best advantage of their members.

Since there are many legal matters to consider in an organizing campaign, it helps to be familiar with the laws and to know how to find them and how to refer to them. Laws are found in Acts (sometimes referred to as "statutes") that are passed by the Legislature, for example, the Ontario *Labour Relations Act*, R.S.O. 1990 c.L.2. R.S.O. means Revised Statutes of Ontario, the published volumes of books which contain all the Acts that have been passed by the

Ontario Legislature. The year 1990 refers to the date the statutes were last compiled into a set of volumes. The abbreviation c. refers to the Chapter number in the Revised Statutes.

> PEOPLE ARE SO SCARED. THEY'RE AFRAID THEY'LL LOSE THEIR JOB AND WON'T BE ABLE TO SUPPORT THEIR FAMILY. THEY KNOW THE BOSS IS REAL SMART, THEY KNOW THE BOSS CAN'T FIRE THEM FOR JOINING A UNION, BUT THEY THINK HE'LL FIND ANOTHER WAY. I'M NOT AFRAID. I KNOW THE LAW. I ARGUE WITH THE BOSS.
>
> A LOT OF PEOPLE WHO ARE HERE ON WORK PERMITS THINK IT'S ILLEGAL FOR THEM TO JOIN A UNION. BE SENSITIVE TO THAT REAL FEAR. ASSURE THEM THEY CAN'T BE DEPORTED FOR JOINING A UNION.

ONTARIO LABOUR LAWS AND WORKPLACE LAWS

There are a number of laws or Acts that give workers minimum protections in certain work areas whether they are unionized or not. Some give even greater protections to unionized workers.

Although workplace laws are supposed to be enforced by agencies such as Ontario's Employment Standards Branch and Pay Equity Commission, often it is not until workers are unionized that employers follow these minimum laws.

Aside from certain minimum government standards such as paying the statutory holidays, maintaining health and safety standards, and observing non-discrimination laws, the employer is free to do much as he likes — the employee, on the other hand, is only free to quit.

If, however, the workers have unionized, they can use the labour law that prohibits the employer from making deals with workers individually.[1] Then the employer must bargain with the union designated to represent all of the employees. This bargaining, which must be done in good faith, usually results in a legally binding collective agreement between the union and employer that sets out the employees' wages and working conditions.[2]

WORKPLACE LAWS AND HOW THEY AFFECT ORGANIZED AND NON-ORGANIZED WORKERS

RIGHT TO MINIMUM EMPLOYMENT STANDARDS

The *Employment Standards Act,* R.S.O. 1990 c.E.14 in sections 23 to 58, says that all workers are entitled to minimum wage, pregnancy and parental leave, equal pay for work of equal or comparable value, notice and severance pay. This law applies to both unionized and non-unionized workers.

RIGHT TO A HEALTHY, SAFE WORKPLACE

The *Occupational Health and Safety Act,* R.S.O. 1990 c.0.1, gives many workers the right to question an employer's workplace practices for health and safety reasons. Although non-unionized workers can apply this law, workers with a union have more rights and can get backup if they refuse to work.

RIGHT TO PAY EQUITY

The *Pay Equity Act,* R.S.O. 1990 c.P.7, as amended, sections 1 to 21, says that women workers should get non-discriminatory compensation, but only unions have the right to negotiate with the employer what the terms of the pay equity plans will be for their women members.

RIGHT TO EQUAL TREATMENT

The *Human Rights Code,* R.S.O. 1990 c.H.19, section 5(1), says that workers should have terms and conditions of employment free of discrimination based on race, ancestry, place of origin, colour, ethnic origin, citizenship, creed, sex, sexual orientation, age, record of offences, marital status, family status, or handicap. With a union, workers who experience discrimination can get help in making a human rights complaint.

RIGHTS TO WORKERS COMPENSATION BENEFITS

The *Workers Compensation Act,* R.S.O. 1990 c.W.11, provides benefits to workers who are injured on the job. Many unions provide their members with representation to make sure they get the benefits they are entitled to.

RIGHT TO EMPLOYMENT EQUITY

The *Employment Equity Act,* or Bill 79, gives women, racial minorities, aboriginal peoples, and persons with disabilities the right to have their workplaces examined for discriminatory barriers to their equal enjoyment of workplace opportunities and the right to have these barriers removed. Like the *Pay Equity Act,* unions are given the joint responsibility with the employer to negotiate employment equity plans.

ONTARIO LABOUR LAWS AND THE RIGHT TO FORM A UNION

In Ontario, the labour law that covers most unionized employees is the *Labour Relations Act.* This legislation also outlines the rules for organizing employees into a union and protects employees who are organizing.

For a wide range of people, special laws provide the right to organize. There are, however, some occupations that are not covered by one specific law and it is not clear what the rights of these employees are. They can still organize, but they have only their collective strength with which to force their employers to bargain with them. The law doesn't require these employers to bargain in good faith, and collective action against the employer may be illegal. If you are not covered by labour relations law, then you should consult a lawyer before taking any action.

LAWS FOR PUBLIC SECTOR WORKERS

Many public sector workers are covered by special legislation and organizing rules. Their rights to belong to a union are covered completely, or partly, by laws specific to their occupations. These laws and the sections of the law that apply are noted below.

- Police officers and civilian police employees — *Police Services Act*, R.S.O 1990 c.P.15

- Firefighters — *Fire Departments Act*, R.S.O. 1990 c.F.15

- Teachers — *School Boards and Teachers Collective Negotiations Act*, R.S.O. 1990 c.S.2

- Provincial government employees — *Crown Employees Collective Bargaining Act*, R.S.0. 1990 c.C.50

- Fee for service physicians or interns and residents — *Ontario Medical Association Dues Act*, S.O. 1991, c.51.

- Employees in industries regulated by the federal government, which include the federal civil service, banking, and transportation systems that do business between the provinces or territories, such as airlines, seaports, trucking firms, and what's left of the railways — *Constitution Act*, 1867.

- Hospital employees have the right to organize under the *Labour Relations Act*, and also come under a law called the *Hospital Labour Disputes Arbitration Act*, R.S.O. 1990 c.H.14. This law prevents hospital employees from striking. If they can't bargain a collective agreement, an arbitrator decides on their contract.

THE *LABOUR RELATIONS ACT* AND OCCUPATIONS THAT CAN ORGANIZE WITH SPECIAL RULES:

[New] Lawyers, architects, dentists, and land surveyors can now organize, and, if they wish, form a bargaining unit separate from other employees in their workplaces.[3]

[New] Security guards can choose any union they want, though the Labour Board will give them a separate bargaining unit if their duties put them in conflict with their co-workers, such as having to search co-workers who are leaving the building.[4]

[New] Domestic workers can organize if they work with another employee in their workplace. This is because the labour law requires that there be at least two employees in a workplace before you can form a union.[5] This means that domestic workers often cannot organize unless they are employed by an agency.

THE *LABOUR RELATIONS ACT* AND OCCUPATIONS THAT CAN'T ORGANIZE

• Trappers and hunters.[6]

• Self-employed people or "independent" contractors. "Dependent" contractors, however, are covered by the *Labour Relations Act*.[7] (See Appendix A for further details on the difference between the two types of contractors.)

• Managers or supervisors and employees with regular access to confidential labour relations information.[8] (See Chapter 8 for a review of whom this includes.)

• Under the old *Labour Relations Act* people who worked on farms or for tree and plant nurseries could not organize but the Ontario government has now introduced special legislation that, if passed, will allow these workers to organize.[9]

• Any employee who works by herself — for example, some domestics, secretaries, dental hygienists. You need two or more employees at a workplace to get a union.[10]

ORGANIZING A UNION AND THE
LABOUR RELATIONS ACT AND ONTARIO
LABOUR RELATIONS BOARD

Ontario's *Labour Relations Act* and the Ontario Labour Relations Board's Rules of Procedure set out the basic steps for establishing a union in your workplace. To ensure workers freedom of choice, the *Labour Relations Act* bans certain conduct during the organizing campaign.[11] It provides remedies for action against unfair labour practices such as rehiring employees fired because of their union activity.[12]

The Ontario Labour Relations Board (Labour Board), a tribunal appointed by the government of Ontario, interprets, administers, and enforces the *Labour Relations Act* and the Rules of Procedure.[13]

Once the organizing campaign is over, the union applies to the Labour Board for certification. According to the *Labour Relations Act,* the union must show the Labour Board that:

- it meets the Labour Board's requirements and constitutes a trade union or has "status."[14] This means showing the Board that your union has been certified before or, if not, that your union can function as an organization with a proper constitution;

- it represents a majority of the employees. To demonstrate this majority support, workers will have signed union membership cards, which are then handed into and counted by the Labour Board, or will have had a vote for the union at the workplace, or sometimes will have done both;

- it has organized a group of employees who can suitably bargain together, that is, it has an "appropriate bargaining unit."[15]

The *Labour Relations Act* prevents the Labour Board from certifying a trade union that discriminates against anyone on the basis of race, national or ethnic origin, colour, religion, sex, sexual orientation, marital or family status, age, or handicap, as specified in the

Human Rights Code or the *Charter of Rights and Freedoms*.[16]

Not all the answers to your questions will be found in the *Labour Relations Act* and the Board's rules. Many other guidelines can be found in the written decisions of the Labour Board or in Practice Notes issued to the public by the Board. The *Labour Relations Act,* for example, simply states that a trade union must be "an organization of employees," but in some of its decisions the Labour Board has interpreted this to mean that a new union is required to select officers and produce a constitution.

1993 AMENDMENTS TO THE *LABOUR RELATIONS ACT*

In November 1992, the Ontario Legislature passed Bill 40, which contains wide-ranging amendments to the *Labour Relations Act.* The new amendments came into effect on January 1, 1993 (referred to as the "1993 amendments").

Organizing laws had been widely criticized by the labour movement as inaccessible to many workers and too weak to promote wide-spread organizing, especially in difficult-to-organize workplaces. The 1993 amendments have made these organizing laws more accessible and give substantially more protections to workers organizing a union.

For example:

- many of the restrictions on the organization of part-time workers have been removed [17]

- anti-union petitions which are often management-inspired have been restricted [18]

- if the employer fires or penalizes an employee during organizing activities, the trade union can get help more quickly for the employee by requesting an immediate or a "fast-track" hearing that is held within 15 days with the Board making its decision within 48 hours after the hearing has ended [19]

- unions can enter private property normally open to the public to persuade employees to join a union. For example, going into malls to reach retail workers [20]

A QUICK NOTE ON PROVINCIAL
AND FEDERAL LABOUR BOARDS

Labour boards regulate and administer labour laws. This book mostly deals with the process of unionizing a workplace that is covered by provincial labour relations laws and labour relations boards. This is because most workers are covered by provincial labour laws.

However, if your workplace is in the federal government, or part of a federal Crown Corporation, then it is governed by the federal labour relations law, the *Canada Labour Code,* and by the federal Canada Labour Relations Board. An example is the Canada Post Corporation.

The federal rather than the provincial government also has the power to control your labour relations if you work directly for a "federal work, undertaking or business." These include activities that are governed by federal laws such as banking, inter-provincial commerce, inter-provincial railways and buses, inter-provincial communications, and inter-provincial trucking, transportation and airlines. A national telecommunications company is an example of a federal business. If you work for a business which supplies work or services for a federal undertaking, you may or may not be covered by federal labour laws.

Usually, it will be fairly clear whether your employer is covered by federal or provincial laws. However, if you work for a business that, let's say, provides services or products to a federal undertaking, then it may be more difficult to know which law governs and which labour board to apply to. Some of these businesses try to argue that they are under federal jurisdiction to avoid more progressive provincial labour laws. To determine where you stand,

• first identify the core federal undertaking (for example, Canada Post Corporation) and the subsidiary operation (for example, a company that provides technical services for postal equipment),

• then ask whether that subsidiary operation is vital, essential, or integral to the core undertaking. Do this by looking at the "normal relationship" of the subsidiary undertaking and the "practical and functional relationship of those activities to the core federal undertaking."[21]

If you are not sure whether your workplace falls under the provincial law or the federal law, you can seek assistance from the Ontario Labour Relations Board or the Canada Labour Relations Board. They are both listed in your telephone book under your provincial government listings, or Government of Canada listings. If you are still not sure after speaking with one or the other, you may want the advice of a lawyer. It is important to know which laws apply before proceeding with your application for certification.

GETTING LEGAL ASSISTANCE

If the union you join is an established one, it will probably have a lawyer or a staff representative who is skilled in labour relations law. But if you're organizing your own union, you will need a lawyer or someone experienced in labour law to help you.

To make sure that you choose a lawyer who acts for unions and not for management, you can ask unionists for recommendations. And keep these three questions in mind when considering a lawyer:

- Does the lawyer have any experience with the types of problems you will encounter in the certification process? Such experience is especially important if you are organizing in the clerical, technical, professional, retail, or social service sectors. These areas of labour law are relatively new and developing rapidly.

- Does the lawyer act for any unions that might oppose your application for certification? If the lawyer does, he or she shouldn't act for both of you.

- What fee does the lawyer charge? Don't be afraid to ask. It is important to get this matter straight at the beginning, even if the lawyer can give only an estimate.

Although you need your lawyer's advice, it is important that one (or more) of your members become familiar with the law. This is a valuable process, but certainly is not a substitute for having an experienced person help you through the certification process.

Legal research in this field can be done if you consult the publications listed under the Selected Bibliography.

◆

CHAPTER FOUR

CHOOSING A UNION

IN THIS CHAPTER you'll find:

- how to look for a union
- questions to ask union representatives
- a warning about unions under management's thumb
- pros and cons of forming your own union
- disadvantages of employee organizations that aren't unions
- how to change an organization into a union
- steps necessary to form your own union
- advice about changing unions

HOW TO LOOK FOR A UNION

If you know the names of the unions you're interested in, you can look them up in the white pages of the telephone directory. If you don't have names to start with, the Yellow Pages of many city telephone directories lists some unions under the heading "Labour Organizations." We've listed a number of the major labour organizations on page 418, but that's only a start. There are hundreds of different unions in Canada.

Central labour organizations, such as the Canadian Labour Congress, the council of labour unions in your region, or provincial labour groups, such as the Ontario Federation of Labour, will be able to give you names of their member unions. Some community information centres and legal aid clinics may also have lists of unions.

Friends and neighbours who belong to unions are another source of information. Ask if you can see a copy of their contract, union newsletters or educational material that they might have. Ask them about union elections, membership meetings, and educational programs.

Invite the unions that interest you to send representatives to meet with your group, and to bring written material about their union. You can ask them to bring along a copy of the union constitution, local by-laws, policy papers, and sample collective agreements they've signed in workplaces like yours.

Most unions say it's better not to question representatives from several unions at the same time. Interviewing them one at a time means you'll probably get clearer answers.

QUESTIONS TO ASK UNION REPRESENTATIVES

Unions have different styles, structures and ways of serving their members. Your group can make a list of questions to ask when you meet with the union representatives.

Choose questions that are important to your particular committee. Don't be afraid to ask *any* question that's on your mind, no matter how small it seems, or how uncomfortable it might make someone. You have a right to know. Here are some suggestions.

WHAT HELP WILL YOU HAVE GETTING STARTED?

Will the union assign a staff organizer to help with the union campaign at your workplace? Will the person be able to take evening and weekend telephone calls when you need urgent advice? Will that person be able to meet regularly with your group?

Where does that person fit in the union's organization? If you need a leaflet, or more time to organize, will the person helping you be able to deliver? Ask for an estimate of how long the campaign is likely to take, and why, so that you can judge whether the answer is realistic, or part of a sales pitch.

Does the union offer workshops or other help for workplace organizing committees? Will the union prepare leaflets? Will the union translate leaflets into other languages? Will the union help mail or distribute leaflets?

What will the union do if the employer disciplines or fires someone while you're trying to organize a union?

Will the union assign a staff person to help with or lead your negotiations for a first collective agreement?

HOW MUCH ARE DUES AND
WHERE DOES THE MONEY GO?

How much dues do union members pay? Is there a formula used to calculate dues? How much would a typical employee at your workplace pay? Do part-time employees pay the same dues as full-time employees? What do call-in casual employees pay? Is there an initiation fee? Do you pay anything before you get a contract?

Ask if the union has information that tells, or a chart that shows, how much of each union dollar is spent where.

How much is the union's strike pay? Is there a strike fund? Who decides whether or not you get strike pay if you go on strike? Once a strike has begun, does anyone have the authority to cut off strike pay?

HOW ARE DECISIONS MADE?

How much say will your local have in making decisions that affect you? How often are membership meetings? How will members of your negotiating committee be chosen? Does the union hold a vote to approve the collective agreement? What process does the union use for a vote on whether or not to strike?

Ask the representative to show you a diagram that explains how your local would relate to other locals, and to any regional, provincial, national, or international levels of the union. Who votes for the officers and/or delegates at each level? How often does the union hold general meetings and conferences?

If the union is an American-based union, which decisions are made by Canadian members and which are made at an international convention or at the head office? Can the Canadian wing of the union take an independent position from the American union on issues like free trade?

Does the union co-ordinate the bargaining process for locals in workplaces like yours? Will your local be bargaining with other locals? Who decides?

Who sits on the union's executive board? Is there diversity? For example, are women, people of colour, and immigrants represented?

WHAT SERVICES DOES THE UNION OFFER?

Does every member get a copy of the collective agreement? Who helps with grievances? Who decides whether to take a grievance to arbitration?

Does the union send regular newsletters to members? Does the union have education programs such as health and safety training, English as a second language and literacy classes, or workshops on issues of the day? Who can attend? Does the union have films and videos that local unions can use for special meetings and workshops? Does the union have staff or members who have special knowledge of fields such as health and safety, job evaluation, pensions, pay equity?

Does the union arrange for interpreters and translate information into the languages people use? What about child care at meetings and conferences? Are there sign language interpreters at meetings so that deaf members can participate? Are meetings accessible to the workers with disabilities?

WHAT'S THE UNION DONE TO STOP DISCRIMINATION?

Has the union taken a public stand on problems such as racism and discrimination against women, aboriginals or persons with disabilities?

Are there women and people of colour in elected positions at every level of the union? What's the proportion, compared with the number of women and people of colour in the union?

Does the union have a system to ensure that women and people of colour sit on union boards and committees?

Are there experienced members or staff to help with issues such as employment equity, anti-racism, sexual harassment, and barrier free workplaces for persons with disabilities? What's the union's record in these areas? Does the union have policy papers or statements on these issues? Ask to see examples of collective agreement wording on the issues that are important to you.

What's the union done to get equal pay for work of equal value (pay equity) for women? Has the union supported gay and lesbian workers in their struggle to end discrimination and obtain spousal benefits?

Does the union have a committee that's working on employment equity? Does the union have any examples of places where it's bargained (or tried to bargain) with the employer to set up a joint committee on employment equity?

IS THE UNION ACTIVE IN THE COMMUNITY?

Most unions do more than bargain collective agreements covering wages and benefits, or "bread and butter" items. These unions are part of a movement for justice and equality for all members of the community, and not just for union members. You'll want to know how broadly or narrowly the union sees its job.

Does the union support activities that affect workers who don't belong to unions as well as helping organized employees?

Has the union lobbied governments on issues such as health and safety, equal pay, employment equity, unemployment insurance, free trade, and child care? Does the union have policy statements or papers on these issues? How is the union's position decided?

Does the union support or give money to a political party? How are decisions about party politics made? Is the union a member of a labour council or federation? What services do these organizations provide?

AFTER THE INTERVIEW

The most important question is the one you ask yourselves after the interview with each union representative: "Do we feel comfortable with the discussion?" Mutual respect is what you're looking for.

Creating a union is about building trust, and your "gut-feeling" is where you begin. One way to check this out is to go around the table after each union representative has left and let each member of your group give a short "yes," "no," or "maybe" with reasons before your discussion begins.

> THE FIRST MEETING WE HAD ABOUT THE UNION, EVERY WORKER HAD A HORROR STORY ON HER MIND ABOUT UNIONS. AN UNCLE WHO GOT SHAFTED, ETC. YOU HAVE TO ADDRESS THOSE STORIES HONESTLY AND DIRECTLY, RIGHT AT THE START. WRITE IT DOWN. TAKE NOTE.
>
> A LOT OF PEOPLE OUTSIDE ARE LOOKING AT US AND SAYING WELL IF YOU WERE TO ORGANIZE ME WOULD YOU REALLY BE REPRESENTATIVE? OR WOULD I JUST BE SWALLOWED UP? UNIONS HAVE TO DO A LOT MORE OUTREACH. WE DON'T SEE OURSELVES REFLECTED IN THOSE ORGANIZATIONS AND QUESTION WHETHER THEY'RE GOING TO REPRESENT US.

UNIONS UNDER MANAGEMENT'S THUMB

If your employer, through supervisors or other management staff, helps in your campaign, the Labour Board won't certify your organization. The law doesn't allow "unions" that management controls.[1] This common-sense rule may sometimes work against you. Be wary of sympathetic supervisors who offer to help.

There are cases where an employer has asked the Labour Board to refuse to certify a union because staff who handled the company's labour relations were involved in organizing.[2]

That's reason enough to keep personnel managers and others in confidential jobs away from your planning meetings. You don't want them collecting cards or participating in any way in your campaign.

You should politely refuse offers to help. Don't even accept something as simple as a supervisor's offering to arrange for a room to meet in. (You shouldn't be meeting on your employer's territory, in any case.)

SHOULD YOU JOIN AN EXISTING UNION OR FORM YOUR OWN?

IF YOU DECIDE TO JOIN AN ESTABLISHED UNION

• You will probably be able to get help from an experienced organizer who can call on the union's lawyers for advice if necessary.

• If the employer interferes illegally while you are organizing, an existing union can provide you with free representation at the Labour Board.

• An existing union will probably assign a staff representative to help you bargain for your first collective agreement. If your employer stalls and you're unable to bargain an agreement, the staff representative can help you apply to the minister of labour to set up a board to decide on your first agreement.

• An existing union will probably have members or staff who can advise your new local on such issues as employment equity, sexual harassment, health and safety, and accessible workplaces.

• The parent union will have put money into a strike fund over the years, so that if your local ever votes to go on strike you'll be able to get strike benefits.

- In an existing union you'll meet other union members from workplaces like yours and also people from very different work environments.

- If you're in an existing union your employer will know that although you're negotiating your first agreement you have the benefit of years of experience to guide you. He also knows you'll be able to call on a network of support if needed. You'll be stronger than you'd be on your own.

- If you choose to join an existing union you may become a part of one of the union's existing local unions, or you may form a new local.

- If you're forming a new local in a union, then your organizer can advise you on what the parent union's constitution says about the steps for forming a new local. This is important information because you have to prove to the Labour Board that you're a trade union.

ON YOUR OWN...

- You may decide to form your own union if you can't find an established union that's willing to help you.

- You may want your own union if the unions you've considered don't meet your needs.

- Forming your own union will give you and your co-workers direct control over how you organize and bargain.

- Many groups who have formed their own union say the biggest obstacle was lack of resources, both money and experienced help.

- If you decide to form your own union you will need to decide how you'll raise money if you need legal advice. You also need to work out a financial plan.

- The old saying "There's strength in numbers" is still true. If you form your own union, you'll be stronger if you can make links with other unions and community organizations.

EMPLOYEE ORGANIZATIONS:
SOME ARE UNIONS, SOME AREN'T

You can't tell whether or not an organization is a union by its name alone. Many employee groups or staff associations do some form of bargaining with their employers. Some are unions and some aren't. The difference is important.

Some of these associations are certified as unions, or have gained voluntary recognition as the bargaining agent under the *Labour Relations Act*.[3] Their members have the same rights and protections that other union members do.

Members of organizations without union status are at a disadvantage. For example, they aren't protected if their employer discriminates against them for union activity. If the employer decides not to bargain one year, the organization can't use the *Labour Relations Act* to force negotiations.[4] Employers know that members of these organizations have little true bargaining power because the *Labour Relations Act* doesn't apply. If they're not covered by the Act, employers don't have to bargain fairly and employees can't strike. And, if an employer chooses to break an agreement with a non-union association, the association can't use the *Labour Relations Act*'s grievance procedure to enforce the agreement.

As well, if a member of a non-union association is fired, he or she can go the expensive court route and possibly receive a cash settlement but the court won't give the member his or her job back. A union member who's wrongfully fired will be represented by the union and can get his or her job back, as well as money for lost pay.

If you belong to an employee organization and are interested in gaining union status, you can contact existing unions for help, or you can take the necessary steps to convert your organization to a union on your own.

Before you begin, it is important that management employees who may be a part of your organization not be involved when you convert an organization into a union.[5] The Labour Board would see that as management interference, even if the employees meant well.

CONVERTING A STAFF OR EMPLOYEE
ASSOCIATION INTO A UNION

If your staff already has a constitution and officers, you don't have to adopt a whole new constitution unless you want to. You just have to ensure that your constitution complies with the Act's requirements. This means, for example, excluding managerial and confidential employees, and defining the purpose of the organization as being the regulation of relations between employers and employees. If your constitution isn't adequate, you should call a meeting of the organization according to the rules in your existing constitution and give any required notice to the members of the constitutional amendments you want to make. At the meeting, follow the rules in your constitution for passing the amendments.

If your organization is an informal one, without a constitution, and if you've chosen not to join an existing union, then follow the steps below for founding a union.

FOUNDING A UNION

Here are the steps to take to set up your own union:

1. Draw up a short but clear constitution. You can use the model constitution found in Appendix B and change it to meet your specific circumstances. Make it as simple or detailed as you need. To be considered valid by the Labour Board your constitution must:

    a. include a clause stating that the union is an organization of employees formed for purposes that include the regulation of relations between employees and employers;[6]

    b. not exclude from membership anyone whom you should represent;

    c. not discriminate against any person as prohibited by the *Human Rights Code* or the *Canadian Charter of Rights and Freedoms*.[7] The Code prohibits discrimination on grounds of race, ancestry, place of origin, colour, ethnic origin, citizenship, creed, sex, sexual orientation, age, marital status, family status, or handicap.[8] The grounds of discrimination prohibited by the *Charter of Rights and Freedoms* are discrimination of race, national or ethnic origin, colour, religion, sex, age, mental or physical disability, or other similar grounds.[9] We suggest you include in your constitution a specific section stating that there will be no discrimination on the above grounds;

d. make provisions for operating the organization on a daily basis, that is, electing officers, calling meetings, and making decisions;[10]

e. exclude "managerial" and "confidential" employees.[11]

2. Prepare membership cards for your new union. (See Chapter 5 for a model membership card.)

3. Hold a meeting of the main union supporters. Have enough copies of the draft constitution and the membership cards available for the meeting. At the meeting appoint one worker to be chairperson and one worker to take complete minutes on all that takes place, including the date, time, place, and the names of those attending. After the meeting is called to order, the following steps must be taken in this sequence:

a. Adopt the constitution. Usually this is done by first having a general discussion of the draft. After all changes have been agreed upon, a vote is taken and the results recorded.

b. Adjourn the meeting after the adoption of the constitution. Delegate one or two supporters to distribute membership cards and collect signatures. Make sure you follow all procedures in your constitution for bringing in new members. If your constitution says workers are not members until they take an oath of allegiance to the union, take the oath at this time.

c. Reconvene the meeting. Now that the persons present are members of the union, you must ratify the constitution, that is, put the adopted constitution to a vote again and record the results.

d. Now the members elect the officers according to the procedure that you established in your now ratified constitution. Usually a member at the meeting nominates another member also present at the meeting to stand for a union position. After all the nominations have been made, the vote is taken and you have duly elected officers who can administer the union.

e. You have now legally founded your union. You may apply for certification if you have signed enough members for your bargaining unit. If not, you can start organizing to sign up the necessary number of members in your workplace.[12]

Keeping Records

The Labour Board will recognize your organization as a trade union without a hearing if your employer agrees, and you submit records which show that you have followed the necessary steps and rules. Your records should include a copy of notices of any meetings, minutes of meetings, the constitution, and so on.

If the employer objects, the Labour Board will schedule a hearing and someone from your group will have to be a witness and give evidence about the steps. It is important to keep a record of each step so that it can be filed with the Labour Board and, if necessary later, help to prepare one of your group to be a witness.

Changing Unions

Sometimes employees who belong to a union talk about switching to another union, forming their own union, or doing away with the union entirely.

Some employees may start an association to try to replace a union that is taking a strong stand about a workplace issue. These groups feed rumours that play on people's fears. Sometimes a new group appears during a strike, undermining people's confidence. They give the impression that they have a painless formula for success in dealing with management. Anti-union employers sometimes encourage these kind of takeovers.

When one union tries to convince people in another union to change unions it's called "raiding." The labour movement has taken a forceful stand against raiding, largely in reaction to takeovers by employer-inspired unions.

The Canadian Labour Congress is an organization made up of more than 90 central unions, called affiliates. Unions that are members of the Congress must follow the Congress policy that says that affiliates can't raid or interfere with each other's local unions.[13] The organization's constitution outlines a process for handling disputes between its member-unions.

Changing unions is a serious decision. Be alert to campaigns that will leave you without any union or without strong representation. Remember that if you vote to give up your union status, that is, if you vote to "decertify," you're on your own if management disciplines, transfers, or fires you.

At the same time, local union members don't have to tolerate poor servicing and indifferent negotiating. If you think you're not getting good service from your union, first try to change the union from within. Attend membership meetings, join a committee, get active, nominate someone who will work for change, or run for office yourself.

Call or write to the provincial or national or international president of your union, setting out the problems you're having. If the problem is that your servicing representative has an impossible workload, then his or her superiors need to look into the union's staffing policies. Or, the problem may be one of personalities. There are bad apples in every field of life, and if that's your situation, then the solution is to deal with the particular person.

If you can't build a more responsive union, and want to change, then you must follow the rules outlined in the *Labour Relations Act*. These rules are summarized in Appendix C.

Generally you can only change unions during an "open

period," which varies from province to province. In Ontario, the open period is usually the last two months before your current collective agreement ends.[14] You must follow a process that's similar to signing up members for the first time.

WE FORMED OUR OWN FEMINIST UNION, AND WORKED COLLECTIVELY. OUR PROBLEM WAS MONEY. WE HAD A LONG STRIKE AND NO STRIKE FUND. AFTER THE STRIKE WE JOINED A MAINSTREAM UNION BECAUSE WE NEEDED THE RESOURCES THEY COULD GIVE US.

OUR UNION REP IS WONDERFUL. SHE GIVES US THE SCOPE TO DO WHAT WE WANT, BUT THE TECHNICAL STUFF...WHENEVER I WANT IT SHE GETS BACK TO ME IMMEDIATELY. I USE HER AS A RESOURCE, I TRUST HER. THEY'RE NOT ALL LIKE THAT.

I WAS VERY ACTIVE IN MY UNION BACK HOME IN GUYANA, SO I WAS HAPPY WHEN I FOUND OUT THAT THE HOSPITAL OFFICE HERE WAS UNIONIZED. I WAS SURPRISED TOO BECAUSE NO ONE EVER SPOKE ABOUT THE UNION.

WHEN I'M A WORKSHOP LEADER AT A UNION CONFERENCE THE UNION PAYS MY WAGES SO I CAN GO TO THE TRAINING SESSION THE DAY BEFORE. THEY ARRANGE FOR ME TO STAY OVER AT THE CONFERENCE HOTEL. I DON'T HAVE TO WORRY ABOUT BOOKING WHEELTRANS BACK AND FORTH.

◆

CHAPTER FIVE

THE CAMPAIGN
FOR A UNION

THIS CHAPTER describes how to organize a campaign to form a union. The process is called an "organizing drive," or an "organizing campaign," and involves having co-workers sign union membership cards. The signing of union membership cards is the most important part of this process. It is also important to be aware of the fact that once your campaign is under way and made public, the employer or management may react badly to it. The next chapter outlines ways employers react to the prospect of a union in the workplace. There's no magic formula for organizing a union. How you apply the steps described in this chapter depends on your particular workplace.

After the organizing drive, the next step is to win bargaining rights for your union. Applying for certification to the Labour Board is the most common way. Chapter 9 explains how to do this. Another method discussed in Chapter 9 is called "voluntary recognition," sometimes used in workplaces where the employer is not opposed to workers unionizing.

Another choice to use when the employer is sympathetic is the co-operative approach known as the "waiver process," which the Labour Board uses to help everyone reach agreement on your application for certification. Chapter 9 explains why we recommend the certification route with the waiver process, rather than voluntary recognition route in situations where the employer is sympathetic.

This chapter describes the steps to take to organize your campaign:

- how to form your inside organizing committee
- how to put together the list of employees
- preparing for the signing of cards
- how to sign cards
- answers to questions people ask about unions
- how to build unity through leaflets and letters, house calls, and phone calls
- solutions to common problems: the anti-union petition and interviews with the boss
- keeping up the momentum
- getting to the home stretch

THE INSIDE ORGANIZING COMMITTEE

SECRECY AND CONFIDENTIALITY

Keep any thoughts of forming a union secret until you know for sure what you're going to do. Deciding when to "go public" is an important part of any organizing plan.

Often the best campaigns are ones that the employer doesn't hear about until the union has taken the application to the Labour Board.

There are good reasons for this. For example, the law forbids employers to discipline or fire people for union activity.[1] If the employer disciplines or dismisses someone before a campaign even begins, it's more difficult for a union to prove that the action was taken because of their union work.

If your employer is the kind who's going to fiercely oppose the union, then the less time he has to make trouble, the better.

Keep total and absolute secrecy until the organizing committee decides to let everyone know there's a union campaign under way. If the campaign can come out into the open with a rush of support, then you've got an advantage over the employer, who'll be caught off guard. If your employer decides not to oppose the union when your campaign is made public, then you and your employer can use the Board's waiver process when you apply for your certificate.

THE FIRST STEPS

Forming your inside committee is the place to begin. Ask two or three people to meet privately to talk about the idea. These people must understand the importance of keeping the discussions confidential. You have to trust and respect each other.

At the meeting, discuss the reasons people want a union and list the main problems at work.

Decide what work is to be done and assign tasks. Talk about ways to get the names of all employees. Who will take responsibility for getting those names? Who will find out about the law on organizing and get a copy of the *Labour Relations Act* from a government bookstore or a library?

If you're not in touch with a union at this stage, the group should consider the steps and choices outlined in Chapter 4, "Choosing a Union." Then decide whether or not to meet with union representatives. If you do choose to work with a union, the union representative will help you plan your campaign.

SAMPLE AGENDA FOR AN ORGANIZING
COMMITTEE MEETING

4:30	Meeting begins: Introduce new committee members
4:35	Reports from work areas
4:45	Organizer's/co-ordinator's report
4:50	Discussion of co-ordinator's recommendations
5:00	Plan next steps
5:10	Tasks: Who does what, questions and answers
5:20	Education (how to sign cards, what dues will we pay, and so on)
5:30	Meeting finished

WHO THE MEMBERS ARE

The seeds of your new union are in your organizing committee. It's up to the first people who meet to include and welcome a variety of new members to the group and to be on the lookout for sympathetic people from other groups in the workplace and to get their support. Your committee should be representative of your workplace. It's also important to be on the lookout for natural leaders. The real leaders may not be the people who always speak up. Some respected leaders are soft-spoken people. When you identify the leaders, ask them to join the committee.

By the time you're ready to start the campaign, the organizing committee, ideally, should include both men and women, workers from all the shifts, and a selection of leaders — all of whom are from each of the major job groups, departments or sections, age groups, and racial and cultural groups. With a variety of members, you'll be stronger as a committee and as a union.

WHAT THE MEMBERS DO

The organizing committee members co-ordinate the union campaign in the workplace. They may work with an outside union organizer to plan the organizing strategy. They collect the information that's needed to create a list of employees before they begin to sign people up. They encourage people to sign union application cards, and keep records of people to contact. They learn about the law so that they can spot violations and follow up on these violations.

WHEN AND WHERE THE MEMBERS MEET

The committee's choice of a meeting place is important. Even if there is a private room or staff lounge that's available at work, the committee should meet somewhere away from the workplace.

Sometimes committees hold their first meetings in a convenient restaurant. Some get together in a room in a nearby school or community centre. Others want to take fewer risks in being seen and prefer to have the meeting at someone's house or apartment.

Some union organizers arrange for a meeting room in a hotel. For long campaigns where there are hundreds of employees involved, outside union organizers may arrange to rent a house as organizing headquarters.

COMMITTEE MEETINGS

• Meet at a convenient time, right after work is often best

• Meet in a neutral quiet place where you won't be observed

• Arrange child care or interpreters or accessibility aids ahead of time

• Keep the meeting short, no longer than an hour

• Have an agenda

• Choose one person to chair the meeting

WHY MEET?

• To pool information

• To plan what's next

• To divide up the tasks

• To get training (for example, how to sign cards)

The meetings should take place in a location where everyone feels comfortable. If there are people at work whose religion forbids them to drink alcohol, then a bar isn't the place for you. It's best not to meet in a bar anyway.

Do what you can to make it easier for people to be a part of the campaign. Keep people's family responsibilities in mind when you set a time and date. If some people have children to care for, arrange for a babysitter to come along and help. Bring snacks and toys for the kids.

If committee members are part-time students, arrange meetings around their course times. If there's a committee member who is disabled, make sure that the meeting is in an accessible, convenient place, and help arrange for any aids he or she needs to participate.

If there's a committee member who speaks a language other than English, take steps to ensure there is someone who can interpret.

The committee should try to meet regularly, at least once a week. The members should put together an agenda — a description of the topics to be discussed — for each meeting.

HOW TO PUT TOGETHER THE LIST OF EMPLOYEES FOR YOUR WORKPLACE

The most important information is an accurate list of the names and addresses of the employees at your workplace who are eligible to form a union. This information is often hard to get.

If you can't get a ready-made complete list of employees from your workplace, then the committee must put the list together, name by name. When you are putting your list together, try to get the addresses and phone numbers too.

Addresses are useful if you want to mail information or visit people at home. Phone numbers are useful too, so that you can contact people privately and answer their questions confidentially.

Use discretion and your imagination. You can get the names of people from shift schedule forms, timesheets, work assignment sheets, health and safety committee lists, memo routing sheets, birthday lists, social committee contacts, coffee club reminders, lottery pools, sports pools, Avon representatives, charity fund-raising lists, workplace sports teams, minutes of meetings that list the names of people who attended, and so on. You may need help from several people in order to get the names of part-time employees and employees who work on call. You may feel like a secret agent at this stage. Organizing would be easier if lists of employees were more public.[2]

Be sure to list all the workers you can. One way to keep track of the task is to make a chart of each work station. Check off each work station as you get the name of the employees who are located there.

You may find it helpful to buy a large binder and keep the list of employees and other information in one place under different tabs.

Remember that people in management jobs and confidential jobs *are not* part of your employee list. They are not eligible to be union members.

COMPILING INFORMATION

After you have made a list, put the following information beside each name, where possible:

- full-time, part-time, temporary, casual
- usual shift
- phone number and address
- job and department
- communication aids required

Now you can compile the "big picture." Don't get stalled just because you can't find out all you want to know. Compiling your list of employees and figuring out the type of work each employee does are your most important tasks. Once you know what each employee does, you can work out which jobs belong in your union or unit. This process is called "defining the bargaining unit." Defining the bargaining unit is key to deciding who and how many members you have to sign up in your campaign. (See Chapter 8 for more detailed information about the law.) Here is a list of the information you'll need:

THE NUMBERS OF EMPLOYEES AND THE JOBS THEY DO

How many are there?

How many full-time, part-time, and casual employees in each area and on each shift? Are there students?

What are the jobs they do? Are job duties spelled out in writing? Which employees work in jobs where they see confidential information about other employees?

INFORMATION ABOUT THE EMPLOYER

What's the exact name of the company or the organization? Is it a part of another, larger organization, or does it have smaller companies or warehouses that are a part of the business? How many management positions are there? Who reports to whom? Which employees have access to confidential labour relations information? Is there a company lawyer? Does the organization use consultants? (In the case of services or agencies, ask yourself similar questions.)

LEGAL ADVICE YOU MAY NEED

If there are people who work at other locations but who are a part of the same organization as your group, you'll need advice to help you decide whether you have to include them in your campaign. Who is the real employer? Is the employer affiliated with other related businesses in the industry? Is the employer a supplier to a larger firm? Will the Labour Board insist that workers there be a part of your new bargaining unit? Or, can you unionize alone? Are you dealing with a familiar warehouse where employees move back and forth to and from the plant? Or, are you part of a fast food chain where you have both a franchisee owner and a head office? You need advice from experienced people to help you decide what to do in these situations.

ORGANIZING INFORMATION

There are other facts to find out that can help you plan your organizing drive, and that will help you when you prepare to bargain your first contract.

Have employees tried to organize before? Why wasn't the campaign a success? How did management react? Do you know anyone who was a part of that campaign? Will they be sympathetic? Which people have worked the longest and which are new? Are there significantly different age groups?

Is there a formal complaint procedure at work? Who has the final say? Your employee guidelines or handbooks are a good source of information. What are the rules about sick time? lateness? Do any people have special arrangements like free parking?

Summarize the benefits employees have — vacations, profit-sharing, and insurance plans. Can you get copies of memos about workplace rules?

Are there employee committees? Make a list of them. Is there an active health and safety committee? What's the record on health and safety?

THE CAMPAIGN TOOK A YEAR AND MANAGEMENT DIDN'T KNOW A THING UNTIL THE DAY WE APPLIED FOR CERTIFICATION. I CALLED UP THE PERSONNEL MANAGER AND INTRODUCED MYSELF, OUTLINED WHAT HE COULD AND COULDN'T DO UNDER THE LAW. HE WAS FLOORED.

WHEN WE STARTED GATHERING THE NAMES OF THE CASUALS WE THOUGHT WE WERE LOOKING FOR 200 PEOPLE. SIX WEEKS LATER WE HAD MORE THAN 800 NAMES. WE COULDN'T BELIEVE IT. NEITHER COULD MANAGEMENT WHEN WE SIGNED THEM UP IN LESS THAN A MONTH.

SOMETIMES WE SPEND MONTHS PLANNING AND GETTING NAMES. WE WON'T HAND OUT CARDS UNTIL WE'RE ALL READY. IT MINIMIZES THE TIME MANAGEMENT HAS TO PRESSURE PEOPLE. WE TRY TO SIGN EVERYBODY UP IN A VERY SHORT TIME.

THE WAY A MEETING IS RUN IS A FOREIGN LANGUAGE FOR IMMIGRANTS, AND FOR MANY PEOPLE WHOSE FIRST LANGUAGE IS ENGLISH TOO!

FINALIZING YOUR LIST AND PREPARING FOR THE SIGN-UP CAMPAIGN

Signing membership cards is the next step in your campaign for a union. When you apply to the Labour Board for a union at your workplace, the Labour Board requires these cards, signed by people who want a union, as proof that you have enough members.

This is why a complete list of employees is crucial. You need an accurate list so that you know who is eligible to sign membership cards and so you can figure out your position at the Labour Board. The Labour Board decides on a union application based on the proportion of employees who have signed a union card by the date you file your application.[3]

Keep the list up-to-date as new people are hired, and others resign, transfer, are promoted, and so on.

The Labour Board will count the number of people who have signed cards and compare it with the total number of eligible workers.

Based on this information the Board will make one of the following decisions.

- If more than 55 percent of the employees have signed a union card, the Labour Board normally issues a union certificate *without a representation vote* (called automatic certification), or they may order a vote.[4]

- If between 40 percent and 55 percent have signed a union card, then the Labour Board *must* order a representation vote.[5]

- If 35 percent or more sign a union card, the Labour Board *may or may not* order a "pre-hearing" representation vote to see if the majority wants a union.[6]

To win a representation vote, the union must receive at least one more than half of the votes of the people voting, that is, one more than 50 percent.

WHO CAN SIGN?

Make sure you include each person in every job on the list. The Labour Board says that *all* people in *all* potential union jobs are part of the union list, whether you've included them or not. The people in these jobs together form the potential "bargaining unit." If you've left some people out, the numbers you're aiming for will be too low and your campaign won't be successful.

Be especially careful to include all full-time employees, even if they're working on a short-term basis, and people from agencies who get their paycheques from your employer.

PART-TIME AND CASUAL EMPLOYEES

See Chapter 8, "Defining the Bargaining Unit," for detailed information about including employees whose jobs are not full-time, year-round jobs. The Labour Board will include both part-time and full-time employees in the same bargaining unit if you get the required number of signatures from each group, full-time and part-time. If you don't have enough support from both groups, then the Board can certify the unit that has the required support.

NEW HIRING OR LAY-OFFS

If the employer is hiring a lot of new people you will have to make a judgement about whether to go ahead with your campaign or wait until all the new hiring is done. The same is true if your workplace is facing a series of lay-offs. You may want to wait until the lay-off situation is over.

When the Labour Board makes its count of employees, it considers all those who worked at some time 30 days before, or, are expected to work 30 days after the date the union files its application. That means you must include employees on short-term lay-off, workers' compensation benefits, sick leave, or official leave, and so on. See Chapter 10 and Chapter 15 for more detailed information on eligible employees.

The 30-day rule is one reason why unions try to avoid organizing part-time and casual employees during holiday or vacation time, when the numbers of eligible employees fluctuate. Also, if an employer knows about an organizing campaign, it's relatively easy to bring in a large number of part-time employees on a temporary basis, just to inflate the numbers. This is called "flooding the unit."

In your campaign, aim to sign up a good many more than 55 percent, to allow for mistakes, miscalculations, and people who have a change of mind. A good rule is to strive for 60 to 75 percent, and to try to reach that percentage as quickly as possible.

CHECKLIST FOR MANAGEMENT JOBS

Management staff should not sign cards. The committee has to decide which jobs are management jobs. This is important because you have to aim to sign up everyone who belongs in the bargaining unit, and you have to avoid help from people who are in management jobs, no matter how friendly they are. See Chapter 8, page 174.

The duties of some jobs aren't always that clearly cut. This list of factors will help you decide if a person is part of management. Does this person do any of the following — hire, fire, discharge, transfer, lay-off, write performance reviews, sign evaluations, discipline, interview for promotion, promote, reward (merit pay, perks), give time off or recall to work?

Also consider the place of the job in the organization's hierarchy. Who does the person in the job report to? For instance, if the person in the job makes the recommendations to hire, promote, or fire an employee to a manager who usually acts on them and who actually does the deed, neither job belongs in the bargaining unit.

Also, jobs where people make independent policy decisions for the employer are excluded from a union. Staff who handle the employer's labour relations and jobs where a person regularly handles confidential information about other employees, such as secretarial duties that include taking minutes of management discussions about firing someone, are also not included in a union.

If you decide that a job does belong in the bargaining unit then count the number of people in that job as part of the total for the bargaining unit.

PREPARING THE CARDS

If you are joining an established union, the union will give you cards to use. If you're forming your own union, or converting an association to your own union, you can follow the sample card on page 104 as a model.

If you're going to use a language other than English or French on your union cards, then you should make sure that the translation is absolutely accurate. To be on the safe side, assume that your employer or an anti-union employee is going to cause trouble about the other language. Ideally, you should be ready to show that this is a translation approved by a certified translator.

If there are blanks on the card for a local union name or number, put that information on the cards ahead of time so that it's not left blank by mistake. (But don't fill out the date until the employee and you are actually putting your signatures on the card.)

HOW TO SIGN THE CARDS

The Labour Board accepts as proof of union membership a card that shows that an employee is a member of the union or has applied to become a member, and wishes the union to represent her or him in collective bargaining.[7]

The card is a "union membership" or "application for union membership" card. Each card must be filled out accurately, or it doesn't count.

Generally, it takes two people to make a valid signed card: the employee (called the "applicant") and the "collector" or "agent" (who will be a committee member, union organizer, or a person helping the union). The collector should see the employee sign the card. The union has to be ready to prove to the Labour Board that there was a witness present, someone watching, when each employee signed a card. (Note: Technically, the collector does not have to sign as long as her or his name is clearly identified on the card as the collector. The name can be printed on. Because it's necessary to be able to prove that the collector witnessed the applicant's signing the card, it's good insurance to insist that all collectors sign too.)

Have a practice session with sample cards before the campaign begins.

Go through the steps first as an applicant and then as the collector. (Rip the practice cards up when you're finished so they don't get mixed up with the real ones.)

It's very important to sign up people properly:

- Ask the employee joining the union to sign the card on the front.

- You, the "collector," sign the card *at the same time* and date the card. Make sure the date is correct. It's safer to use the name of the month, rather than a number (May 6, 1994, rather than 05.6.1994).

- The employee must *sign* the card, with the same signature as she or he uses at work or on cheques. The employee shouldn't just print his or her name. When the Labour Board receives the cards, a labour relations officer will compare the signatures on the union cards with the copies of employee signatures, which the employer must give to the Labour Board.

- An employee who can't write may sign with an "X." The name must be printed clearly on the card. A relative or friend should sign the card as an additional witness.

- If you make a mistake while filling out a card, tear it up and make out another one.

- Fill out the personal information on the back of the card — the employee's address, phone number, job, department, and so on. This information isn't a legal requirement, but it's useful to have it. If the committee has people's addresses and phone numbers, then they can keep in touch.

- Put the cards in an envelope and keep them with you until you can give them to your committee co-ordinator. Don't leave them at work. Once the union application is filed with the Board, it's a legal requirement that the cards be kept confidential (section 113, *Labour Relations Act*).

- Keep the names of people who have signed cards *confidential.* That way people who are thinking about joining will learn that they can trust you and will be encouraged to join.

DO'S AND DON'TS WHEN SIGNING CARDS

- Be careful.

  There are legal limits on union activities during working hours. You can sign people up before work, during official breaks, or after work. Don't sign people up in their work areas. Keep to the locker rooms, the washrooms, the cafeteria, the parking lot or bus stop, or arrange to meet people at their homes.

- Be discrete. There are people who will want to sign but won't want their friends to know. Don't assume anything but absolute secrecy!

- Don't pressure anyone to sign.

- Don't use the names of other people who have signed as a way to convince others to join, unless you have permission to do so.

- Don't talk about "jobs." Some people might think you're promising (or threatening) their job if the union is successful. That's not legal.

- Don't promise that a vote will be held so that people can have a "final say." If you sign at least 55 percent, the Labour Board can give the union a certificate without a vote. If you promise a vote, the Labour Board may order a vote because of your promise, even though more than 55 percent sign a card.

SIGNING CARDS: QUESTIONS AND ANSWERS

When you're asking people to sign a union card, they'll have many questions. If someone asks you a question and you don't know the answer, you should say so, and tell the person you'll get back to them with an answer.

It's important for members of the organizing committee to let one another know about hard questions that come up. You may want to put out a leaflet that addresses the issues that bother people. Here are some general questions and statements about unions you may hear, and responses you could give. Chapter 2 gives some answers to common myths about unions.

SAMPLE MEMBERSHIP APPLICATION CARD

Front of card
[Name of Union]
MEMBERSHIP APPLICATION

I have signed my name below:

to apply for membership in the _____[name of union] to show that I agree to abide by its constitution and by-laws and to authorize the union to be my only bargaining agent.

Signed _____

Date _____ Signed (Witness)_____

Back of card
[Name of Union]

Local number _____ Full-time _____ Part-time ____

Name _____

Address_____

Phone _____ Employer _____

Job title_____

WHAT DOES SIGNING THIS CARD MEAN?

It means you want a union to represent you. It means you are applying for membership in a particular union. If more than 55 percent of the people at your workplace sign cards, the Labour Board will normally give the group a union certificate without a vote. If fewer sign, the union can apply for a vote at your workplace.

CAN I BE FIRED FOR SIGNING A CARD?

It is illegal for an employer to fire anyone for signing a card or for being part of an organizing campaign.

The law puts the responsibility ("onus") on an employer who fires a worker during an organizing drive to prove that union membership or activity had absolutely no part in the firing.[8]

If the employer can't prove that, the Labour Board will order the employer to take you back, and to pay you for the time you lost from work. (See Chapter 13 for more information on employee organizing protections.)

[New] In Ontario, if an employer disciplines or fires you during an organizing drive, the Labour Board must schedule a hearing within 15 days to hear the case from Monday through Thursday consecutively every week until the hearing is done. Then the Board must give its decision within two days.

Unions provide legal advice and representation if someone is fired during a campaign. Some unions give strike and defense benefits to employees who have signed cards and have then been fired, and financial aid to activists while the complaint is at the Labour Board.

You are also protected between the time a union gets certified or recognized and the union is able to bargain a first collective agreement.

[New] It's against the law for an employer to fire or discipline anyone during that time "without just cause."[9] (See page 284.) A "freeze" on existing working conditions and practices also applies during this period.[10]

If you're an immigrant or here on a work permit, you cannot be deported for joining a union. It's against the law to discriminate against employees who are not citizens.

WILL WE HAVE TO GO ON STRIKE?

In most unions, the local union members are the only people who decide on a strike.

Unions have to hold a secret ballot vote before they can strike. Educating clients or customers, holding rallies, handing out information to the public, and making links with groups in the community are examples of other ways unions choose to show their power and influence.

I'M LUCKY TO HAVE A JOB.
I CAN DO WITHOUT A RAISE FOR NOW.

The union won't ask for a raise unless the members vote to ask for a raise. Having a union will mean that you can bargain for a fair process around keeping your job, and you'll have free legal representation if the employer should fire you. Even the pay you get now isn't guaranteed unless it's written into a legal contract. Otherwise the only protection you have is the legal "minimum wage."

CAN THE UNION DO ANYTHING ABOUT FAVOURITISM?

Fairness is the most important part of a good union contract. The rules are there for everyone to see. By law the employer has to follow them. Union members can file a grievance if there's a problem. If the union decides that a grievance isn't resolved fairly, then they can take the problem to an arbitrator. Management is no longer both judge and jury.

I'M ONLY A STUDENT. I DON'T WANT TO GET INVOLVED
AND ANYWAY STUDENTS DON'T NEED UNIONS.

Students can benefit from a grievance procedure, overtime pay, and fair scheduling just as permanent employees do. Who knows, you may be working here permanently someday. Because you're an employee now, the employer has to put you on the list that goes to the Labour Board. You're involved whether you want to be or not because if there's no union card to go with a name on that list, it's the same as voting against the union. That's why the more senior workers care about your decision.

I'M JUST A CASUAL. I DIDN'T KNOW CASUALS COULD BE IN A UNION.

Today both casuals and part-timers are getting together in unions. There are some union locals made up of only casuals or part-timers, and other union locals that include casuals and part-timers with the full-timers. A union contract can set out fair rules for call-in work, and can give casual employees benefits. Many casuals really want a full-time job. A union contract can set out a fair process so that casuals can move into vacant permanent or part-time jobs.

THE BOSS SAYS WE'LL LOSE THE BENEFITS THEY GIVE US NOW IF WE FORM A UNION.

The opposite is true. Without a union, the employer can take away your benefits anytime. It's against the law for employers to retaliate against the union by taking away what you have now. Having a union contract and bargaining for improvements is one way of securing the benefits you've gained so far.

It's against the law for management to threaten employees with loss of benefits during an organizing drive. See page 143 on how to fill out an incident report.

WHY SHOULD WE PAY DUES TO THE UNION?

The people at your workplace will be part of "the union." The dues you pay are for union services and benefits, such as handling grievances at arbitration, providing educational programs, contributing to the strike fund, and so on. Depending on the union, your local may be able to call on free health and safety experts, pension specialists, lawyers, and trained professional staff.

As a union member you will have a say in how your money is

spent. Union account books are audited regularly, and the union treasurer is accountable to the membership.

Most unions don't begin to collect dues money until *after* the local has voted to approve their first collective agreement. You can deduct the amount of union dues you've paid from your income when you complete your income tax return.

If someone can satisfy the Labour Board that he or she objects to joining a union or paying dues to a union because of a religious conviction or belief, the Board can order an alternative. The Board can make an order saying the person does not have to join the union or pay union dues, but an amount equal to the required union dues must be given to a Canadian charity. The union and the employee have to agree on the charity, and if they can't agree the Board will choose one.[11]

THE SUPERVISOR SAYS IF THE UNION COMES IN THEY'LL BRING IN NEW PEOPLE AND I'LL LOSE MY JOB.

That's not true. No one can take your job away for not signing a card, and neither the supervisor nor the union can treat you differently if you oppose the union. If we have a union you can vote on our first collective agreement even if you don't join.

If our union negotiates a "union shop" in your first contract then everybody will have to join the union. (Some unions bargain for a union shop with a special provision for employees who were working at the time the union was organized. They don't have to join. They can vote on the contract and the union must represent them as if they were members. All new employees must join.)

The organizing committee should make sure that no one talks about keeping (or losing) jobs when signing cards, or when talking about the union. The employer or anti-union employees might use that to complain to the Labour Board saying that people signed only because they were afraid they'd lose their jobs, that they felt threatened and intimidated. If proved, this kind of charge could mean that other cards collected by the person promising jobs would be invalid, and your campaign jeopardized.[12]

WON'T QUALITY OF CARE AND SERVICE SUFFER IF WE HAVE A UNION HERE?

On the contrary, we can show that unionizing means better service, better care. Having a union means we'll have new resources to help us make the case for better funding or budgeting, better work organization and workplace improvements. Having a union means we'll be protected when we speak out about problems.

THE BOSS SAYS HE'D RATHER MOVE THE FACTORY TO MEXICO THAN DEAL WITH A UNION.

This is a common threat that employers make during an organizing drive, even though it's against the law to threaten employees' jobs this way. Many employers have moved jobs south to the United States and Mexico already, but not because of unions. Employers who are planning to move to Mexico will make the move anyway — with or without a union.

If the company is planning to move, then a union can help you and your co-workers. If you have a union, the boss will have to answer for what he's doing. You'll have an advocate to fight for you and what you're due under the law in severance pay, back pay, and unemployment insurance. Unions can also arrange retraining and other educational programs for laid-off workers.

DURING THE CAMPAIGN

KEEPING RECORDS: KEEPING COUNT

One of the most important jobs of a union organizer and of the committee is keeping confidential records.

The committee needs a system for assigning individual committee members to approach specific people or groups of people, and also a system for collecting the signed cards. Choose one person, usually the organizer or the committee co-ordinator, to keep the signed cards and to be the record-keeper.

That person must keep track of every employee, every potential union member, through a very confidential system that shows whether they've signed a union card or whether they're likely to. *This list is secret and confidential and only one person should have it.*

Computerizing information can be useful, especially in workplaces where there are hundreds of employees. You'll need to keep track of the same information whether your records are on computer files or in file folders or in a three-ring binder.

There are many ways to keep lists and keep count: by work area, by job titles, by name of committee member assigned to a group, or by shift. What's important is that there be a system to follow what's happening. Whatever system you use should include a way of evaluating the degree of support from people who haven't yet signed cards. A common system lists four different levels of support for the union: strong yes, maybe yes, maybe no, strong no. Others use a simple, yes, no, or maybe system. (See the contact card on page 114.)

Even when the campaign is open and public, committees usually choose to keep the numbers secret, in order to keep the employer guessing. They want the employer to be caught by surprise when they take the application for certification to the Labour Board. If several people know the count you can be sure that the news will travel all the way to the supervisor.

A note of caution: People who sign a card may change their mind, so you'll need to know more than just the number of signed cards on hand to judge the outcome of your campaign.

BUILDING UNITY

What can the workplace committee do to develop a strong union? There's no secret recipe for building unity, but there are ways that can help bring people together.[13]

AT MEETINGS

Begin and end meetings on time. It's easier for people to come if the time is predictable. If the meeting's taking longer than planned, and there's still important work to do, don't let it drag on. The group should decide whether to stay past the set time or wait until the next meeting to finish the agenda.

Bring problems out in the open. People should feel comfortable enough to talk about things that are bothering them. Perhaps begin each meeting by listening to one another's complaints and problems. Then you can build solutions into the work ahead.

Make it easier for each person to take part. Encourage people who are shy and soft-spoken. Go around the room and find out what each person thinks. You build trust and respect by talking together as equals.

Rotate who's going to chair the meeting on different days, or divide the meeting into sections and have a different person lead each section. The chair should make a "speakers' list," which is a fair way of keeping track of the names of people who want to speak, and the order in which they've signalled that they have something to say.

When you're chairing a meeting be specific when it's time to make a decision. Don't ask if people agree "with what was suggested," instead say exactly what you're reaching an agreement about. You should ask people to say whether or not they agree. Don't ever assume that silence is agreement.

If there are strong disagreements, discuss them openly. Being open about conflicts can lead to creative solutions.

Many groups that are working for change (and not only union organizing committees) go through a common pattern of development. At the beginning people may be very excited and confident. Then as they learn more about obstacles in their way, some become pessimistic about the task ahead and don't think they can do it. People may feel uneasy, and think about pulling out of the committee. If they don't feel comfortable with the group, they may keep their worries to themselves, and simply stop coming. The committee can get through this phase if you've created a structure and atmosphere that lets people talk freely from the very beginning.

It is at this stage, when people are facing up to the amount of work to be done, that the best planning can happen, because it will be based on a realistic evaluation of what's to be done.

Just as there is no place for harassment or discrimination in the

MAKING IT EASIER TO PARTICIPATE

WE PAY CHILD CARE EXPENSES SO IT DOESN'T
COST WOMEN EXTRA TO COME TO MEETINGS.

POWER-SHARING. WE ROTATE POSITIONS. THE WOMAN
WHO WAS VICE-PRESIDENT LAST YEAR IS PRESIDENT, AND
LAST YEAR'S PRESIDENT IS VICE-PRESIDENT. SHE'S RIGHT
THERE IF THE NEW PRESIDENT NEEDS HELP.

FOR WORKING PARENTS IF YOU CAN PROVIDE AN
EVENT THAT GETS THE KIDS FED, THAT'S ANOTHER
REASON FOR THEM TO COME.

BE ON TIME. REMEMBER WHEN THEY MEET WITH YOU THEY'VE
ALREADY DONE ONE SHIFT, THE MEETING'S A SECOND SHIFT,
AND THEY'RE GOING HOME TO A THIRD SHIFT. IF YOU LET THE
MEETING RUN OVER, HOW CAN THEY BE SURE YOU'LL TAKE THE
EQUITY ISSUES TO THE BARGAINING TABLE?

EVEN IF YOU HAVE ENOUGH PEOPLE ON YOUR COMMITTEE
BUT THERE AREN'T WOMEN, GO BACK AND TAKE THE TIME
TO FIND WOMEN AND ENCOURAGE THEM TO COME ON.
EVEN IF IT'S HARDER AND TAKES LONGER, YOU HAVE TO DO IT
IF YOU REALLY BELIEVE IN EQUITY.

WE NEED TO CHALLENGE THE MACHO BARGAINING STYLE, LATE
NIGHTS. ALL OUR MEMBERS ARE WOMEN, MOST HAVE KIDS.
WE BARGAIN DURING NORMAL WORKING HOURS.

A LOT OF GAY AND LESBIAN WORKERS FEEL SILENCED.
IT'S UP TO THE UNION TO RAISE THEIR ISSUES, THAT'S
THE WAY TO INCLUDE THEM.

workplace, there is no place for them in an organizing drive. The organizing committee should deal with any harassment problem as soon as it occurs. You can get printed material and advice from unions, community centres, women's shelters, human rights organizations and government agencies.

TALKING WITH CO-WORKERS

People sign union cards for many reasons, but no one signs a card unless they trust the person who's offering it. Promise confidentiality and keep the promise.

Questions are better than arguments. Listening goes further than making speeches. Ask the person about problems at work, don't assume that you know the issues that others care most about. Ask people what they think about unions, if they know anyone who's been in a union.

If they've heard negative stories about unions, listen carefully. A successful campaigner listens to people's fears, and knows how to offer reassurance. Don't argue. Look for points of agreement, and build from there. Be honest and polite about where you disagree.

Don't make a sales pitch. Forming a union is not the same as selling insurance or buying a manufactured product. You and the other employees will be the union, making decisions about what's important all along the way.

Don't make promises you can't deliver on. Employers like to manufacture anti-union campaigns based on unions' pie-in-the-sky promises. Don't say things that make the employer's pitch believable.

If the person is sympathetic, ask them to sign a union card right then, and see if they're willing to help out. Ask for suggestions about other people who might want to join. Say you won't use their name unless you have their permission. Ask them to help by talking carefully to one other person. The more help you have, the faster and more successful your campaign will be.

Keep track of whom you have spoken to by filling out a contact card as soon as the conversation is over. You can also indicate the person's support of the union on this card.

CONTACT CARD

Name _Sue Student_   Department _Storeroom_
Address _123 Home Street_ Job Title _Clerk_
Home Phone _987-6543_   Full-time/~~part-time~~/casual
Date 1st contacted _February 8_ Contacted by _Laura_
Date 2nd contacted _____ Contacted by _____

Issues _wants benefits for part-timers, says boss
discriminates against part-timers, worried about
cost of dues._
Supports union? Yes   No   (Maybe Yes)   Maybe No
Follow-up _get sample contract language for
part-timers as soon as possible_

Will help with_ ? _

MAKING HOUSE CALLS

Should you call on people in their homes? It depends. The advantage of visiting people is that you can talk in private. House visits are easier to make in smaller towns than in large cities. It's hard to co-ordinate visits when employees live over a wide metropolitan area, but it's often worth the extra effort.

Some unions deliberately avoid contacting people at or near the workplace. As soon as they have a list of names and addresses, they communicate with people by telephone or in person. House calls are sometimes crucial towards the end of a campaign when there are just a few more signatures to get to achieve the numbers you're aiming for.

Some employees don't want anyone at work, even people on the organizing committee, to know they've signed a card. They prefer a secret visit at home from the union organizer. Some organizers go alone to people's homes, especially in situations where people are very frightened and may not trust someone from work to keep the visit private. In other situations, an organizer or committee member brings along a translator. If you don't know the area, it's best to go in pairs for safety's sake.

A male organizer or male committee member shouldn't go alone to visit a female employee at her home. He should take a woman from the committee along. There are two reasons for this. The first is that her family members might not approve, and you're putting her in a very difficult situation. The second is that you don't want to put the campaign at risk by feeding the rumour mill. Appearances can be more important than reality. Don't give anti-union employers or employees a chance to make up stories about the union's representatives.

When you visit someone at home, introduce yourself, explain that there's a group trying to make some changes at work and you'd like to know what the person thinks. Ask if you can come in for a few minutes.

Listen and ask questions and follow the advice in the previous section. Talk to family members who may be there. (A strong pro-union or anti-union relative may have a lot of influence.) Try not to stay longer than half an hour. Remember you're a guest, and you also have other visits to make. Try to get a decision there and then. If there are still serious questions, ask if you can return at another time. Thank the person for letting you visit, and fill out the contact card as soon as you leave.

MAKING PHONE CALLS

For some, making a phone call is easier than talking to someone in person. Phoning has drawbacks, though, and is always second best. It's better to talk to people directly, in person, so that they see how attentive and serious you are, and so that you can judge if they mean what they say.

Some people won't sign a card but will whisper that they'd like a phone call at home so that they can get answers to some questions.

Talking to people on the telephone is another way to keep

private your conversations about forming a union. Try to get telephone numbers at the same time you're collecting names and addresses. If possible, put a number on every leaflet where people can call if they want information about the union.

Some committee members won't be able to make house calls, but they can be a part of the campaign from home. They can help search out phone numbers and do the calling.

> FEAR USED TO BE A QUESTION OF 'DO WE HAVE TO GO ON STRIKE?' WE DON'T GET TO THAT QUESTION ANYMORE. THE QUESTION IS 'WILL THEY CLOSE US DOWN AND MOVE TO MEXICO?' THAT'S NUMBER ONE.
>
> I TRIED ALL THE USUAL EDUCATION APPROACHES. BROUGHT LEAFLETS, TALKED ABOUT THE UNION'S POLICY. HE PERSISTED WITH RACIST COMMENTS. FINALLY I MET WITH HIM ONE ON ONE. IF YOU WANT OUR UNION, THIS IS OUR POLICY, YOU HAVE TO ADHERE TO IT. HE BASICALLY BACKED OFF.
>
> WE DID IT THE 'EACH ONE TEACH ONE' WAY. THE THREE OF US TALKED TO OTHERS UNTIL WE HAD 20 PEOPLE. I WAS ON A WORK PERMIT BUT NOT LANDED YET. I WAS SCARED A LITTLE BUT I THOUGHT ABOUT IT AND DECIDED TO CARRY ON. MOST PEOPLE WERE AFRAID. ONLY WE THREE, WE KEPT EACH OTHER GOING. THEY WATCHED ME, EVERYTHING I DID. I FELT MAD. I DIDN'T KNOW I WOULD GET CAUGHT UP IN IT LIKE THIS.

Fill out a contact card after each call. Promise confidentiality and ask sympathetic people for the names of others to contact.

Two cautions. Your list of employees may include some unlisted telephone numbers. Don't use them, don't call those people, respect their desire for privacy. If you do decide to call an unlisted number in a pinch at the end of a campaign, listen carefully to the tone of voice of the person you are calling. If the person is hostile, apologize, thank them politely, and say goodbye. You may be asked where the number came from. The answer, of course, is that the number was given in confidence, and just as you're not going to tell anyone about this telephone conversation, you're not going to give out any names.

The second caution is about phoning women with families. If a woman works a full shift and then has a family to care for, it's hard to find a time when a phone call at home isn't going to interrupt dealing with the kids, or supper, or bedtime, or the dishes. It's best not to call, but to try and speak with these busy women in private.

HOLDING OPEN OR CLOSED MEETINGS

If you're trying to run a secret campaign you won't be holding open, public meetings. Union supporters are vulnerable because word always travels back to the boss.

The organizing committee decides whether or not and when to hold open meetings or confidential, closed meetings of particular groups of workers, such as all clerks, or all people on the afternoon shift.

Don't call a meeting unless you're sure there's going to be a good turnout. If not many people come, then word gets around that the union isn't doing well.

If you're sure of strong support, consider holding an open meeting where you can answer questions and explain what's going on. If the committee calls a meeting and lots of people attend, it's a signal to others that the union is gaining support and momentum. A well-organized meeting is a show of strength.

Plan in advance. Distribute leaflets, contact people by telephone. Don't take anything for granted. Talk to people so that you know ahead of time who's coming and who can't come.

Choose a nearby place for the meeting. Make sure the room is accessible for employees with disabilities. Plan to have any necessary language interpreters present. Arrange for child care. Better to have a hall that's too small than one so large that people feel lost and isolated. Keep the meeting short, have an agenda, provide time for questions and answers.

If there are key issues, such as sexual or racial harassment, lack of pensions, or favouritism, try to provide printed information that people can take home and read.

There may be some employees there who will report back to management. Don't let that put you off. Be direct, don't make promises you can't keep, and show your confidence that coming together in a union will make life at work better for everyone.

> YOU DON'T WANT TO HOLD AN OPEN MEETING EARLY IN THE CAMPAIGN. IT EXPOSES THE PEOPLE ON THE ORGANIZING COMMITTEE. AND IF WE GET 20 OUT OF 100 OUT WE KNOW THAT'S A GOOD TURNOUT, BUT THE BOSS WILL SAY, SEE, THE UNION JUST DOESN'T HAVE THE SUPPORT.
>
> PEOPLE DON'T COME TO MEETINGS ANYMORE. THEIR LIVES ARE TOO BUSY.
>
> OPEN MEETINGS? TOO RISKY. THE ONLY TIME WE EVER CALLED AN OPEN MEETING WAS WHEN WE WERE DESPERATE.

DISTRIBUTING LEAFLETS

It's an old organizing truism that leaflets don't sign people up, people do. Still, there are times when leaflets can help an organizing committee do its job.

Putting out a leaflet may be part of the committee's decision to go public. The leaflet can be in the form of a flyer that members of the committee hand out as people come in to work, or as a letter that's signed by each member of the committee and sent to each employee's home. Many employees won't want to be seen with a union leaflet at work, but they'll read one at home. A flyer or letter signed by everyone on the committee tells co-workers that you're not afraid, and that you are confident enough to go public. Some committees, however, don't circulate anything in writing until they announce that they've applied to the Labour Board for a union certificate.

Listing the members of the organizing committee in a public way is also a form of insurance. The employer can't get away with firing anyone for union activity, and he can't claim he didn't know about the union if there are union leaflets everywhere.

Sometimes you'll want to give out information to counter an employer's misinformation campaign. An example is dealing with the question of dues. Some groups put out a leaflet about dues at the very beginning so that employees have the facts before the employer attacks. Try not to be defensive, and don't fall into the trap of a paper war with the employer.

Leaflets should be short, simple, and to the point. Facts and figures, charts, photos, and humour can show that you're confident and that you understand the issues. A cartoon of an unpopular manager is always a hit. Proofread carefully for errors. The appearance of the leaflet can reflect on the union's credibility. Include a phone number to call for people who want to talk confidentially.

If there's an issue that many employees are asking about, such as the union's record on pensions, strikes, or pay equity, then people will probably welcome a leaflet on the topic to read at home.

Get your leaflets translated into the languages that your co-workers speak. Make sure the translation is accurate. One group found too late that the person they'd engaged to do a translation really didn't like unions, and so he'd changed their message! Making the effort to give out information in someone's first language is a good message about the union.

Put out a victory leaflet the day you get your union certificate. Make sure the message is that the union's going to work to include everyone, whether or not they signed cards.

> I HATE LEAFLETS. I DON'T WANT THE EMPLOYER TO KNOW. THE ONLY LEAFLET WE PUT OUT IS AT THE TIME OF THE VOTE TO INFORM PEOPLE ABOUT THE LAW.
>
> WE PUT OUT LEAFLETS IN PORTUGUESE, CANTONESE, VIETNAMESE, PUNJABI. PEOPLE TAKE IT HOME AND READ IT IF YOU PUT IT IN THEIR LANGUAGE.
>
> THE NOTICES FROM THE UNION WERE WAY OVER PEOPLE'S HEADS, PRECISE LANGUAGE ABOUT CLASSIFICATIONS.

SENDING OUT LETTERS FROM THE UNION
AND THE ORGANIZING COMMITTEE

The committee and the union organizer make the decisions about sending letters to employees. Who signs depends on what's in the letter. People on the local organizing committee have more credibility with other employees than strangers do. They're often the best people to sign letters about campaign issues. On the other hand, a union official should sign a letter that describes a legal matter.

Here's a list of topics for letters:

Announcing the campaign: Do this only if secrecy is impossible and you've made a decision to make your campaign public from the start. It's been used to organize part-time and casual workers. Mark the letter "personal and confidential" and mail it to people's homes or deliver it by hand just before or after work. Consider enclosing a leaflet about the law and the rights to organize and be protected.

Welcome to the union: This letter goes to each person as soon as they sign a membership application card. It may explain what happens next. Some unions send a temporary union membership card with this welcoming letter.

Survey of issues: This letter asks new members to tell the committee which issues are most important for bargaining. Some unions include survey questions in the welcoming letter. Others send out a survey questionnaire with a letter the day they apply for certification at the Labour Board.

News of the application for certification: This letter tells employees the union has applied for certification. It describes what happens next. Some unions send two different letters at this time, one to people who have signed cards, and one to those who haven't signed.

Voting day: If there's a representation vote, you have to make a judgment about the degree of union support when you decide who gets a letter, or whether to send two different ones. If the vote's going to be very close it's not smart to encourage opponents. On the other hand, this letter is another chance to communicate with people who haven't decided yet.

Results of the survey: Informing people about the issues they care most about is good preparation for bargaining.

SEEKING COMMUNITY HELP

If your organizing committee has decided to make the campaign public, look for support from local groups. The most obvious people to contact are leaders from unions in other similar or nearby workplaces. See page 418 for a list of labour organizations that might help you get in touch with these unions. Ask them to write a letter, sign a flyer, answer questions at a meeting.

Build on the connections members of the organizing committee have in their communities. Have a discussion about where your allies might be. Don't assume that community groups will automatically support your campaign for a union.

If you belong to an activist organization, like an immigrant women's group, ask them for help. If you're working for a service organization, think about ways having a union could improve service to your clients, and let the client groups know what you're doing and why. Call your community newspaper to ask them to write an article about your campaign. Speak to your local legal aid clinic. Ask if they will prepare a leaflet explaining that people have a legal right to form a union.

Before other groups can show their support for you publicly they'll need information. Prepare an outline of the facts about the workplace and a summary of the issues to give to groups and individuals whose support you want. Arrange to attend a meeting and present your case.

Many unions work with other organizations, such as churches, environmental groups, and seniors. Some unions have formed coalitions with several organizations to work for alternatives to free trade, to help refugee groups, to improve the environment, and so on. Ask to attend a coalition meeting.

Hand out leaflets at public events. Think of ways to make vital links between your workplace and the community. If racism is an issue, sponsor a panel discussion or a public forum on racism. Show people at work that the union is prepared to provide resources and lead the fight against racism.

COMMON PROBLEMS: COMMON SOLUTIONS

Chapter 6 outlines various ways that employers will react to organizing campaigns. Your committee will want to be prepared from the start for any negative responses from management. Two common tactics that management uses to hurt organizing campaigns are encouraging petitions and summoning union activists to a meeting with the boss.

PETITIONS

Petitions are supposed to be a formal way for employees who have signed union cards to tell the Labour Board that they've changed their minds. But they are not always used this way. Petitions have been a convenient way to delay and even kill union organizing campaigns.[14] Anti-union employees, frequently instigated or encouraged by management, ask people, especially those who may have signed union cards, to sign a petition saying they are opposed to having a union. Before the 1993 amendments, there was a process for filing petitions with the Board after the union put in its application.

[New] Now the Labour Board accepts petitions only up to and including the day that employees put in their application for certification, not after.

Petitions are still a problem, even though the rules about timing have changed. Warn each person who signs a card that a paper called a petition may appear and ask them to let you know if there's a petition around. Let them know so that they won't be caught by surprise. The petition may come during work time (though that's illegal), it will probably be on a clipboard, and someone will suddenly stick it in front of them and say, "Sign here if you don't want a union." It's a difficult situation because it's natural for workers to think that if they don't sign the petition everybody's going to guess that they've signed a union card.

Warn people that this is one of those times when they have to stay strong if they want a union. If enough people sign the petition the chances of having a union may disappear. Anti-union rumours usually circulate along with petitions, and workers may face stories about how everyone is deserting the union. Challenge those stories! Often the people with the petitions try to get support for the petition by telling people that they have more signatures than they really do. They hope in this way to create a stampede or snowball effect away from the union. Stop the stampede in its tracks by letting people know that the organizing campaign is going forward.

What can workers say when the petition's under their nose? They can say they're not interested, that they're staying out of it, they don't want to talk to anyone, they don't want to sign any papers. They could even say, with a smile, that they never sign papers without their lawyer! Or, that they're here to work, not to sign papers!

If a petition shows up at your workplace before you have filed your application, take the petition seriously, and be sure to take steps to deal with it.

Since many of the union's best supporters will never be approached to sign a petition, you may have to ask others to carefully look at it. They should check the wording, that is, what are the people who are signing the petition agreeing to or asking for. They should also check which union members have signed. Your organizing committee should then contact these people to talk to them about why they signed. Remember, if someone who signs a membership application card willingly signs an anti-union petition, their card doesn't count for the union. Your count of people who have signed cards won't be accurate if some also sign petitions.

People have often signed petitions because they felt pressured and were worried they would be reported to management as union supporters if they did not sign. They may be too embarrassed to tell you they've signed a petition. If you suspect that this may have happened, privately speak with the person about signing a new card with a new date just before you put your application in. Signing a new card cancels the effect of an earlier signature on a petition. You then submit only the second card to the Board.

There is another approach, but we do not recommend it. You can also ask employees who signed a petition to sign a reaffirmation form. This is a document that states that the employee or employees signing it confirm that they wish to apply to be a member of the union and have that union represent them to the employer.

The Labour Board accepts the last voluntary signature made by the employee as standing for her or his wishes, so long as it is filed by the application date.[15]

The problem with this approach is that the union will have to prove the employee signed the form voluntarily, which is not necessary with the re-signed card. This exposes employees to being identified as union supporters if they have to testify.

If your committee decides to ask someone to sign a second time, remember your pledge of confidentiality. Have the person who witnessed the first signature offer the card the second time.

In response to the new rules about petitions, some anti-union groups are testing an approach where many employees file charges that the union intimidated or coerced them into signing a card. This danger is good reason to be very careful when asking people if they will sign a second time. Don't put pressure on anyone or make promises you can't keep. Make notes of your discussions with people about this. Pressuring someone to sign could be used against the union as evidence later at a Labour Board hearing.

Don't wait to find out from the Labour Board if a petition has actually been filed with the Labour Board. Then it will be too late to get employees to sign new cards. Take steps beforehand and follow through by filing the new cards or reaffirmation forms with your other membership evidence when you file your application.

Rules 47, 48, and 49 of the Labour Board's Rules of Procedure require that all membership evidence, such as membership cards, petitions and reaffirmation forms, must:

- be in writing
- be signed by the employee concerned
- include the date on which each signature was obtained by the employee concerned
- include the name of your union, including the local number if applicable, if known
- be accompanied by the name of the employer involved, and the name, address, telephone number and fax number (if there is one) of the person who is submitting the evidence — in your case, the contact person for the union

MANAGEMENT INVOLVEMENT IN PETITIONS

Sometimes management has a hand in helping petitions circulate. If you have information about management involvement in a petition, tell your co-workers and let them know that management involvement will cause the Labour Board to reject the petition as evidence since it is "tainted."[16]

Union supporters who are approached about the petition can ask the person carrying it if management will back them up if they sign. If the answer is "yes," then this statement could be evidence of management support.

If you have any facts suggesting that the petition is not a voluntary statement or that the employer is involved, you may want to bring an unfair labour practice complaint. An example of the form used for this is found in Appendix E.

You may want to plan the timing of this complaint to go in with your certification application if you are almost at the point of filing the application. Remember, violations of the *Labour Relations Act*, such as intimidation of employees, may be grounds for automatic certification under section 9.2 even when your membership support is 55 percent or less.

On the other hand, if your organizing campaign still has some time to go, you may wish to file the complaint earlier. For more discussion about unfair labour practices and timing the complaint, see Chapter 13.

MEETINGS WITH THE BOSS

If the employer finds out about the campaign, you or one of your committee members may be summoned, one-by-one, to a private meeting with the boss. It's common for management to put people who are active in union campaigns to the test in hopes that they'll be frightened and back down.

Be prepared for unexpected meetings. If you're called, ask if you can bring a co-worker along, as a witness. Don't be surprised if management says no, but it's worth a try. Have each person on the organizing committee carry a small notebook and pencil in their shirt pocket or purse at all times. When you're called in for a meeting, take out the notebook so that it's clear that there's going to be a record of the interview. When the supervisor or manager makes a strange statement, politely ask him to repeat it, and slowly write it down. It's good insurance against threatening or intimidating remarks.

This kind of response normally works well, if people get over their initial fear. As a backup, be prepared to turn the tables and ask questions yourself. You could ask, "Won't you get in trouble for asking me questions that have nothing to do with my work? Why am I here instead of working? Why can't I have one of my friends here as a witness?"

If the campaign is out in the open you might say, "Yes, I'm working for the union campaign, do you have a problem with this?" Or, play dumb and say, "My husband (or my friend) says this happened to him and I shouldn't talk without a lawyer."

Always try to complete your notes immediately after the meeting so that you have a good record of the interview.

Taping the interview is another method that has worked in some places. The inside person co-ordinating the campaign carries a pocket tape recorder at all times. When committee members are called in for an interview they take the tape recorder along. If the boss objects to having the meeting recorded, the committee member takes out the notebook and says, nicely, "Pardon me, I didn't quite get what you said?" It works. Management is less aggressive and more careful.

For further details on whether conduct in these meetings may be an unfair labour practice, see Chapter 13.

KEEPING UP THE MOMENTUM

If your campaign is more than a couple of weeks long, you'll probably find that there's a slow period, a lull following the rush of enthusiasm when people are first signing cards.

It will seem like everyone is asking how many cards are signed. Some will simply be excited and impatient. Some supporters will begin to worry about whether the union will have the support it needs. If management staff know about the union, they will want to find out the numbers so that they can tell the employer and try to arrange a raise or promotion for the person passing on valuable information to them.

This is the time to contact the people who are undecided: people who are afraid, those who say they are neutral, and those who want more information. You can also make an extra effort with the group who have told committee members they're leaning towards the union. Tell them now's the time to add their name to the count.

This is a difficult time. The committee should meet regularly to exchange tips and ideas, and for inspiration and support. Let other employees know that you're well-informed about how campaigns work, and that people are signing up just as you expected.

Sometimes you need to decide to go public and do something to encourage the undecided people. In one large plant where the campaign was dragging on, the committee decided to have a union T-shirt day. They chose a Friday so that they had the weekend to recover if it was a failure. The day was carefully planned, committee members had the shirts in their lockers and began distributing them in the morning. As expected, the foreman began writing down the names of people who were wearing the union shirts, but so many workers put on the union shirts that he couldn't keep up. The open show of support and management's confusion were just what the organizing committee needed to bring in enough cards to apply for automatic certification.

Sometimes a bold action like this one gets more support than you expect. There are risks in being so public, but people don't feel alone. It can give employees a tremendous sense of confidence.

In the drive to organize Eaton's in 1948, union supporters passed out paper bags containing five peanuts ("Don't Work For Peanuts") to employees on their way into work. The gimmick gave people a good laugh together, and an easy way to begin a conversation about poor wages. The union also gave out helium balloons to children and then enjoyed the manager's dismay as he tried to get the balloons, marked with the union's name, down from the ceiling.

Old Cards

The Labour Board calculates the "age" of union cards from the date each card is signed. Cards that are more than a year old aren't valid, and are known as "stale cards." The Labour Board won't include cards that are between six months and one year old in the count to decide on granting automatic certification, but does include them in the count to decide whether or not to order a representation vote.

If you're applying for certification with cards that are more than six months old, consider asking the people who signed these cards to sign new, up-to-date cards.

DECIDING WHETHER TO STOP THE CAMPAIGN

A good organizing committee has a timetable and sets specific goals. Examples are deciding how many names and addresses to collect before beginning or how many cards to sign in the first week. Other measures might be how many people you'll need to contact each employee individually or how long you expect to take to sign up 35, 40, 55 percent and so on. These targets can't be set in stone, but are a useful way to measure how you're doing.

Occasionally, a campaign just doesn't seem to be working the way you expected. Signposts like those mentioned above can help committee members evaluate how they're doing. Other questions to consider include: How strong is your organizing committee? Are people solid in their support, or are they wavering or uneasy about the campaign? Look at situations that affect the numbers of employees you're working with. Is the employer doing a lot of hiring of new employees? Are people you had hoped you could count on quitting and moving on? Is the holiday season coming where things are sure to slack off?

If the committee's working with a union organizer, then his or her experience will help you judge whether you should stop because you've miscalculated the support for a union, or whether you simply misjudged the time and work involved in getting people to find their courage and sign up. If you've misjudged the time and work involved, carry on.

If support for the union isn't strong enough, you may decide to stop the campaign.

If you decide to stop the campaign, do so with your heads up. Send everyone who signed a card a thank you letter. If the campaign's been public, send a letter to each employee or circulate a flyer, explaining the decision and letting everyone know that a union will come at another, better, time.

Don't discard the information you've collected. Put it in a safe place, so you have it on hand when the time is ripe to try again.

THE HOME STRETCH!

When you decide on when to put your application in to the Labour Board, you must take into account how much support there is for the union, and also the degree of present and potential opposition from your employer.

The degree of support for the union and the strength of the employer's opposition to the union are directly linked. That's why most organizers want to keep the campaign secret. If between 35 and 40 percent of your co-workers have signed cards and the employer doesn't know about the campaign, then you'll want to continue to aim for more than 55 percent before you put in the application. On the other hand, if you're just under 40 percent and the employer's putting out scary stuff, then you may want to put in the application and try for a representation vote quickly.

If you decide not to take the automatic certification route, remember that it can take many weeks between the time you submit your application and the time the Board orders and conducts a representation vote. The more time employers have to send personal letters to employees, to post information against the union, and to campaign against the union, the more likely employees are to vote against the union.[17] The workplace is the employer's territory, it's his ground, and many workers are afraid. Even though a vote is secret and conducted by a labour board official, employees often think that the boss will know how they marked their ballot. (Page 98 describes what the Board may do, depending upon the percentage of signed cards, and Chapter 10 tells how to submit your application.)

VICTORY

Unionists describe the day they get the good news that the Labour Board has certified their new bargaining unit as one of the happiest in their lives. However you decide to celebrate your victory, remember that your task is to build an effective bargaining unit. Be joyful, yes, but immediately begin working to include everyone, especially those who stood on the sidelines. Send a welcoming letter or leaflet to each employee, explaining what's going to happen next. Sometimes employees who argued against the union turn out to be good union leaders, once they have the protection of the union and don't have to rely entirely on the boss's approval to get along.

> NEVER PLAN A DRIVE THAT RUNS THROUGH THE
> CHRISTMAS SEASON, ESPECIALLY WHERE THERE'RE
> WOMEN WORKERS. THEY'RE TOO BUSY. YOU LOSE
> TWO OR THREE WEEKS, AND THERE GOES ANY
> MOMENTUM YOU'VE ESTABLISHED.
>
> IF YOU HAVEN'T GOT THE CARDS IN THREE MONTHS, HAVE
> THE COURAGE TO WALK AWAY. DON'T LET IT DRAG ON.
>
> SIX WEEKS. IF YOU CAN'T DO IT IN SIX WEEKS
> IN A SMALL WORKPLACE, YOU HAVEN'T GOT IT.
>
> WE HAD 48 PER CENT OF THE PEOPLE SIGNED UP
> AND THEN THE COMPANY STATED PUTTING OUT SCARY
> STUFF. SO WE PUT IN OUR APPLICATION AND WENT FOR
> THE AUTOMATIC VOTE. IT CUT DOWN ON THE TIME
> THE COMPANY HAD TO INTIMIDATE PEOPLE.
> SEVENTY PER CENT VOTED YES.
>
> WHEN THE NOTICE CAME FROM THE BOARD SAYING THE
> UNION HAD APPLIED FOR A CERTIFICATE PEOPLE WERE
> SCARED. THEY DIDN'T KNOW WHAT IT MEANT. THEN THE
> EMPLOYER TOOK THE NOTICE DOWN. ALERT PEOPLE TO
> WATCH FOR THE NOTICE, AND MAKE SURE IT STAYS UP.

◆

CHAPTER SIX

THE CAMPAIGN:
MANAGEMENT
REACTIONS

IF YOUR COMMITTEE has decided to ask for "voluntary recognition," your employer will be someone who respects and under-
stands the role of unions. This chapter describes what to expect
from employers who are against unions. This chapter outlines:

• ways management reacts to organizing

• advice anti-union consultants give to employers

• what supervisors can and can't do during a campaign

• how to keep a record of problems with management

• letters you can expect from the boss

• how to deal with anti-union employees

Be prepared. Experienced organizers learn to expect the unexpected. If your organizing committee can predict what's likely to
happen, you can take some of the sting out of your employer's anti-
union drive.

If you know that the supervisors have probably been given a
list of questions and answers to try out at coffee breaks, then you
can warn co-workers to be wary of supervisors bearing doughnuts.

If you expect management to send a letter about union dues

and strikes, then your committee can act first and put out its own information.

This chapter will help your committee tailor an overall strategy to your workplace, and it will help you anticipate daily events.

Refer to Chapter 13 for advice on what to do if you think your employer is breaking the law.

WHAT WILL MANAGEMENT DO?

There are exceptions, but nine times out of ten a union will want to keep an organizing drive a secret from the employer for as long as possible, ideally until just after it files the application for certification.

A study in the United States shows that the earlier an employer finds out about an organizing drive, the less probable it is that the union will win. This is because employers often fight unions by creating a climate of fear in the workplace. The more time they have to do that, the more difficult it is for employees.[1] Labour laws are different in Canada, but there are tough and nasty employers (as well as good ones) on both sides of the border. The authors of *Confessions of a Union-Buster* estimate that in the United States "At a billing rate of $1,000 to $1,500 a day per consultant and $300 to $700 an hour for attorneys, the war on organized labor is a $1 billion-plus industry."[2]

Deciding when you're ready for your employer to know you're unionizing is an important part of your organizing committee's plan. You should also be prepared in case your employer discovers what you're doing before you want him to.

Some employers don't believe it when they hear rumours that their employees are talking about a union. When they hear the news for certain, some employers are upset, some are astonished, and some try to carry on as usual. Others push the panic button. Some will immediately think of how a union may affect profits and budgets, how a strike could affect customers, whether head office will fire them.

No matter how the boss reacts, once the campaign becomes public you can expect some kind of opposition from management.

Even if it's silent, you'll feel it in the air. If you've kept your campaign secret and the first time your employer hears about it is when the notice from the Labour Board arrives, you can be sure he will phone a lawyer immediately.

> WE PREPARE THEM ABOUT WHAT THE COMPANY'S GOING TO SAY. THEN WHEN THE COMPANY SENDS THE STUFF AROUND IT'S ALREADY FAMILIAR. NO SURPRISES.
>
> ONCE YOU'VE GOT 20 CARDS SIGNED, YOU CAN BE SURE THE BOSS IS GOING TO KNOW. PEOPLE TALK.
>
> THEY PLAY UPON WOMEN IN PARTICULAR WITH A WHOLE GUILT SYNDROME THAT YOU ARE PART OF A FAMILY AND THAT YOU ARE DISLOYAL.
>
> THE EMPLOYER WAS VERY CLEVER, VERY SOPHISTICATED. THEY OPERATED JUST WITHIN THE FRAMEWORK OF THE LAW, RIGHT ON THE EDGE. SUBTLE INTIMIDATION, ALL THOSE THINGS THEY'RE NOT SUPPOSED TO DO. I SPENT HALF MY TIME RUNNING TO OUR LAWYER.

MANAGEMENT TYPES

Managers, supervisors, foremen, nursing directors, administrators, presidents — all have different personalities and different ways of dealing with people on the job. Some are more decent than others. Management personnel will have individual and different reactions to the idea of a union. You may have to deal with many layers of bosses, and you may find that some are sympathetic and some are strongly opposed to what you're doing.

Whatever these individuals might think, the employer will usually direct the way the firm or agency or factory will respond as an institution. Usually that response is in character; it fits with the way the organization has been managed all along.

Here are three management "types" that you might see during an organizing drive. Your boss may be like one of them.

ALL IN THE FAMILY

Some employers respond like hurt parents. They are often unaware of problems and just assume that employees feel like part of one big family. Sometimes these employers do very little to counter an organizing drive. They may sit back and watch because they can't believe that their employees will really get together in a union. They're sure that in the end everyone (except a troublemaker or two) will agree that father knows best.

They may put out gentle reminders. The management of one office supply company sent a letter to each employee listing all the benefits of working for the company, including the "FAMILY ATMOSPHERE."

They may hint that all the benefits they've given to employees could disappear overnight with a union.

An employer who's been throwing his weight around like big daddy may repent, for the moment anyway. One furniture chain store executive posted a typical memo: "...employees are voicing their displeasure by joining a union.... It is disappointing that this is happening to us as retaliation for the fact that we have made a few mistakes.... I am asking those employees to not sign a union card just because you want to get even with us for our mistakes.... I don't think any of us is perfect."

This company arranged "breakfast with the boss" meetings for employees, and promised to bring in the supplies the employees had requested months before. A sudden flurry of promises and improvements is normal, but most organizations revert back to the old ways if the threat of a union goes away.

A business column about employee focus groups recounts one consultant's advice to make "one highly-visible change" soon after holding a focus group. The consultant observed, "Unfortunately, some companies follow up focus groups by developing communications programs designed more to convince employees everything is all right...."[3]

THE BALLISTIC BOSS

This employer will go to any lengths, even break the law, to keep employees isolated and frightened. Unfair labour practices seem more likely to happen in organizations that employ recent immigrants and pay minimum wage or less.

One expert on unions and management says that these aggressive anti-union bosses may be "driven by ideology and emotion rather than rational reflection."[4] They're used to being King of the Castle, 110 percent in control, and don't want to give up even a shred of their power.

The ballistic boss puts the organization on full alert, ordering managers to clamp down on all employees. He knows people are afraid and he's used to getting his way. Employers like this will do anything to cause delays and wear people down.

You need lots of courage and a union lawyer to deal with this type. The best strategy is to keep the campaign secret for as long as possible, and to take notes and keep detailed records of any problems with supervisors. (See page 143, "Report of Incident.")

Employers who try to fire workers who support the union have two goals in mind. First, they want to get rid of activists, and second, they want to use the firing to scare other workers away from the thought of organizing.

It's against the law to fire people for union activity, but in the past employers in Ontario have risked breaking the law because they could count on the Labour Board taking months to hear a union complaint. Now the 1993 changes in the law mean that a union can get a quick hearing and decision when someone's fired during an organizing drive. The union may also get an interim order within a week that says the employer must take the person back to work while the Board is making its decision.[5]

SMART AND SYSTEMATIC

The third type is the employer who's invested time and effort in being prepared. While the others have only a short-term strategy to fight the union, he's got a long-term plan too.

He's paid for professional advice from management lawyers

and human resource consultants. He's tried the newest personnel management techniques, quality circles, management by objectives, process mapping, focus groups, attitude surveys, total quality management. He says he's using "positive employee relations" that guarantee a union-free environment.[6]

He's sure he's done everything in his power to keep things going his way, and so he's astonished and angry when he hears about the union. But he takes the professionals' advice and doesn't over-react. He calls his lawyer who will be in the background every step of the way during your campaign.

He's weeded out prospective supervisors who might be pro-union. The supervisors are going to be the centrepiece in this employer's response. They've been trained to keep him informed about what's going on. They know to ask leading questions like, "How are things going?" and "Anything bothering you?" They're going to be friendly, they'll join you for coffee, and they'll be very good listeners. Be wary.

AN AD FOR ANTI-UNION WORKSHOP

$795 : POSITIVE EMPLOYEE RELATIONS
FOR THE UNION-FREE WORKPLACE

"It is a timely opportunity to train, sensitize, motivate and arm key members of your management team with the tools they require to keep the workforce on side...a systematic, methodical and comprehensive approach."[7]

WAYS TO KEEP OUT UNIONS

Employers who attend seminars about keeping a union-free workplace trade stories and get advice from management lawyers and consultants. Your employer may have tried some of these suggestions on WAYS TO KEEP OUT UNIONS:

Distribute an employee handbook. Outline the rules using pleasant language. Design the handbook to look like a union contract. Use a personalized computer letter to remind employees about how much their benefits cost the company. Have a real open door policy. Walk about and keep in touch with your staff. Post a "seniority list" with names and dates, then workers will be happy because they will think they have seniority. Do a survey to detect problems. (One survey can even provide the employer with data by using a "diagnostic alienation scale" that is supposed to warn when employees are thinking about a union.) Send birthday cards and flowers. Invite staff to special breakfast, lunch or dinner meetings with the boss. Organize sports or social activities. Get them drunk and then listen to what they say. Use information from the company's counselling program. The employees think the counsellor's neutral and don't seem to understand that she is really management. Set up an employee committee to discuss problems. Set up your own Employee Complaint Feedback Mechanism.

UNION AVOIDANCE PLAN APPROACH

One large department store has an anti-union plan with written advice for supervisors. Your union committee may want to keep their advice in mind and watch for managers who are watching you! This "Union Avoidance Plan Approach" instructs supervisors to meet regularly with staff, to encourage lots of questions, to post minutes of meetings along with notation of actions taken within 48 hours, to be on the alert for new leaders among employees, to watch for employees who stop talking when a supervisor or manager approaches, and, finally, to watch for employees acting very busy or excited at break times or at meal periods, employees who were previously "relaxed and aimless."

THE LAW AND YOUR SUPERVISOR

Just as you and the union have to follow the rules when you're organizing, the employer and management must also follow certain rules while you are campaigning. Watch for unfair labour practices.

The law says that the employer, and that includes all management people, including your supervisor, can't threaten, intimidate or coerce, or use undue influence to keep employees from joining a union.[8] See Chapter 13 and Appendices E and F for further details on unfair labour practices and filing procedures at the Labour Board.

What A Supervisor Can't Do

A supervisor can't question you about your feelings about a union, or ask whether you've joined or are thinking of joining.

A supervisor can't ask about union meetings or activities.

A supervisor can't call someone into the office to talk about the union, unless that person asks for the meeting.

A supervisor can't spy on someone who's taking part in union activities.

A supervisor can't give employees who support a union the dirty work as punishment.

A supervisor can't discipline a union supporter for doing something employees who don't support the union also do but get away with.

A supervisor can't put all the union supporters in the same work area to keep them from talking to other workers.

A supervisor can't visit employees in their homes to talk about the union.

A supervisor can't promise wage increases or other benefits if employees won't join, or say they might lose benefits if they're for the union.

A supervisor can't tell you the organization will close down, or lay people off, or say that management will refuse to deal with a union if the employees choose to organize.

A supervisor can't help or even encourage employees who are organizing against a union.

A supervisor can't ban ordinary union buttons from the workplace if jewellery and buttons are normally allowed.

WHAT CAN A SUPERVISOR DO?

Under the law the employer, and that means all management
people, including supervisors, can tell employees what they think
about a union so long as the employer doesn't use threats or undue
influence.[9]

The employer can make a pitch for the company or organization, and say how good the working conditions are. He can guess
the questions about the union that might be on your mind, and
give you his own answers. The employer can call a meeting. But he
can't pressure or force you to attend the meeting or make you listen
to his opinion. The Board has found such "captive audience" meetings to be illegal.

Management can tell you their opinions about the downside of
union membership, for example, that you have to pay dues. They
may say they don't think unions are really democratic because not
everybody bothers to attend membership meetings.

The employer can give you a new benefit or a raise during an
organizing drive, and some do. (If only talking about a union can
get you a raise, think of what really having a union might do!) The
employer can increase your benefits, start to hold monthly, or
weekly, or daily meetings to solve problems. Problems that have
irritated employees for years sometimes get resolved almost the
minute an organizing drive begins. However, once you apply for
certification, the *Labour Relations Act* states that the employer can't
alter workplace conditions without union consent.[10]

The employer can tell you that he treats each and every person
fairly, without bias or favouritism. The employer can remind you
that unions don't create jobs, companies and organizations do.
Management can tell you the door is always open, though you can't
be sure if it's open for you to come in for a talk, or whether there's
a hint there about showing you the door.

THE SUPERVISOR IS THE KEY

Consultants tell employers that the supervisor is the key to
preventing unions and to stopping a campaign once it begins.
From the union's point of view, understanding the role of the

supervisor can help you plan a more effective campaign.

One anti-union consultant tells employers to deal with supervisors by weeding out any pro-union supervisors. He advises that a new supervisor may be confused because he's still loyal to his former co-workers, and suggests employers give their supervisors special management training so that they learn to identify with management, and not with their beer-drinking buddies. Also, employers must teach supervisors what it will mean to them to have a union. Finally he says, "A successful union organizing campaign usually means that there have been personnel relations problems in the store — frequently attributable to one or more managers. Where the manager cannot learn to improve his people management skills he/she may need to be replaced."[11]

He says that if that fails, and the employees are signing union cards then further action is necessary. If an employer doesn't have confidence in the mental abilities of supervisors, then he should muzzle them during an organizing drive. He warns that if supervisors are silent, employees may think they approve of the campaign. So, employers must prepare supervisors to answer employees' coffee-time questions. One idea is to keep a file of press clippings with unfavourable stories about unions. Hand them around and discuss them with employees. Seek the testimonial of the former union member who has become disenchanted with the union perhaps because of plant closures, lay-offs, strikes. Supervisors should try to find out what's on the other guy's mind and ask, "What is it about unions that interests you? their leadership? strikes? their promises?" If the employee wants a frank discussion about unions, the supervisor should not bad mouth the union, but, rather, show that union organizers often promise a lot more than union negotiators actually deliver.

> LETTERS FROM THE BOSS? WE OFTEN HAVE A LEAFLET
> READY TO GO OUT BY THE NEXT DAY. MAYBE ON SOME-
> THING DIFFERENT. BUT OUT RIGHT AWAY. IT'S A REMINDER
> THE UNION'S THERE AND NOT AFRAID.

KEEPING RECORDS OF PROBLEMS WITH MANAGEMENT

THE INCIDENT REPORT FORM

The organizing committee needs a way to keep track of problems from management during a campaign in case it needs to file a complaint with the Labour Board. *[New]* In Ontario when you file a complaint, you must file all of the information you want to use for a hearing at the same time that you file the complaint. Keeping a record of questionable comments and events will:

- remind management that there are rules they must follow

- allow you to record details while they're fresh in your mind

- keep a record until the committee can get legal advice after work

- be a written record the union can use if it decides to file an unfair labour practice charge at the Labour Board

If a union organizer or other union staff person is helping with your campaign, the committee should tell him or her about an incident the same day that it happens.

REPORT OF INCIDENT

1. Date of Incident   *February 4, 1994*
2. Time of Incident   *10 a.m.*
3. Location of Incident   *Cafeteria*
4. Description of what happened *Supervisor told Maria Brown he'd block her promotion if the union got in*
5. Who acted improperly *Dave Snipe, supervisor*
6. Names and phone numbers of people who were there (witnesses) *Tony Lee 765-4321 Helen Hew 876-5432*

     Your signature *Tony Lee*
     Date recorded *February 4, 1994*

MESSAGES FROM THE BOSS

THE THIRD PARTY LINE

Employers like to say that forming a union means bringing an outside "third party" into the workplace. The three parties, they say, are the employer and the employees who are the insiders, and then the union, the outsider. They use this argument over and over again, suggesting that if you choose to have a union you'll have two bosses to contend with, the union, as well as the employer. They say that the union's trying to do something to you, like levy dues or impose a strike.

A union is not an outside "third party." In the workplace, the union is the employees united, who have chosen to deal with the employer with one voice. Employees in a union are insiders who have chosen to work together.

Employers most often use the "third party" line in personal letters to each employee, warning them that having a union means management will no longer be able to deal with employees one-on-one as individuals.

What worries people about this "warning" is how it implies that having a union means there won't be any flexibility for employees in times of personal or family emergencies. That's not so. Having a union can mean that leave for special circumstances is built into the contract so that everyone (and not just certain favourites) is treated fairly. Having a union can also mean having a steward to help you make your case when a problem arises.

LETTERS DURING YOUR CAMPAIGN

You can expect a flurry of memos and letters from your employer at every step of your organizing campaign.

Anti-union consultants warn employers to avoid meetings and debates with union supporters. Question and answer sessions are dangerous, too, they say. Why? Because management might get stuck with questions they don't know how to answer, and because there's a real risk of embarrassment. Written communication is safer, and cheaper, too, because employees don't lose any time from work.

One management consultant told an anti-union seminar that he keeps 25 sample letters for his employer clients to send. He advised participants to be careful who signs the letter, to use the person who has the most credibility with employees. Better to have a popular supervisor sign than the distant big shot at the top.[12]

He told participants to send three letters: the first letter is sent as soon as they hear that employees are signing union cards. The idea is to bring the campaign out into the open immediately. This letter should warn employees that the union will say almost everyone's signed and that that's not true. His advice to them was not to deal with the issues. "Three times out of four this letter kills the campaign" because then the workers think the union is conning them.

He advised employers that if they have to do another letter they should use a question and answer format to keep out of legal trouble. (Question: "What can I do if union supporters bother me?" Answer: "Report it to a supervisor.") He suggested writing only one page, using short sentences, and saving the ammunition for letter number three.

In the third letter, the consultant advised, employers should talk about strikes. (Question: "What difference does it make to the company if the union is certified?" Answer: "Production and your pay could be stopped because of a strike.") And to tell employees that unions are like politicians, they make promises they can't keep.

THE LAST LETTER FROM THE BOSS

If the Labour Board orders a representation vote, expect to get another letter right from the top. This is a good reason to aim to get a majority of employees to sign cards so that you can get automatic certification. If there is a vote, employers will often send out personal letters to each worker just before the day of the vote. There are some common themes that employers use in this last letter.

One theme is that voting day is one of the most important

dates in your life, and that you can make your decision by secret ballot.

Another describes the union as a third party and asks the employees whether they want to be represented by the union or if they want to deal directly "with us through our open door." The employer warns that if employees vote to unionize, the employer can't deal with their "particular needs and problems in the informal, flexible and personal way which has thus far worked well."

Often there's a message about union dues. "Only management can grant wage and benefit increases. The union won't represent you for nothing. It needs your money to operate."

Finally, the last letter urges everyone to vote. "Don't let others make a decision for you.... The decision you make can change your relationship with us forever."

Tell your co-workers to expect this letter and that it will be slanted to portray unions as outsiders, rather than as your own organization. The employer wants to convince those who are indifferent or undecided to defeat the union by voting "no."

If the letter is coercive or intimidating you may be able to get the Labour Board to order your employer to withdraw it. Chapter 5 makes suggestions about letters your committee can send before the vote to counteract management's influence.

DEALING WITH HECKLERS

If your campaign is public, be prepared to deal with situations — in a coffee shop, in the cafeteria, at a public meeting — where someone tries to pick a nasty argument with you.

People express their opposition forcefully for different reasons. How you handle these conflicts depends on the situation and on your quick assessment of what the real problem is.[13]

Some people just have a critical perspective on everything. Their challenge may be a sign of a lively mind, even though it sounds like trouble for you. (They often make good stewards!)

Some opponents may be afraid they'll lose the little control they do have over their work day, that union bosses are going to come and take away their flex-time, or take them out on strike. Or some may feel the burden of family responsibilities, and fear deeply for their jobs and the future. For them, the union's just one more unknown to reckon with.

Others may be making speeches that they hope management will hear about, a desperate signal that they're on the side of the boss.

No matter what the motivation of the person who is challenging you, others will be judging your reaction. How you react will be a sign about how the union responds to differences.

SUGGESTIONS FOR DEALING WITH CONFLICT AND HECKLERS

1. Always give the person the benefit of the doubt.

2. Don't belittle the person.

3. Be alert to the "real" question or problem on his or her mind.

4. Choose one point to answer, and do so in a concise way, and move on to the next person or the next item on the agenda.

5. Try not to be defensive.

6. Agree to disagree.

7. The question being asked in an antagonistic way may be the one that's holding back a potential union supporter. Answer the question respectfully.

8. Look for agreement on the process, on the next step. "Can people agree that we'll have two more questions and then break for coffee?"

9. Diversion. Say you'd be happy to take time after the meeting to have a lengthy discussion. Or suggest that the person go to the back with someone from the committee during the break.

10. If you don't know the answer, say so, and arrange to find out or have someone else contact the person as soon as possible.

11. Remember that if the organizing drive is successful, the opponents will still be alive and well. Try to answer in a way that includes, rather than excludes them and their fears. Your union will be their union too.

ANTI-UNION EMPLOYEES

Don't be surprised if a group of employees who oppose the union post a memo or send a letter to all employees. Their letter will have many of the same themes as information put out by management. It's sometimes hard to see any difference.

They'll assert that they're not afraid to stand up and be counted, and sign their names at the bottom of the letter for all to see, especially for the employer to note.

Don't answer these letters with more letters. It's you who should choose the issues to debate. Just be open and upfront about what unions can and can't do when you're talking with people. Employees who sign letters like this will probably never support an organizing drive. Leave them alone and concentrate on the people who haven't made up their minds yet.

Another thing that may appear at your workplace is a sheet of paper listing 13 "guidelines for employees opposed to union organization drives." It's obviously been put together by a company lawyer, but begins with this warning: "First and foremost, employee activities directed against trade unions must not be, nor perceived to be, prompted, authorized or condoned by the Company." It reads like a pep talk to encourage anti-union workers to speak out against the union. It also tells employees they "can report any union attempts to threaten, coerce, bribe or intimidate employees into signing union cards to the Labour Board." This is a good reminder for organizers not to pressure people into signing cards.

GREAT CHANGES, GREAT CHALLENGES

To organize a union is no "little thing." It means great changes and challenges for employers. Why do employers get so upset? The stakes are big. Having a union means that employees have more power over their daily working lives. With a union the employer no longer has complete and absolute control.

Some employers will fight your efforts, as if you don't have a right to organize. But whether or not you join a union is none of their business. You don't have a say, or even care, if your employer joins the Chamber of Commerce, the Business Council on National Issues, or a central service association. Your decision to join a union should be no different.

> AS SOON AS SOMEBODY ASKS YOU ABOUT DUES YOU KNOW
> THEY GOT THE QUESTION FROM THE COMPANY. THEY
> NEVER ASK ABOUT DUES UNTIL THEY GET THAT LETTER!
>
> WE CALL THEM 'RUNNERS.' THE ONES WHO TELL THE BOSS
> EVERYTHING. ONCE WE PRINTED JUST ONE LEAFLET AND
> MAILED IT TO THE RUNNER. NEXT DAY MANAGEMENT
> PUT OUT A LETTER TO EVERYONE ABOUT THE LEAFLET.
> THE REST OF THE WORKERS SAID, WHAT'S ALL THIS,
> WHAT ARE THEY SO UPSET ABOUT?
>
> ONE ANTI-UNION GROUP WAS CALLED STOP THE
> UNION NOW — STUN — VERY APPROPRIATELY
> SPELLED NUTS BACKWARDS.

◆

CHAPTER SEVEN

THE ONTARIO LABOUR
RELATIONS BOARD

A LABOUR BOARD has the role of enforcing the rules found in labour legislation that specify when and how employees can unionize and that protect the rights of employees and their unions during and after unionization. In Ontario, this legislation is called the *Labour Relations Act* and the board is called the Ontario Labour Relations Board.

Ontario's Labour Board was established in 1944, when the *Labour Relations Act* first came into effect. From that time forward companies had to accept and bargain with certified unions, and employees who wanted to form unions had to follow a defined set of rules. So even though workers had gained the right to organize under the law, that same law limited their powers.[1]

One of the rights that workers gained was the right to have their complaints heard at a Labour Board hearing. The members of the Board who are responsible for hearing cases are a neutral chair and alternate chair and vice-chairs, and members appointed to represent the employer and employee point of view.

The Board has the power to decide on such issues as union certification, whether a representation vote should be ordered, unfair labour practices, first contract arbitration, and unlawful lockouts and strikes. A ruling by the Labour Board is usually final.

In making decisions, the Labour Board must follow the *Labour Relations Act*. However, the Act gives Board members a fair amount

151

of leeway to use their own special knowledge to help them decide what needs to be done to make sure the Act is not violated.

Although the Labour Board is set up as an independent tribunal and functions as an independent body, the provincial government does fund the Board, appoints the decision-makers to the Board, and sets and amends the law. This gives the government a way of influencing the decisions and operations of the Board.

The Labour Board does, however, set its own practices and procedures. Detailed Rules of Procedure and Practice Notes govern how cases are dealt with and what forms must be used.[2] A new set of Rules was issued in January 1993 that changed many of the Board's procedures. You can obtain a copy of the Rules, the Practice Notes, and the forms from the Board. Since these documents can change frequently, make sure you get up-to-date copies from the Board.

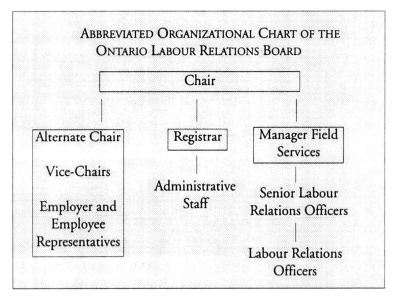

ABBREVIATED ORGANIZATIONAL CHART OF THE
ONTARIO LABOUR RELATIONS BOARD

Chair

Alternate Chair

Vice-Chairs

Employer and
Employee
Representatives

Registrar

Administrative
Staff

Manager Field
Services

Senior Labour
Relations Officers

Labour Relations
Officers

WHERE IS THE LABOUR BOARD?

Ontario's Labour Board is in Toronto. The Board may schedule a hearing outside Toronto if that is more convenient for everyone involved and if its budget allows the expenditure. Many kinds of hearings may only be heard in Toronto. If you feel it is very important that the hearing be held in your area, then it is a good idea to include a few arguments in favour of that request in your application. For example, you can demonstrate the inconvenience and cost of coming to Toronto by listing the number of your witnesses who would have to travel or by pointing out the lack of overnight child care, and so on.

LABOUR BOARD ORGANIZATION AND HOW IT WORKS

THE REGISTRAR

The Registrar and her staff handle all the applications for union certification and supervise representation votes if they are necessary. All the paper work regarding certification is sent to the Registrar. She also sets hearing dates, decides other administrative matters, and deals with special requests.

EMPLOYEES WITH DISABILITIES

If you are disabled and find that the Labour Board is not accessible to either you or your disabled co-workers, contact the Registrar and ask her to accommodate your needs where possible. For example, you can ask that the Act and Rules be sent to you on an audio tape if the written material cannot be understood.

INTERPRETERS

If you need an interpreter for a witness at a hearing, contact the Registrar.

LABOUR RELATIONS OFFICERS

The Labour Relations Officers work in the Field Services Department. They attempt to settle disputes between the employees and their employer that are related to the *Labour Relations Act*. They may also be asked to conduct fact findings about issues such as appropriateness of the bargaining unit, or whether an employee's in a managerial job.

THE DECISION-MAKERS AND
THE DECISION MAKING PROCESS

The people who make the decisions about your case are called the adjudicators. They are composed of the chair and alternate chair, the vice-chairs, who are mostly lawyers, and an equal number of employee and employer representatives, sometimes referred to as members.[3] These adjudicators are appointed by the government and work full-time or part-time.

Cases are usually heard by a panel of three of these adjudicators — the chair, alternate chair or one of the vice-chairs, an employee representative, and an employer representative. A majority vote decides the case.[4]

A hearing can be oral, where you attend before the panel, or non-oral, where your application is decided by this group without an oral hearing and on the basis of the written material filed with the Board.

There are certain cases the chair or a vice-chair may hear alone, such as expedited unfair labour practice hearings. This can also happen for other cases if the parties agree or where there is the possibility of undue delay or other prejudice.[5]

When an oral hearing is scheduled in Toronto, it is held at the Labour Board's offices in a room set up to look like an informal courtroom. The panel hearing the case listens to witnesses and considers the arguments from the parties about what should be done to solve a problem.

During the hearing, the Board will only accept the oral testimony of witnesses and decides the case based on the evidence it hears. Therefore, you will have to be ready to bring forward the witnesses and documents that you need. Remember that your witnesses cannot just sign a document stating their evidence and not come to the hearing. They must be present. (See Chapter 12 for further details on what happens at a hearing.)

APPLICATIONS FOR CERTIFICATION

Most applications for certification are decided without the need of an oral hearing. This is because of the Board's Waiver Program and the pre-hearing Labour Relations Officer meeting. A Waiver Officer or Labour Relations Officer helps employees and employers settle any disagreements between them so that an oral hearing is not necessary.

Once the Labour Board has received all the evidence and documentation it needs to make a decision about an application, it has the power to decide whether or not to certify based on the written materials filed with it.

THE DECISIONS

For the most part, the Labour Board's decisions are final — for both oral hearings and non-oral hearings.[6] Occasionally the Labour Board agrees to reconsider a case, particularly when there is newly discovered evidence.[7] Sometimes it is possible to go outside the Labour Board to the courts on limited questions of law.

The Labour Board does not have to follow the decisions it has made in the past, but it usually does because it tries to apply the law consistently so that everyone knows what rules they have to follow.

If you want to get an idea of the decision the Labour Board might make about your union campaign, you can read the cases listed in the endnotes at the back of this book that discuss the problems your union may have at the Board. You can find these decisions at the Labour Board's library or at any law school in Ontario. Unions often have a set of the decisions as well.

Ontario Labour Relations Board, Law and Practice, by J. Sack and C.M. Mitchell, and *The Annotated Ontario Labour Relations Act, 1993,* by Daniel Randazzo, also provide summaries of cases that have been heard by the Labour Board.

ENSURING THAT THE LABOUR BOARD IS EFFECTIVE

[New] The 1993 amendments to the *Labour Relations Act* have given the Labour Board a new mandate (contained in the "preamble" at the beginning of the Act) to interpret the *Labour Relations Act* in a more pro-active way.[8] Overall, this means any decision, rule, or procedure of the Board should be judged by whether it helps more employees to engage in collective bargaining and removes barriers facing employees.

Using the preamble, you can argue that the Board should decide any issue in your case so that:

1. workers in your workplace can freely exercise their right to organize by protecting their right to choose, join and be represented by a trade union of their choice and to participate in its lawful activities;

2. workers are encouraged to engage in collective bargaining that will give them

   • a better chance to negotiate terms and conditions of employment with their employer;

   • an opportunity to participate and co-operate with their employer, which will help everyone in the workplace adapt to changes, develop new skills, and promote productivity;

   • a better chance of avoiding harmful conflicts with their employer;

3. differences are resolved in an effective, fair, and speedy way.[9]

Union and community activists have criticized the Labour Board in the past for lengthy delays in hearing cases and making decisions, and for being too legalistic and complicated. For example, when people are fired illegally, delay in reinstating them in their jobs can result in the loss of valuable leadership at a critical stage in a campaign. Labour relations delayed is labour relations denied.[10]

A process which is not easily understood and not easy to use will not be effective. Procedures that favour legal technicalities over making a just decision will benefit company lawyers, who will use them to defeat the organizing drive.

The 1993 amendments and the Labour Board's new Rules, including the rules for expedited hearings and interim orders, have gone a long way towards solving some of the problems.[11] The new amendments give the Labour Board new powers that in turn can give workers a better chance at forming unions to represent them. But the Rules can restrict workers' powers. The Board's new Rules are not user-friendly. It is true that requiring those involved in a dispute to think out their case right at the beginning and to write down all the facts does encourage the employer to settle and may shorten hearings. But it also sets up many traps for inexperienced unions or union representatives who are not familiar with preparing detailed documentation and with following technical rules.

Because the Rules are so technical, it is more likely employers' lawyers will be called in and this often leads to more technicalities. The Rules should be fashioned so that non-lawyers are encouraged to file applications and present cases. By doing this the workers will be able to participate more fully in the unionization of their workplace.

Finally, employee representatives on the Labour Board have a role to play in keeping the Labour Board effective. As adjudicators, they need to maintain a strong union perspective and they should be active members of the panel during a hearing to try and make sure that management lawyers do not abuse witnesses or use delaying tactics. And, if they can't win the panel chair to their point of view, they must be prepared to write vigorous dissenting opinions that clearly state why they disagree with the decision. It is important to have these views on the record as they can influence future decisions and they will be helpful if the matter does go before the courts.

KEEPING UP THE PRESSURE

With such an important mandate, everyone has to keep pushing the Labour Board to make sure it operates to encourage and help employees to organize. The Labour Board has been trying harder to be more accessible. The Waiver Program is an important improvement which has meant that many employers and employees are able to define and agree on issues and reach settlements without the need for a hearing. But the Board still falls short of its goal. Its new Rules are very technical and may complicate the process even more than before.

> I'M NOT A LAWYER. I HANDLE MOST OF OUR UNION'S ORGANIZING CASES AT THE LABOUR BOARD. YOU JUST HAVE TO KNOW A FEW BASIC RULES. DON'T GET BOGGED DOWN IN LEGALESE, IT'S ONLY CAMOUFLAGE. MIND YOU, YOU HAVE TO PREPARE, SPEND TIME ON YOUR CASE.

♦

CHAPTER EIGHT

DEFINING THE BARGAINING UNIT: RULES AND GUIDELINES

IN THE END, certification of your union comes down to a matter of numbers, the number of members you have signed up and if you have enough members in the right job categories. The Labour Board must be satisfied that your union represents a sufficient number of workers for it to be certified as the bargaining agent for the group of workers. The Board's decision to automatically certify your union or to order a representation vote is based on the amount of support found amongst the workers in this group and on the types of jobs found in this group. Once certified, the employees in this group will be the only ones your union is entitled to represent.

In order to know whether or not it is time to file your application with the Board, you must know which employees are in this group and the total number of employees in this group.

This group is called the "appropriate bargaining unit." Bargaining unit is defined in the *Labour Relations Act* as "a unit of employees appropriate for collective bargaining, whether it is an employer unit or plant unit or a subdivision of both."[1] The Labour Board decides what the "appropriate bargaining unit" will be based on the rules set out in the Act and on the Labour Board's past decisions.[2]

Your application for certification must name the bargaining unit that you are proposing to represent. Even if you and your employer agree on the unit, the Labour Board can still order a different one.[3] Your employer must respond by naming its proposed bargaining unit.

In rare cases, where the evidence in support of each of two or more proposed bargaining units is so evenly balanced, the Labour Board may conduct a vote of the employees to find out what bargaining unit description they prefer.[4] This is different from a representation vote, which determines if all workers want a union.[5]

If the union and the company can agree on the description of the bargaining unit, the Board normally accepts that agreement unless it seriously violates the Act or Board policy. For example, the Labour Board could not agree to a unit including managerial employees.[6]

You will want to think about the kind of bargaining unit that will likely be approved by the Board even before you start organizing, so that you know who to sign up and how many to sign up.

Often, the union organizer your committee is working with will be able to help you determine the best bargaining unit for your union. It is not a clear-cut process. For example, if you include jobs in your proposed bargaining unit which end up being excluded, the Labour Board will not count the membership cards signed by workers in those jobs. This could lead to your membership numbers falling below the level required for automatic certification, forcing you into a representation vote, or leaving you with too low a number to even get a vote.

But you also have a problem if you have too few members. If the Labour Board includes more jobs than you planned to have in the bargaining unit, you may not have signed up enough members to be certified or to get a vote.

An additional complication is when employers, who want to defeat a union's certification, propose a different bargaining unit description in the hope that the union will not have sufficient numbers to fit that description. For example, the description may exclude workers whom employers suspect signed union cards and include professional employees who may be opposed to unionization.

As you can see, winning your certification means defining your bargaining unit with a good idea of which jobs the Labour Board will include in it. This chapter gives you the information on the Labour Board's rules and guidelines to help you make that decision.

For more help in deciding how to define your bargaining unit, check the back pages of the Labour Board's Monthly Report to see how other unions like yours have successfully defined their bargaining units.

DEFINING THE APPROPRIATE BARGAINING UNIT

Some of the Board's rules and guidelines that help determine an appropriate bargaining unit are set out in the *Labour Relations Act,* and others have been developed over the years by the Labour Board in its decisions that interpret what "appropriate" means.

How important each guideline will be depends on the Labour Board's view of each situation. As long as the union's proposed unit is appropriate, the Board will not investigate whether another narrower or broader unit is more appropriate.[7]

The 1993 amendments have changed many of the rules and policies that determine an "appropriate" unit. Since there have not been many decisions written under the new rules, it is not yet possible to say with any certainty what final approach the Board will likely take on these new amendments. It is important that you read up on the most recent cases to keep informed.

SHAPING COLLECTIVE BARGAINING

The Board looks at the appropriate bargaining unit description as an opportunity to set up the collective bargaining process. This may help avoid later labour relations problems.[8]

The Board asks itself the following question to determine the proposed unit's collective bargaining potential and, as a result, whether it is appropriate:

Does the unit which the union seeks to represent encompass

a group of employees with a sufficiently coherent community of interest that they can bargain together on a viable basis
without at the same time causing serious labour relations
problems for the employer?[9]

In simpler words, you must be prepared to answer the question, "Do employees in the group have enough in common to
bargain well together without causing their employer serious problems?" This is called the "Hospital for Sick Children Test" and was
first used to determine the appropriate unit for certain employees
at that Hospital when they applied for certification.

Where a union asks for an unusual unit, the Board tries to
balance the importance of letting employees organize with whom
they want and the need for a unit that can sustain collective
bargaining.[10]

COMMUNITY OF INTEREST

An appropriate bargaining unit includes all the employees who
share a "community of interest," or similar work issues or concerns.
You must show that the workers in your proposed bargaining unit
have a community of interest.

To do this, you must be able to persuade the Board that the
interests, skills, working conditions, and so on of the employees in
your proposed unit are similar enough to avoid disagreement over
contract demands and over how to administer the collective agreement. If employees disagree among themselves then they will not
be able to deal effectively with the employer.[11]

The Board's approach to assessing community of interest has
changed over the last number of years. The Board has increasingly
found that there can be a reasonable amount of diversity within a
bargaining unit before labour relations problems are caused.[12]

The Board now believes that all employees of the same
employer share a basic community of interest, although some
groups of employees within the workplace may have a greater
community of interest than others.

The question of how a workplace is organized is closely linked
to the community of interest issue. The Labour Board does not

usually allow a union to organize only one division or department of a company since there is usually a community of interest among employees in the various divisions or departments.[13]

BARGAINING HISTORY

The Labour Board also takes into account the fact that employees dealt with their employer or bargained as one unit or in separate groups in the past.[14] The Board knows that unions often conduct their organizing campaigns and base their proposed unit on what the Labour Board has said in the past. However, this will not stop the Board from certifying a different unit if it believes a particular group of employees should be included in another group's unit.[15]

LARGER BARGAINING UNITS

The Labour Board prefers to include as many employees as possible in a unit as long as it doesn't deny employees access to collective bargaining.[16] The Board believes dividing the employees of a company into a lot of small bargaining units ("fragmentation") would cause difficult, expensive, and continuous rounds of bargaining for the employer and would encourage disputes among the unions representing different bargaining units about which employees should do what work ("jurisdictional disputes").[17]

FULL-TIME AND PART-TIME UNITS

In 1993, a new bargaining unit rule came into effect concerning full-time and part-time units and the consolidation of bargaining units. These new rules will let bargaining units of the same employer bargain together if they want to and allows these units to get Labour Board permission to bargain together even if in the past they would have been in separate bargaining units.

In the past, if anyone requested it, full-time and part-time workers were put in separate units because the Labour Board thought that they did not have a sufficient community of interest.[18] This fixed rule ignored the fact that, generally, these employees often do share the same concerns and interests. It also served to divide part-time workers, the majority of whom are women and people of colour, from their co-workers in the full-time unit, and lessened the bargaining power of both groups. It resulted in many part-time employees being effectively denied their right to organize.

[New] Now a bargaining unit of full-time and part-time employees is considered an appropriate unit.[19]

If the Labour Board is satisfied that the union has signed up enough members in the full-time unit and in the part-time unit to be certified in each of those units separately, then it will combine the bargaining units into one.[20]

If the union does not have enough members signed up, though, the Labour Board may decide to split the full-time and part-time employees into two separate units. This helps the union at least get certified for one unit if it does not have enough support in the other unit.[21]

The Labour Board defines a part-time employee as someone who works less than 24 hours per week.[22] To define a full-time employee, the Board uses a "4/7" test. If an employee works more than 24 hours per week in 4 out of the 7 weeks (4/7) prior to the date of the application, the employee is considered full-time.[23]

SHORT-TERM, SEASONAL, AND TEMPORARY EMPLOYEES

Short-term, seasonal, and temporary employees can all be included in a bargaining unit. The Labour Board is more concerned with the kinds of work employees do in the bargaining unit, than with how long they are going to be employed.

For example, full-time and seasonal employees who have similar work interests can bargain together without serious problems and can be included in the same unit.[24]

STUDENTS

Students may be included in a bargaining unit with full-time employees, if the parties agree. This includes students employed for the summer vacation.[25] Otherwise, they are usually considered to have the same community of interest as part-time workers and will likely be included in a part-time unit.[26]

Usually, students employed in a co-operative training program are excluded from a full-time unit as they are not considered to have the same interests as full-time employees.[27]

SEPARATING PLANT AND OFFICE EMPLOYEES

The Board has said in one of its decisions that the idea that office and plant workers can't share a community of interest is simply out-dated.[28]

The Board can now find a bargaining unit composed of plant and office employees to be appropriate if it meets the Hospital for Sick Children Test. If the history of employee-employer relations and of employee transfers shows that an employer has treated both units as one group, then the unit passes this test.[29]

In one case, an employer asked if the office and sales staff could be included in the warehouse bargaining unit proposed by the union. The Board refused to put them in one unit because it said a warehouse unit was appropriate for the workplace and the employer had failed to show that the warehouse unit would cause serious labour relations problems. The Labour Board felt any problems regarding temporary transfers and job postings across employee groups could be dealt with through the collective bargaining process of the warehouse unit.[30]

COMBINING BARGAINING UNITS

Because of the 1993 amendments, the Labour Board has a new power to combine existing and proposed bargaining units if the units are represented by the same union.[31] This allows larger groups of employees to bargain together and gives them greater power to bargain with their employer. Either the union or the employer can apply to combine two units.

In deciding whether to allow two bargaining units to combine, the Board takes into account the factors it considers appropriate. However, it *must* also consider whether combining the units would:

- make collective bargaining workable ("viable") and stable
- reduce fragmentation of bargaining units
- cause serious labour relations problems[32]

Using this power, the Board combined an outside bargaining unit and an office unit, which had previously bargained separately, because the combined unit would reduce fragmentation. The different interests within the combined unit did not threaten the workability or stability of the parties' collective bargaining. The Board found that the different interests within each existing unit were as great within the existing units as between them.[33]

Large workplaces sometimes make it hard to take advantage of collective bargaining because their size makes them difficult to organize. But this problem does not arise in an application for combination of units.[34] If a unit is already organized under a union then it doesn't matter how large it is.

The Board has also rejected an employer's argument that units should only be combined if there have been previous serious labour relations problems in the past. A history of stable labour relations is no bar to combining units.[35]

The Board does have some restrictions on its power to combine when it comes to manufacturing businesses. The Board cannot combine units at different places if it interferes too much with the business's use of different methods of operation or production at each of those places, or if it interferes too much with the employer's ability to run those locations as workable and independent businesses.[36]

SHOULD YOU CONSIDER APPLYING TO COMBINE YOUR NEW BARGAINING UNIT WITH AN EXISTING WORKPLACE BARGAINING UNIT?

It is very important to know if your union represents other bargaining units in your workplace or elsewhere in your employer's business operations when you make your application for certification. You may want to file both an application for certification and an application for combination with your union's other bargaining units at the same time.

Even if you do not wish to combine, the employer may ask for a combination and you need to be ready with arguments to state your position. Consider the arguments carefully both for and against combination with the other units your union represents.

To help you consider your position, keep in mind the factors and circumstances which the Board has looked at when it has used its power to combine bargaining units.

• The Board combined a newly applied for service unit with an existing maintenance unit because it found that this would avoid separate bargaining, collective agreements, seniority lists, and strikes, and avoid the potential for different trade unions having bargaining rights.[37]

• The Board combined a newly certified part-time unit of employees with an existing full-time unit.[38]

How Does Combining Units Change the Membership Count?

If a new unit is being applied for, and an application is also made to consolidate it with existing units, then the count will include only the number of membership cards signed in the new unit.

But if there are two or more new units being applied for, the question may become more complicated. What if your union has 55 percent support in one unit, enough to be automatically certified, but in the second unit you only have 40 percent support, enough to get a representation vote? You could delay bringing your application for the second unit, but that may not always be possible.

How will the Labour Board count your membership support? It could simply look at the support in each unit, certify one, hold a vote in the other, and if the vote succeeds, then consolidate the units.

On the other hand, the Labour Board could combine both units even before it decides whether to certify or order a representation vote, look at the overall union membership across both units, and decide to hold a representation vote, instead of certifying at least one unit.

GEOGRAPHIC BOUNDARIES

Normally, the Labour Board describes the geographic area the bargaining unit covers in terms of the particular municipality where the unit is located.[39] Any exceptions to this rule must be backed up by very good reasons.[40] The appropriate municipal area for your union may be a city, town, village, township, county, or regional municipality. This identification will usually appear in the certificate as "All employees of the respondent company in the municipality of X."

If your employer opens another business within your union's municipal area, then your union has bargaining rights for that location as well. But if your employer relocates its operations outside the area, your bargaining rights are lost unless the union can establish that the employer relocated to frustrate the employees' collective bargaining rights.[41]

Because of this, you may want to ask for the broadest municipal description possible in your application. And if you do, you will have to make sure your organizing campaign covers all these employees in all locations. If you can't organize such a large campaign, you will have to convince the Labour Board that a smaller unit within the geographic boundaries is the appropriate one. (See "Single-Plant Units".)

SINGLE-PLANT UNITS

It is also important to consider whether or not you should organize into one unit, two or more different plants or offices of your employer that are located in your municipal area.[42] If you decide to do this, you have to sign up employees at all the locations.

Before the 1993 amendments, the Board did certify the different locations of an employer's business in a municipality as separate units unless the operations were highly integrated or there was a sufficient community of interests among employees of the different locations.[43]

In making its decision, the Board considers these factors:

- the community of interest between the employees at the different locations
- the nature of the work performed
- whether there were similar conditions of employment
- the skills of employees
- the administration of the different locations
- the geographic distances between the locations
- the functional coherence and interdependence of the locations
- the centralization of managerial authority
- the economic advantages and disadvantages of the interdependence of the different locations
- the source of work.[44]

If there are not enough of these factors to show that there is a close link between the two plants or offices, then the Board may decide on two separate units.

If you do want a single plant unit where there is more than one plant, you may have to demonstrate that the employees in the different locations do not move back and forth between the locations, that they do not have a community of interest, and that the two locations do not depend on each other for work or employees.[45] If you can't, the Board may deny your application, as it did in a 1993 case in which it dismissed a union's certification application because it found that the two plants — one in Whitby and one in Pickering — together made up the appropriate bargaining unit. The union had only signed up employees at the Whitby plant.

The Board discovered that the two plants had:

- highly integrated operations (common management and sales structure, single payroll, employees performing similar work to produce similar products on similar machinery), and
- extensive intermingling of work and employees through job

postings and temporary transfer of work and employees between the plants.

The Board accepted the employer's argument and found that serious labour relations problems would likely result if the joint operation was broken up into two units because:

- transfers, job promotions and postings would be hindered
- there was a possibility of different unions representing each unit
- it increased the likelihood of jurisdictional disputes and disputes over who could do what work during a strike
- there was only one pay equity plan for both plants as required by the *Pay Equity Act*[46]

The Board stated that the union should have become aware in the course of organizing that the two plants were highly integrated and should have signed up members at both plants. Since they hadn't even tried to sign up the Pickering workers, they couldn't argue that they'd probably be left without a union if enough workers in both plants had to be signed up to win.

While the possibility still existed that they would not be able to organize, the Board felt it was outweighed by the serious labour relations problems that might have been caused by allowing a single plant unit.

The employee representative dissented from this decision. He stated that the employer's problems were not so serious, and that these problems would not create an obstacle to an otherwise appropriate bargaining unit. He felt problems could be resolved through collective bargaining.

SEPARATE UNITS FOR PARTICULAR EMPLOYEES

PROFESSIONAL EMPLOYEES

With some exceptions, most professional employees can be included in a bargaining unit with other employees. The Labour

Board used to think that professional employees, such as social workers, should bargain separately from other employees, such as clerical workers, because it didn't think two such groups shared a community of interest.[47]

The Labour Board now says that just because employees use professional skills, it does not mean they should have a separate bargaining unit.[48] For example, the Labour Board has certified units that include office, technical, and professional employees.[49]

Recently, though, some professionals who have been in units with other employees have tried to get their own unit. The Board has been somewhat resistant to this move. In the case of Registered Nursing Assistants, the Board has said that claims about their increasing professionalization is not enough alone to warrant a separate bargaining unit.[50]

Professionals who are in an existing unit with other employees and want to leave it for their own unit will also have an uphill battle. They will have to show the Board that the all-employee unit has not and cannot advance their particular interests and concerns.[51]

However, some professionals such as registered nurses are allowed to have their own units. Architects, dentists, engineers, land surveyors, and lawyers, who used to be excluded from the *Labour Relations Act*, are now included and can organize and collectively bargain. The Act states that they will be in separate bargaining units *unless* a majority of their members wish to join a bargaining unit with other employees in it.[52]

Now that the Act specifies that only these certain groups of professionals will have separate bargaining units, it is more likely that other professional employees will continue to be put in bargaining units with other groups of employees.

DEPENDENT CONTRACTORS

A "dependent contractor" is a person who is normally not called an employee of the company, but, nevertheless, is obliged to perform work for the company through a contract for services and is dependent on the company for virtually all of his or her work.[53] Unlike self-employed or "independent contractors," dependent contractors can organize because they are considered employees for collective bargaining purposes.

A unit of dependent contractors is deemed to be appropriate unless a majority of them wish to be included in a unit with others.[54] In many campaigns, you will have to decide whether or not to include such employees in your unit or if a separate unit for them is more appropriate. See Appendix A for further information on when a person is a dependent contractor rather than an independent contractor.

SECURITY GUARDS

Security guards who monitor other employees will be put in a separate bargaining unit if either the union or the employer requests it or if their work brings them into a conflict of interest with other employees, for example, if they are required to enforce company rules or discover and report thefts.[55]

CRAFT UNITS

Unions in Canada first started to organize employees into separate units by their "crafts," that is, into groups of employees who practised certain skills such as plastering and carpentry. Craft unions have historically played a significant role in labour relations and continue to do so.

But as methods of doing work changed, it became more common to organize employees in what was called "industrial" or now "all-employee" units. Today, most of the labour movement organizes all-employee units that include skilled labour such as carpenters.

Nonetheless, the *Labour Relations Act* continues to recognize these craft unions and their historic bargaining patterns by allowing them to have their own unit. The Labour Board will also, on occasion, allow a new craft unit to be formed if the skilled workers fulfill the requirements for a craft unit.[56] If they do not, the Labour Board will be very reluctant to grant them a separate unit.[57]

If craft employees wish to break away from an existing all-employee unit, they must show they have been improperly represented by the all-employee union and demonstrate what efforts they made to assert their rights.[58]

If you are a craft worker, you may want to consider a separate unit. However, if you are not, you will also need to know about this area because an outside craft union may intervene in your certification application and argue that certain employees in your unit should be separated because they are craft employees. The Board is then required to consider the craft union's claim for the employees.[59]

To be acknowledged as a craft unit, *all* the following requirements must be met:

- The employees must exercise "technical skills" or be "members of a craft by reason of which they are distinguishable from the other employees" — this means you have to be able to tell them apart from other kinds of employees in your unit because of the kind of work they do.

- The particular craft must "commonly bargain separately and apart from the other employees" — this means that the craft employees have a separate bargaining history than the other employees.

- The union applying for the craft unit must be a union "pertaining to the craft involved" — this means the union must have a history of representing the craft too.[60]

One of the negative effects for non-craft employees of a successful craft application will be making the main bargaining unit smaller and less powerful in negotiations. Remember this point when you are talking about the union to employees in your workplace. If there are craft employees in the workplace, the time to begin addressing their concerns is during the organizing drive. If your union is not a craft-based union, make sure that craft workers know they can count on the union to represent their particular interests.

TECHNICAL EMPLOYEES

With the increasing use of computerized technology in our work-places, it is more and more difficult to draw a clear dividing line between the work of administrative and support staff on the one hand, and "technical" employees on the other. Employees such as data processors, designers, and technicians now often share many workplace concerns and are usually included in the office employ-ees unit, unless they can show a separate community of interest[61] or unless they meet the requirements of a craft unit.[62]

CONSTRUCTION EMPLOYEES

Construction employees are frequently represented by craft-based unions. Their collective bargaining rules are very specialized and are covered by separate sections of the *Labour Relations Act,* which are not discussed in this book.[63] Many unionized construction employees come under a special system of province-wide bargain-ing. This means that an employer who is certified or voluntarily recognizes a union as representing some or all of its construction employees is covered by a province-wide agreement. No matter where in the province the employer operates, he is required to abide by the terms of the collective agreement.

EXCLUDING MANAGERIAL AND CONFIDENTIAL EMPLOYEES

Managerial employees and employees who carry out "confidential" duties involving labour relations must be excluded from your bargaining unit.[64]

MANAGERIAL

Some employees may have great sounding titles, but really don't exercise any managerial or supervisory powers. Others might have job titles that don't sound impressive, but everyone knows they are the managers of the workplace.

It is important that you know how to identify managerial

employees so that you can exclude them from the bargaining unit. The Labour Board has developed certain factors to help you determine what managerial employees do and whether they make enough decisions to affect the economic lives of their fellow employees. If they do, this will create a potential conflict of interest for them if they are in the same bargaining unit as non-managerial employees.[65]

The key factors the Board considers involve decision-making powers. If the employee has independent decision-making power over employees, or independent decision-making power about policies or methods of the company, then that employee is identified as management and excluded from the bargaining unit.[66]

The Labour Board measures the first factor — decision-making power over employees — by looking at the answers to these questions:

- Does the employee spend most of his or her time supervising others with power to significantly affect the working conditions of other employees? For example, does the employee hire, fire, give permission for vacation or changes in work hours, evaluate the work performance of other employees, discipline them, direct the employees in doing their work, make promotions, transfers or demotions, or otherwise have direction and control over the employees?[67]

- Does the employee make *recommendations* about any of these matters that are usually followed by management higher up in the workplace? This is called "effective recommendation" and it has been found by the Labour Board to show that the person is really exercising managerial powers even if he or she does not always carry out the recommendation.[68] However, a person who has no effective control or authority over employees only carries out management instructions.[69]

- Does the employee have terms and conditions of employment that help distinguish him or her from the other employees (for example, a salary instead of wages; a different benefit package; no overtime payments; a private office; the ability to order materials and supplies)? These differences do not, on their own, mean the person is managerial, but in combination with the other facts listed above, they can be evidence of the managerial status of the job.[70]

The second factor — decision-making powers about policies and methods — is included because the Board is aware that not all managers supervise employees. The Board measures these managers' decision-making powers by looking at whether they have the power to make independent policy decisions on their own without having clear directions from a supervisor and the power to carry out those decisions.[71] These managerial positions are often found in the planning, financial, technical, and data-processing departments of the employer's business.

However not all employees working in these areas will be considered managerial. For example, senior technical employees who co-ordinate and direct the work of juniors are not necessarily managers, especially if they perform the same work as the juniors.[72] And employees who only assist others to make those kind of policy decisions by gathering information or by making policy recommendations are not necessarily managerial.[73] The Labour Board recognizes that there are increasingly greater numbers of employees whose job it is to assist managers, but who are not managerial themselves.[74]

For example, supervisors who carry out all of the following duties are considered managerial employees by the Board:

• do not do bargaining unit work

• are expected to report employees who break company rules

• have authority to grant casual time off, schedule and assign overtime

• ensure that there are enough employees on shift

• assign employees for training, and ensure that employee pay cheques match their hours worked

• work out of lockable offices

• have access to employee records that other employees do not have

- do not hire or evaluate permanent employees
- co-ordinate work at the plant
- issue "disciplinary write-ups" to bargaining unit employees, and make recommendations on disciplinary penalties[75]

CONFIDENTIAL EMPLOYEES

Employees are confidential employees and excluded from the unit if they have regular, hands-on involvement with confidential information that relates to labour relations and if that involvement is an integral part of the work the employee does. Along with managers, this group can include secretaries and other types of administrative assistants who might otherwise fall within the employees bargaining unit.[76]

Secretaries who work for managers who deal with grievances, control finances, or bargain for the employer have been excluded from bargaining units. So have computer programmers who figure out how much different collective bargaining proposals would cost.[77]

But if a secretary or administrative assistant does any of the following type of work, then she *is not* considered to be a confidential employee:

- typing a few letters about negotiations[78]
- knowing the salaries of others, including the president[79]
- receiving and handling confidential documents about non-union matters[80]

"TAG-END" UNITS

Tag-end units are made up of diverse groups of employees who have been left out of previous bargaining units. The Labour Board certifies such units so that employees can exercise their right to organize, even if, strictly speaking, they do not share a community of interest. Tag-end units would be a good example of the kind of unit that could be combined with another larger unit under the new rules.[81]

PREVIOUSLY CERTIFIED BARGAINING UNITS

In the past if workers apply to change from one union to another, the new union usually has to use the old bargaining unit description for the purposes of the application, card count, and vote count by the Labour Board. Again, this might be a situation in which the combination provisions of the *Labour Relations Act* might be used to redefine the bargaining unit.

DESCRIBING YOUR BARGAINING UNIT

Your completed certification application must include a bargaining unit description in it. It is important to follow the rules — you may not always be able to change your application later. You can get help on this by looking at the latest Monthly Report issued by the Labour Board which includes descriptions of the bargaining units that were certified that month.[82]

- Set out the job classifications and not the names of the people who hold the jobs.

- Say "all employees" in a particular classification, such as office and clerical employees in the company. This avoids fragmenting your bargaining unit.

- Set out the geographic location of the town, city, or regional municipality.

- Exclude managerial employees from your unit by referring to the lowest rank of managers and those above that rank.

- If you refer only to "all full-time employees" you won't be able to represent the part-time employees.

THE EMPLOYER WAS FIGHTING US TOOTH AND NAIL.
WE HAD ABOUT 90 WORKERS. THE EMPLOYER SAID IT
WAS ONLY 20, THAT 50 OR 60 OF THE POSITIONS
WERE CLASSIFIED MANAGEMENT!

SOME EMPLOYERS AREN'T JUST ANTI-UNION, THEY'RE
ANTI-EMPLOYEE, ANTI-THEIR OWN STAFF!

THEY'RE AFRAID TO LOSE FLEXIBILITY. THINK THEY'LL
HAVE TO PUNCH A TIME CLOCK. WE TRY TO PRESERVE
FLEXIBILITY IN OUR COLLECTIVE AGREEMENTS. WE TELL
THEM A COLLECTIVE AGREEMENT IS LIKE A POLICY
MANUAL. IT OUTLINES THE RULES. YOU REFER TO
IT IF THERE ARE PROBLEMS.

♦

CHAPTER NINE

WHICH ROUTE?
WHAT EMPLOYER?

AT THE SAME TIME that you are deciding on the best kind of bargaining unit for your workplace, you should also be considering the best route to take to win bargaining rights for your union. There are two ways to do this. You can apply to the Labour Board for certification, or you can try for voluntary recognition from your employer.[1]

This raises another very important question: Who is your employer anyway? We're not kidding — some companies will deliberately try to mix up their workers about who really employs them. In this chapter, we will discuss how to sort this problem out and how to choose your route to winning bargaining rights.

CHOOSING YOUR ROUTE

CERTIFICATION

The most common way to get your union bargaining rights is to apply to the Labour Board. The Labour Board grants a certificate that states that your union is the official and only bargaining agent for your group of employees.

On behalf of your union your representative or lawyer will file an application with the Labour Board to get this certificate. The application must identify the bargaining unit you want, and the signed membership cards must be sent along with the application. The Board will then look at this application, and if necessary hold a hearing to determine if the union should be certified to represent your bargaining unit.

Once the Labour Board makes its decision and issues the certificate, then your employer has to recognize your union,and he has to bargain in good faith with your union for a collective agreement that will set out the terms and the conditions of employment in your workplace.

VOLUNTARY RECOGNITION

Sometimes you can get your employer to recognize your union without making an application to the Labour Board. This is called "voluntary recognition." To get voluntary recognition from your employer, you must have him sign a written agreement with your union, stating that he permanently recognizes the union as the sole bargaining agent for the employees for a particular bargaining unit of its employees.[2]

Voluntary recognition is as binding on the employer and the union as is a certificate from the Labour Board. In fact, once your union is properly voluntarily recognized, the Labour Board won't certify it since there is no point in doing so. Once a collective agreement is signed, the voluntary recognition agreement is replaced by that collective agreement since the agreement also provides for recognition of the union.[3]

Apart from certain restrictions found in the *Labour Relations Act* the same protections under the Act apply to a voluntarily recognized union as to a certified one.[4] But some of these restrictions are significant.

- Within the first year of voluntary recognition or the first year of a collective agreement, if an agreement is reached, any employee or a trade union representing an employee in the bargaining unit can go to the Board and challenge your union's right to represent you.[5] When this challenge is brought to the Labour Board, the Board holds a hearing and the union must prove that it had the membership support to represent the bargaining unit employees on the date the voluntary recognition agreement was signed. If your union fails the test, the Labour Board terminates your union's bargaining rights and any collective agreement ceases to operate.[6]

- During the first year of your first collective agreement, you cannot make union membership a condition of employment in the collective agreement.[7] After the first year, if no challenge is made, the Labour Board treats the union as any other certified union.

- If a voluntarily recognized union hasn't signed a collective agreement within one year after voluntary recognition, another trade union can apply to represent the employees.[8] This union could apply earlier than one year only if it could show that the voluntarily recognized union was not representative.[9]

These restrictions are there to allow other employees to challenge a voluntary recognition agreement if it interferes with their legitimate organizing efforts. This is because, in the past, some employers have tried to head off a union organizing drive by "voluntarily recognizing" a staff or employee association (sometimes called a "sweetheart" union) and quickly entering into a collective agreement that favours the employer. Under the *Labour Relations Act,* employers are required to stay out of the union's business of representing and negotiating for employees.[10]

There is, of course, another major difficulty with this route. It requires the co-operation of your employer. In many workplaces, this is pretty hard to get. Some employers have been willing to co-operate and sign recognition agreements because they want to avoid too much confrontation with their employees. This has happened in organizations that run as co-operatives, for example housing co-operatives, or which have volunteers sitting on Boards of Directors in the non-profit sector with staff operating as a collective, for example, day-care centres. But most employers will not voluntarily recognize a union.

However, with the Board's new waiver process, which

encourages employers and employees to adopt a conciliatory approach to settling any issues without the need for an adversarial hearing, it seems a lot wiser to go the certification route.

With access to the waiver process, friendly employers can demonstrate positively that they are not hostile to the union, and yet the union and its members are given the extra rights and protections that certification can give.

It may be quicker and easier to go directly to the Labour Board, get your certificate and then start bargaining, rather than spend a lot of time trying to get your employer to agree to recognize your union.

If you do decide to follow the voluntary recognition route, the best way to show that your union has adequate membership support is to get employees to sign union cards. However, support can also be shown by more informal ways that reflect the wish of employees to have union representation.[11] We suggest that you still prepare the documents necessary to file an application for certification so that if you can't get your employer to sign a recognition agreement, you are ready to follow this alternative route.

NAMING THE CORRECT EMPLOYER

FIRST AND SECOND COMPANIES

When you submit your application, you have to name your employer. This seems like an easy thing to do, but some employers use different company names than the one they're officially incorporated under, while others hide behind several different companies.

For example, an existing company may set up a second company and hire workers for the new workplace. This second company may take employment applications, pay wages with its own cheques, send letters out to "its" employees on its own letterhead, and even have its own office and manager. But behind the scenes, it's really the original company that's in charge of the business and when an organizing drive starts in the second company, the original company will shut it down.

If you named the second company as your employer, your organizing campaign could be seriously set back, unless you can file a complaint of an unfair labour practice to show that the second company was just set up as a way for the first company to avoid a union.[12] You can also file a "related employer" application to show that you work for more than one employer. The Board can then consider treating these employers as one employer for the purposes of your certification application.[13] (More on this in a moment.)

Another way that companies try to hide the true employer so they can avoid unions is to "contract in" the work done by their own employees who want a union. That is, bring in to the workplace a contract company that is non-union and which will supply non-union labour. This company, however, gets all its instructions from the original employer and hires the workers to do the original employer's work.

For example, a nursing home has a staff of kitchen workers who are responsible for preparing the food for the residents and other staff at the home. When the kitchen staff begin organizing, they are laid off from work and a food services contractor is brought in to do the work they used to do. In fact, some of the old kitchen staff might even be offered jobs by this new food services contractor, although these are non-union jobs. If they accept the jobs, they may find that very little has changed in the kitchen, and they may even be taking directions from the same supervisors and managers who still work for the home.

The main difference is that the kitchen workers' pay cheques now come from the food services contractor, which says it's now the employer. If they try to organize as employees of the food services contractor, they may be quickly transferred to another location with different employees, or even be fired.

[New] Because contracting situations occur so frequently, amendments have been made to section 64.2 of the *Labour Relations Act* to protect employees where there is a contracting-in of cleaning, security, food, and other services by a building owner or manager. Section 64.2 tries to make sure that the employees who do this work do not lose their jobs, or have their working conditions

changed, or have their union or organizing drive interfered with if the new building owner or operator decides either not to hire the original employees or to change the contractor who used to provide the services.

The Labour Board has developed some tests to help identify the real employer in such situations. If you're not clear who your employer *really* is, ask yourself:

- Who controls your wages, hours of work, overtime, work duties, and other conditions of employment?

- Who disciplines employees, by warning them or firing them?

- Who hires new employees and gives out promotions to employees who are already working?

- Who decides how the work will get done, what machinery, equipment and supplies will be purchased and used, what procedures and processes the employees will follow?

- Who does everyone think is their employer? [14]

The answers to these questions will give you the information you need to decide whom to name as your employer and will help the Labour Board if it has to decide this issue.

MORE THAN ONE EMPLOYER

What if you've answered all the questions listed above, and you still can't tell who the single employer of workers in your bargaining unit is? Maybe it's come down to three different companies, which all seem to be involved in some way in employing the bargaining unit members. Maybe the companies all have different, or slightly different names, but they're all involved in the running of a single operation.

If so, you may have a "related employer" situation, and, if your evidence is strong enough, the Board can join the companies together and call them "related employers." Section 1(4) of the *Labour Relations Act* gives the Labour Board the power to look at such a situation and make a decision about whether or not the different companies should be treated as just one employer for the purposes of your application.

This means that you can and should sign up members in all the employer's related operations. The Labour Board will then consider all your membership evidence in one application for all the companies.

The advantage to making a related employer application is that it prevents having the employees and the work moved from company to company by the employer, who may be trying to keep the union out. With one application, all of the employees in the related operations are unionized if you have the membership support.

The more facts you have about how the companies operate, the stronger your case will be and the greater chance you'll have of convincing the Labour Board to join the related employers together.

The first thing you have to prove is that there is more than one company. Then you must determine which facts will show that these companies are linked together so that they carry on related or associated activities, and, finally, that they are under common direction and control.[15] That is, that the companies are connected by what they do and how they are operated.

There are many facts you might try to establish.[16] The Board has found the answers to the questions below to be important in the past. You don't have to prove all of these things, but the facts you do put together must, as a whole, show that the different companies are connected.

Do these companies have:

• the same office, facilities and staff?

• the same lawyers, accountants, and other professional services?

• the same administrators?

• common managers?

• same directors and officers of the incorporated companies?

• the same people controlling labour relations and personnel?

- the same work done by the different companies?
- related work done by the companies, that is, one may make a part of a machine that the other finishes?
- common supervisors on projects?
- issue pay cheques and deduction slips with either or both companies' names on them?
- exchange of staff back and forth between locations?[17]

ESTABLISHING A RELATED EMPLOYER

Once you've collected this information, and you believe that it shows there are related employers, you will ask the Labour Board to deal with this question in your certification application. You must name all the companies that could possibly be related and ask that all the named companies be treated as the one employer for the purposes of the application for certification as permitted under section 1(4) of the *Labour Relations Act*. Once you have filed, the Board sends notices to the employers. Without such notice, the Labour Board will not be able to include them in the certification.

You will also file with your certification application a separate form (Form A-23), required by section 1(4) of the Act. On this Form, you will include a description of all the facts you have found and that make you think the employers are related.

The next step will be to attend a hearing before the Board. At the hearing, the named companies have to produce information that describes the relationship between the named companies, whether it helps their case or hurts it.[18] As well, the companies must call their witnesses first and those witnesses must make efforts to acquaint themselves with all the necessary facts before testifying.

If the companies do not produce all this information at the hearing, you can ask the Labour Board to order them to produce it. You should still try to collect as much information beforehand as possible. Then you can show the Labour Board if and where the companies' witnesses or information is wrong or not complete.

Finally, you should always remember that even though the

companies have to produce the information, the union still has to prove in the end, that the companies are related and should be joined. This means that it is not good enough just to show that the evidence is evenly matched for both sides. The evidence has to "tip the balance" in favour of your argument for you to win.

There is the chance, too, that even if the facts all point to the employers being related, the Labour Board will still refuse to treat them as one employer if it thinks doing so doesn't make labour relations sense. The Board will only do so if it is convinced that obstacles to collective bargaining will be removed and a proper bargaining structure will be created to ensure that the union can deal directly with the organization with real economic power over the employees.[19]

SALE OF A BUSINESS

What if, in the middle of your organizing campaign or certification application, you find that your employer's business, or part of it, has been sold to another company or transferred to another related company? Or your department has been pulled out of the main company and incorporated as a separate company?

The *Labour Relations Act* says that even if there is a sale of a business, the union's organizing campaign or certification application is allowed to continue. The new owner picks up where the old owner left off.

If you cannot get the new owner to agree to stepping into the shoes of the old owner, you can ask the Labour Board to order that a sale of a business has taken place, and that the new owner has all the responsibilities of the old owner. This is very important in the middle of a certification application. You do not want to have to start your application again and name a new employer.

Section 64 of the *Labour Relations Act* deals with a "sale of a business." Although the Act uses the word "sells" to describe the move from one business to another, it defines "sells" as including a lease, transfer, or any other such change.[20]

To decide whether a sale of a business has taken place, the Board has had to determine what a "business" is. It has decided that a business should be defined in an operational sense, that is, it is an economic vehicle that the organization uses to get business done.[21] To establish this, the Board looks at factors such as:

- the continuity of the business vehicle — the greater the extent that the new owner depends on elements acquired from the original business owner the greater the likelihood of a finding of successorship;

- continuity of the character of the business — if the nature of the work performed is substantially the same as that before the transfer, this supports a successorship;

- closure of the original business will not prevent a finding of successorship.[22]

If the new owner already has a business, you may have to decide whether or not you should organize the employees at that business as well. If that business is already unionized, you may find that union seeking the right to represent your bargaining unit as part of the new expanded business. These questions can all be dealt with by the Labour Board on a Sale of Business application.

THE CORPORATE SEARCH FOR THE EMPLOYER'S NAME

An employer can be a person, a number of people operating as a partnership under their own names, or under a special business name, or an incorporated company.

If you are not sure about the correct name for your employer, you can apply to your provincial Ministry of Consumer and Commercial Relations (in Ontario, the Companies Branch of the Ontario Ministry) for a corporate name search to see if your company is a registered business name or partnership or an incorporated company.

If it is listed, there will be additional information you can get from the registration — the address of the business, the names of the directors and officers if the business is incorporated, its lawyer, and the date of its incorporation. This information is also important in a related employer situation where you will want to be able to show, for example, that there are common directors and officers of two or more companies. Remember to have the searches done for all the companies involved in your application if you are in a related employer situation.

There is a small fee you will have to pay for a corporate search. You can find the address of your provincial ministry in your telephone directory under Provincial Government — Consumer and Commercial Relations — Incorporation. You can also get more information about your employer's operations at the business section of your public library.

IF YOU MAKE A MISTAKE ABOUT
YOUR EMPLOYER'S NAME

If you get the employer's name wrong in your application, all is not lost. The Labour Board has the power under section 106 of the *Labour Relations Act* to correct the name of the employer if it seems that the mistake was an honest one. Advise the Labour Board as soon as you discover any mistake. You may have to call evidence at the certification hearing to show how the mistake came about.

> WE DID IT BY VOLUNTARY RECOGNITION. THAT WAS PART OF OUR STRATEGY. WE CREATED A STRUCTURE THAT WOULD PULL PEOPLE TOGETHER. FROM THE FIRST WE BUILT IN A NON-ADVERSARIAL APPROACH. FOR CHILD-CARE WORKERS THAT WAS VERY IMPORTANT.

♦

CHAPTER TEN

SUBMITTING YOUR APPLICATION TO THE LABOUR BOARD

TIMING IS VERY IMPORTANT in an organizing campaign. Since membership is counted as of the date you file your application, you want to plan carefully for the filing.[1]

If there is no union in your workplace yet, you can apply at anytime to the Labour Board, unless you have applied before *and* lost a vote on whether the employees want the union.[2] In that case, the Labour Board may have put a restriction on when you can try again. This restriction is called a "bar" and can only last up to 10 months.[3] While you are waiting, you could use the time to sign up your members again.

If you applied before, and withdrew your application before the Board could deal with it, the Labour Board may refuse any new application, but usually this only happens if you have taken the application forward almost to the point of the hearing.[4]

If you are applying to change unions, specific rules apply to timing which are set out in Appendix C.

FILING AN ACCURATE APPLICATION

The rules for submitting your application are technical and usually the Labour Board will only allow minor errors to be corrected later.

The rules are necessary to ensure fairness in the process.

If you are worried about a procedure or detail, check the Board's rules, call the Labour Board, or speak to a union representative or an experienced lawyer for advice. Don't guess! Failure to follow the rules could lead to your application being refused.[5] Play it safe by getting the information you need *before* you submit your application.

TIPS ON SUBMITTING YOUR APPLICATION

Below, we've set out a chart of the steps to be taken in an application for certification. These steps are taken from the Labour Board's Rules of Procedure and their Practice Notes.[6] You can get an updated copy of these from the Labour Board. You should read them carefully before submitting your application, especially if you are creating your own union.[7] If you are working with an established union, the staff person there will usually assist you and fill out the application.

The procedures for applying for certification are set out below in italics. Following each one, we have listed some helpful tips and points that relate to these procedures.

RULES OF PROCEDURE

1.   Your union files 7 (seven) copies of the application for certification on Form A-1 (see Appendix D for an example, which includes a request for certification under section 9.2).[8]

1.   The Labour Board publishes the forms that are to be used in its cases, and may change these forms from time to time. All necessary forms can be obtained in hard copy and on computer disk from:

The Registrar
Ontario Labour Relations Board
400 University Avenue
4th Floor
Toronto, Ontario M7A 1T7
Send the original and the copies of your application by

registered mail or deliver them in person. You *cannot* file an application by fax. If you have used your union's local number on your membership cards, your application must be in the name of the local and not the parent union.

The "application date" is the filing date on which the Labour Board receives your application, or if you send your application by registered mail, it is the date on which it was mailed.[9]

2. *The following must be included with your application:*

  a. your original membership evidence;

  b. a list of employees, in alphabetical order, corresponding to the membership evidence filed;

  c. a declaration verifying the membership evidence filed on Form A-4 (see Appendix D for an example).[10]

2. You must file all your membership evidence with the Labour Board at the same time as you file your application for certification. The Labour Board will not accept or consider membership evidence filed after the application filing date. Similarly, the Labour Board will not consider any evidence of employees cancelling, revoking, resigning, or re-establishing their membership in the union if it is submitted after the application filing date·[11] (See Chapter 11, Petitions and Interventions, for more information about this.)

Any evidence regarding membership, including your membership cards, must be in writing, be signed by each employee concerned, and be accompanied by the name of the employer and the name, address, telephone number, and facsimile number (if there is one) of the contact person.[12] Your application will contain the information about the contact person for the union, *but be sure the employees sign their membership cards.*

Since all your cards must be filed with the Labour Board when you file your application, do not send in your application until you have enough people signed up!

On the Form A-4, your union representative must state that the membership evidence being filed does represent the recorded evidence of membership employees of the employer who were in the proposed bargaining unit as of the application filing date. The Form also states the number of people for whom cards are submitted and the total number of employees in the proposed bargaining unit as of the application filing date.

If the person who signed Form A-4 (known as the A-4 Declarant) did not personally sign up all the cards, then he or she must find out from those who did witness the employees' signatures on the cards that the information on the cards is true or the Board may dismiss the application. This is because the Board relies on the membership cards to be true.[13]

If any irregularities are found in this process, they must be set out in Form A-4. Depending on the irregularity, the Board may or may not disregard the card or cards.[14]

If you do not file this Declaration, your application will be dismissed.[15] However, unlike membership evidence itself, the Board will accept a late filing of Form A-4, even on the date of hearing, unless the other party can show it was harmed by the late filing.[16]

The Labour Board will not accept photocopies of the membership evidence.[17] Send the original cards in, and keep a photocopied set in your own file for reference.

3. If you are asking for a number of bargaining units to be combined, you must file an Application for Combination of Bargaining Units on Form A-9 at the same time as the Application for Certification.[18]

If you are asking for a related employer declaration under section 1(4), you must file an Application under subsection 1(4) of the Labour Relations Act *on Form A-23.*

3. For more information please see Chapters 8 and 9.

4. The Registrar of the Labour Board sends your union a notice that will fix the date for the hearing and set the terminal date. The terminal date is the last date for anyone to file responses to your application.

4. The terminal date is set by the Registrar, but is usually seven

---

days from the date your application is processed by the Labour Board.[19]

5. The Labour Board sends your employer a notice of the application (Form A-1). A copy of your application is attached but not your membership evidence, which is confidential. Included is the notice of hearing and notices to employees for posting by the employer in the workplace.

5. The notices for posting contain information about your application and the Labour Board's processes for certification applications. The notices tell all the employees when they must file with the Labour Board if any of them want to participate in the application separately from the union.

Your employer must post these notices as soon as he gets them. If he does not, the Labour Board will send a Labour Relations Officer who will make sure they are posted. Contact the Board right away if there's a problem.

Sometimes the employer does not post the notices on purpose, so note the date and time that they go up. The notices must stay up for as long as the Labour Board has said and must be posted where employees will see them.[20]

6. The Labour Board will notify any other union mentioned in the application or in the employer's response to your application for certification. In their documents to the Board, both the union and the employer must name any other trade union claiming to represent any of the employees you have applied to represent.

6. Notified unions have the right to make a claim that they already represent the workers you have organized if they file an Intervention (Form A-3) by the terminal date or other date set by the Registrar. They are then referred to as an intervenor. (See Chapter 11 for more information.)

If they do not file by then, they are considered to have abandoned any claim to represent the employees.[21] If another union files an application for certification after yours, then your application will be considered first.[22]

197

7. *The employer, and any other person receiving notice of your application who wants to participate in any way in the application, must file a response with the Labour Board by the terminal date.[23] If they don't, then the Labour Board will not likely allow them to raise any objections later.[24]*

7. The Labour Board usually acts promptly and sets a terminal date about five working days after the processing date of your application. The processing date is usually one or two days after the Labour Board receives your application.

8. *The employer sends in a form to the Registrar indicating that the notices were posted properly.*

8. The employer must report the date and time that the notices were posted.[25]

9. *The employer sends in Form A-2, the Response to the Certification Application.*

9. If the employer fails to file the Response, then according to Rule 19 of the Board's Rules of Procedure the employer may be found to have agreed to all the facts in your application and the Board can go ahead and make a decision based on your facts.[26]

10. *The employer must file the following documents:*

   a. *schedules of employees listed in alphabetical order;*

   b. *a declaration verifying these schedules;*

   c. *sample employee signatures from existing employee records, arranged in alphabetical order.[27]*

10. The lists the employer must file provide information that will be used to determine your level of membership support in the proposed bargaining unit. They are used to help ensure that the union's membership cards are properly filed. The Board has recently revised and re-organized these.

   • Schedule A — All persons employed in the bargaining unit described in the application on the application date who were *at work* on that date; and

• Schedule B — All persons (including those on lay-off) who were in the bargaining unit described in the application on the application date and who were *not at work* on the application date.

The employer will be required to indicate on both schedules the job classification of each employee listed and whether that employee is employed as a full-time or part-time employee or as a student employed during the school vacation period. For employees listed on Schedule "B," the employer will also be required to indicate the last day worked, the reason for the absence, and the expected date of return/recall.

Essentially, the Board will be requiring the same information as in the past when it used four schedules, but in a more "user friendly" format.

The Labour Board counts as employees in the bargaining unit not only the people at work on the application filing date, but also some people included in the other lists who were at work at some time during the 30 days before the application and who are expected to return within 30 days after the date of the application.

To be counted, even if they are absent on the date of the application, workers must still be considered employees and they must have a sufficient attachment to the workplace. Examples of employees who may be considered to still have sufficient attachment to the workplace are employees on lay-off, sick leave, or official leave.[28]

You should carefully review your employer's lists. They will be part of what determines whether you have sufficient membership support to be automatically certified or whether you have to have a representation vote. Remember that:

• with more than 55 percent membership support you are in an automatic certification position, although the Labour Board still has the power to require a representation vote;[29]

• with 40 percent, but not more than 55 percent support, the Labour Board *must* order a representation vote;[30]

- with not less than 35 percent membership support, the Labour Board almost always orders a pre-hearing representation vote, *if you have requested one in your application.*[31]

For more information on the count and membership support, see Chapter 15, "The Representation Vote."

11. Once the Labour Board gets your application, it checks to see if your union has been certified before. If it has, this is used as proof that your union meets the Act's requirements for a trade union. If your union has not been recognized as a trade union, the Labour Board writes you a letter requiring your union to prove it meets the Board's requirements.

11. See Chapter 4 for details on the necessary steps.

> **WHEN WE APPLY TO THE LABOUR BOARD WE SEND A LETTER TO EACH EMPLOYEE TELLING THEM WHAT TO EXPECT FROM THE EMPLOYER. THEN, WHEN THE INTIMIDATING LETTERS COME THEY CAN SAY, OH YEAH THE UNION TOLD US THEY'D SAY THIS.**
>
> **WE HOLD A DEMAND SETTING MEETING AS SOON AS WE APPLY FOR CERTIFICATION SO THAT THE QUESTION BECOMES NOT WHETHER WE WANT A UNION BUT WHAT DO WE WANT TO GET FROM THE EMPLOYER.**

◆

CHAPTER ELEVEN

PETITIONS AND INTERVENTIONS

THIS CHAPTER EXPLAINS how to deal with objectors and intervenors at the Labour Board. Objectors and intervenors are certain groups that have a stake in the outcome of your application and that may be allowed to present their objections to the Labour Board when your union applies for certification. Dealing with them properly will affect the success of your application.

The most common form of objection by employees is the petition. There is a chance that some of the employees in your workplace will sign a petition against your union (sometimes called a "Statement of Desire") that says they do not want to be represented by your union and have it filed with the Labour Board by the application filing date. If they do, the Labour Board will decide whether or not the petition should affect your application. Employees may also intervene to object to the appropriateness of the bargaining unit, to question or to challenge whether they should be included in the unit, and to charge that they were signed up improperly.

Unions may also file objections and request intervenor status. The reasons a union could do this are:

- another union in your workplace objects because it already holds the rights to represent *some* or *all* of the workers whom you have asked to be included in your unit

- a rival union wants to represent the same bargaining unit, if it can prove it represents at least one employee in the unit[1]
- the existing union is attempting to change unions

A company or an employer organization may also intervene if its interests are affected by the application. For example, a company may intervene to say that the union has named the wrong employer in the application.

OBJECTORS AND PETITIONS: A PROBLEM OF THE PAST?

Will petitions continue to surface in organizing campaigns? Probably, but with less effect. The 1993 amendments significantly restrict the use of petitions, as discussed in Chapter 5. Under section 8(4) of the 1993 amendments, the Labour Board is prohibited from considering petitions if they are filed after the application filing date.

However, the Labour Board still retains the right to consider petitions that revoke union membership or reaffirmations, to determine whether membership evidence was obtained by intimidation, coercion, fraud or misrepresentation, or whether a pre-application petition or reaffirmation was voluntary, or to verify written evidence filed by the application date.[2]

The reason for this change in the law is simple. Most of the petitions submitted to the Labour Board in the past have been rejected. But these rejections only came after costly and time consuming hearings into whether or not the petitions were valid expressions of the employees' true wishes. Since most petitions in the past were circulated after the workplace was notified of the application, this new rule in the law will go a long way to deal with the problem.

Employers will try to find out as early as possible about your organizing campaign so that, in turn, they can organize, directly or indirectly, the circulation and signing of the petition before your union applies for certification. If the petition is filed in time, it may still cause a chilling effect on your campaign, and if it is found to be a voluntary petition it will still affect whether or not you get automatic certification or whether or not you have to hold a representation vote.

There is a chance, however, that a petition filed or presented by the application date may not affect your application. Remember that the Labour Board can only consider the petition for the purpose of deciding whether the signatures on it cast sufficient doubt on the membership evidence to reduce the union support to less than the required more than 55 percent support for automatic certification. If a petition is "successful" in this way, all that happens is that a representation vote will be ordered.

There are a number of situations where a petition will be filed but will never be considered at all because it won't make a difference to whether or not a representation vote should be ordered.[3] For example,

- if your union has already requested a pre-hearing vote
- if your union already only has enough cards to get a representation vote and not automatic certification
- if there are not enough signatures on the petition to bring your membership support to 55 percent or below
- if your union is willing to agree to a representation vote being ordered

Even if the numbers on the petition could affect your right to automatic certification, the petition may be dismissed if the Board is not satisfied that the petitioners signed voluntarily.

In any case, you should be prepared early in your campaign for the possibility of these petitions circulating. It is very important that you consider what your response will be and that you are prepared to deal with this evidence if it comes before the Labour Board.

DEALING WITH PETITIONS
AT THE LABOUR BOARD

If employees file a petition with the Labour Board, your union will receive from the Board a copy of the petition — the petition heading and the dates of each signature will be left untouched, but the names of the employees or "petitioners" will be removed to protect the confidentiality of the employees and replaced by a number. You only need to be concerned with the employees who signed before the application filing date and who already signed union cards. This is an issue that will be dealt with at an oral hearing.

If the Board finds that enough employees have signed the petition so that it may affect the union's entitlement to automatic certification, it will call on a representative of the petitioners to prove at the hearing that the petition meets the *Labour Relations Act* requirements and

- was filed on or before the application filing date

- is in writing, is signed by the employee concerned, includes the dates on which the document was signed by the employees concerned, is accompanied by the name of the employer involved, and includes the name, address, telephone number and fax number (if there is one) of the person who is submitting the evidence[4]

- is a *voluntary* expression of the employees' wishes[5]

- and that management was not involved

If the representative fails to call witnesses and prove these points, the petition is disregarded.[6] Only if the petition is found to be voluntary, will it call into question the union's right to automatic certification or to a representation vote.[7]

To prove all of these, the petitioners' representative will call witnesses (petitioners themselves) whose firsthand evidence must show how the petition started, how it was circulated, who was involved, and when and where all this was done. The representative must also call witnesses to explain the process of getting each signature on the petition, to explain where and when the signatures were obtained, and that this was done without company help and without intimidating or misleading any of the petitioners.

The Labour Board questions the witnesses for the petitioners first, after which the union's representative has a chance to cross-examine the witnesses. The union representative is not shown the actual signatures on the petition. Everyone refers at the hearing to each signature by the number assigned by the Labour Board.

If the petitioners and their representatives do not attend or do not provide first-hand evidence about their petition, the Labour Board will be unable to determine these issues and will dismiss the petition.[8]

MANAGEMENT INFLUENCE AND VOLUNTARY EXPRESSION

The Labour Board's past experience with petitions shows that the creation and circulation of most cannot stand up to scrutiny and are rejected as being dominated by management and involuntarily signed by the petitioners.

The Board recognizes that employees are financially dependent on their employer and therefore can be easily influenced and pressured into opposing a union the company does not want.[9] That is why the petitioners must show that their petition was completely voluntary on their part, and free of any management involvement. The burden of proof is on the petitioners, not the union.[10]

Most petitioners are not successful in proving that their petition represents a voluntary expression of all the employees' wishes and that it is *completely free* of any employer influence. As well, many petitioners fail to provide evidence on every part of the petition process. This creates a gap period, which usually leads the Board to dismiss the petition since it cannot be sure the petition did not fall into management hands during this period.[11]

At the hearing, how can your union show that the petition was influenced by management? What will the Board consider to be valid evidence? In questioning employees who have signed the petition and when preparing your evidence, keep these questions in mind:

• Was the employees' "change of heart" genuine, or was it based on fear about their job or fear that the employer would find out who had not signed the petition?[12]

• Did the employer create a work environment that was so hostile to the notion of a union that the employees' freedom of expression to say "no" was unlikely?[13]

- Are there facts which would lead the employees to associate the petition with management and believe that management started the petition? For example, did management have a meeting with some employees to talk about labour relations just before the petition appeared? If so, the Labour Board may refuse to consider it.[14]

- Was the petition circulated during working hours and were the people circulating the petition agents or favourites of the employer? Did the employee think they would show the petition to the employer?[15] If the petitioners were allowed to circulate a petition during working hours or were perceived as managerial employees, the petition will be "tainted" and dismissed.[16]

- Has the employer held so-called "information meetings" with some of the employees and frightened them with talk about job losses and wage cuts if the union is successful? If such a "captive audience" meeting was held just before a petition circulated, the petition will be tainted.[17]

- Does the petition really disown or reject the union or is the language so general or unclear you cannot tell if the signers really were rejecting the union?[18]

- Are there indications of management approval of the petition? For example, did management agree to allow a meeting about the petition to be held on work premises or during work hours?[19] Did management let anti-union leaflets circulate in the internal mail? Did management recommend the lawyer who is representing the petitioners?[20] These kinds of "silent support" can taint a petition.

- Was the petition circulated in such a manner that management knew it was being circulated and who was signing or not signing?[21]

In one case, the Board rejected a petition because it found that the circumstances would lead an employee to worry about whether his or her failure to sign the petition would become known to management and result in reprisals.

At that plant, the union organizing campaign began at the beginning of February. The two main organizers were fired on February 15 and 16. The Board usually finds that firings of union organizers just after a campaign starts will have a chilling effect on employees and will make it hard for petitioners to show that they signed an anti-union petition voluntarily.

The petition process in that case was also suspicious and would likely lead employees who were asked to sign it to think that management wanted them to sign and would come to know whether they signed or not. The petition originated on February 16 and was circulated on the shop floor, during working hours, and discussed by employees involved in the petition during a lunch break. Their lunch break extended beyond the normal lunch period and the foreman, when told that they were having a meeting, made no attempt to have them return to work.

The petition circulator left the meeting to speak to the general manager and asked him to reinstate the fired employees in exchange for him getting the employees to sign the petition. Though the manager refused to speak to him about the matter, the Board found this incident to be very important as proof that employees would think there was management involvement.

In addition, typed at the bottom of the petition was an instruction that said "This petition will be posted on the bulletin board in the shop." This would mean that employees who signed it would have been under pressure because they knew their views would be made known to the employer.[22]

PRESENTING YOUR CASE AGAINST A PETITION

Be prepared to ask a lot of questions at the hearing. Collect as much information as you can before the hearing. The Labour Board takes into consideration many factors in deciding whether or not to accept a petition. These questions may help you prepare for the hearing and cross-examining of the witnesses. It's important that you try to prove that petitioners signed involuntarily and, as just pointed out, that management was involved.

By preparing these questions in advance of the hearing, you

will be able to ask the question knowing what the answer will be. And you will be able to ask those questions that will support your argument. Two very important rules to remember.

You can also call your own witnesses to provide new information about the origin and circulation of the petition or to show that the petitioners are not telling the truth.

MANAGEMENT ADMINISTRATIVE SUPPORT

• Was the petition typed or photocopied on company machines or computers?

• Is it printed on the company letterhead?

• Who typed the petition? was it the office secretary?

• Was the petition composed on company time or on company premises?

• Is the language in the petition legalistic? Is that because the company lawyer or a lawyer recommended by the company was involved in drafting it? Ask the supposed writer of the petition what the words mean exactly, and where he or she got the words from.

• Did the company refer the petitioners to a lawyer? Who paid or is responsible for the lawyer's fees?[23]

• Where was the petition kept before it was filed with the Labour Board? Was it locked on the company premises for "safekeeping"?

SUPERVISOR'S INVOLVEMENT

• Was a supervisor at any level or from any part of the company involved in circulating the petition?

• Did a supervisor sign the petition? Ask the Labour Board to examine any names that have been scratched out. The Labour Board usually discounts any names that appear after a supervisor's name.

THE PETITIONER AND THE PETITION

- What was said to employees when they were asked to sign? Was there any intimidation or misrepresentation? Did the employees who were circulating the petition suggest, for example, that union members would be fired if the union were certified?

- Did the petitioners get special privileges to move around the company on work hours to collect signatures?

- Was there another petition during the campaign? Why wasn't it submitted? Was it obvious that the company was involved? If so, employees may have been influenced to sign a second petition.[24]

- How did the petitioners know they had a right to circulate a petition? How did the petitioners know that the petition had to be into the Labour Board *before* the certification application? How did the petitioners know that certain kinds of information had to be included with the petition?

- Does the petition clearly state that the signers are opposed to the union or does it just state that they want a chance to vote? A petition that says "We the undersigned oppose certification of _____ Union without a vote" will not be accepted by the Labour Board as retracting membership in the union.[25]

INTERVENTIONS BY ANOTHER UNION

As discussed at the beginning of this Chapter, you may encounter another union during your organizing campaign which objects to what you are doing. To make any kind of formal objection, the union must file a Form A-3 Intervention by the terminal date and set out its objections in that document.

RIVAL UNION

If another union is also trying to sign up members in the bargaining unit you are organizing, then the first union to file an application for certification will have their application dealt with by the Board.[26] The union who files second will only be able to intervene in the first union's application and will not be able to apply for certification.

Before the 1993 amendments, a union could only win intervenor status in a hearing if it had filed its application for certification by the terminal date and had provided evidence that it represented some people in the bargaining unit, either through having a certificate or collective agreement for them already, or through a membership card or written authorization from at least one employee.[27]

Now, section 8 of the new amendments requires that all membership evidence that is to be considered by the Labour Board be filed on or before the application date. It is not certain whether this will mean that another union must file at least one membership card with the Labour Board as soon as it has it in order to make sure that it is filed on or before the date another union makes its application.

ANOTHER UNION OBJECTING TO THE
BARGAINING UNIT DESCRIPTION

If another union in your workplace objects to your bargaining unit description because it says that you are including employees already in that other union's bargaining unit or for any other reason, they can also file a Form A-3 Intervention and come to the Labour Board hearing to state their objections. See Chapter 8 for more discussion of this.

♦

CHAPTER TWELVE

THE HEARING PROCESS

THIS CHAPTER OUTLINES what a hearing involves, should you have to attend one. Hearings can be about your application certification or about unfair labour practice charges. Although this chapter focuses on the certification hearing, many of the rules discussed apply to all types of Board hearings.

Not all applications for certification result in an oral hearing. The Labour Board certification process has become more streamlined in response to the great number of applications it receives and the need to process them quickly. These days, it is more likely that you will never actually appear before the Labour Board panel itself. It is more likely that you will have worked out all the issues between the union and the employer with the assistance of a Board Officer in the pre-hearing discussions. We will explain this waiver process and how it works below.

Recognizing that labour relations delayed is labour relations denied, the Labour Board has also introduced a system for "fast tracking" certain hearings. This means that certain cases are scheduled to start on a certain date and continue from day to day with no interruptions (except for Fridays and holidays) until the case is completed. Depending on the availability of resources, the Board will likely schedule the following applications dealing with union organizing on a fast track basis:

- applications for certification

- applications for termination of bargaining rights

- applications for interim relief under section 92.1

- applications and complaints concerning organizing and picketing under section 11.1
- expedited unfair labour practice complaints under section 92.2 of the Act [1]

Whether or not you will eventually attend an oral hearing, you will receive a Notice of Hearing once you have filed your application for certification or your complaint or whatever. This Notice will tell you three important things:

- the terminal date — if your union has to prove its status, you must file any documents you are relying upon by this date;

- the date of the meeting with the Labour Relations Officer — this one-day meeting is to try and settle all or as many issues as possible prior to the hearing. It is usually scheduled on the Wednesday prior to the hearing date and all the parties must attend;

- the hearing date — the purpose of the hearing is to hear evidence and representations concerning all the issues which were not settled prior to the hearing. The hearing will probably follow the fast-track schedule and is usually scheduled approximately several weeks after your application filing date.

THE WAIVER PROCESS

PROCEDURE

Before you even get to your Labour Relations Officer meeting or Labour Board hearing, you will receive a telephone call, letter, or fax from the Waiver Officer assigned to your application. This Labour Relation Officer's job is to try and get the union representative, the employer, and any other party (for example, the objecting employees' representative or an intervenor union) to agree on all the issues so that there is no need for a meeting or formal hearing or so that the issues are defined for that meeting or hearing.

The issues dealt with by the Waiver Officer are those with which the Board is concerned: if your union has trade union status, if the bargaining unit description is appropriate, if the employees were in the bargaining unit at the relevant time for the count, and if the membership evidence and support are valid. The officer will also deal with your union's A-4 Declaration, any petitions filed by objecting employees, as well as any other issues raised by the parties.[2] A more detailed review of the issues which are reviewed by the Waiver Officer are set out below under the heading "Agenda of the Labour Relations Officer Meeting."

If all the issues can be settled and the union is in an automatic certification position, the officer will ask the union and the employer if they waive their right to a hearing and ask them to sign a Form A-5 Application for Certification — Waiver of Hearing. If you have enough membership support, a certificate is then issued by the Labour Board and sent to the union.

If the union is in a representation vote position and there are no other issues in dispute between the parties, the officer may again ask if the union waives its right to a hearing in favour of going directly to a vote (see Chapter 15 on how votes are held).

If the parties can't agree on all of the issues with the Waiver Officer, then they attend a pre-hearing meeting with a Labour Relations Officer. If that meeting doesn't result in a settlement, then the officer will report back to the Board panel. Officers will not disclose the "off the record" discussions other than to tell the panel what each party's final position on an issue was. This is to make sure that the parties can talk fairly freely about what they would be willing to agree to without being held to that proposal if the talks break down.

If the parties agree on some but not all of the issues, then the Waiver Officer or the Labour Relations Officer writes up a report to the Labour Board about these agreements.

The Labour Board will then hear evidence and argument about the issues in dispute, keeping the hearing going for as many days as it takes to finish listening to the evidence and arguments of each side.

THE MEETING WITH THE LABOUR RELATIONS OFFICER

At the meeting, the officer deals with the issues in the following order, giving everyone an opportunity to participate and give their position.

TRADE UNION STATUS

If this is an issue, the officer will examine the documents supporting the union's status as a trade union under the *Labour Relations Act* and discuss any objections to the documentation.

BARGAINING UNIT

The officer asks the parties what they think the bargaining unit description should be, and if necessary, will refer to Board policy if the description seems at odds with that policy.

If the parties are unable to agree on whether a certain job description should be excluded, for example a managerial or an independent contractor position, the parties may agree to proceed directly to setting a date for an examination of an incumbent of the job by the officer. (See Chapter 14 for further details on these examinations.) Or the parties may agree to just refer a dispute directly to the Board and make arguments to the Board in writing or at an oral hearing.

REVIEW OF THE EMPLOYEE LISTS

The officer then moves on to review and discuss the employee lists (the lists of employees for the bargaining unit). (See Chapter 10 for information on these lists.) The Board will not provide the union with a copy of this list prior to this time unless the employer agrees to releasing it earlier.[3] Some unions always request a copy of the list at the earliest opportunity as some employers agree to its release. If this discussion takes place with the Waiver Officer, then the officer can, at this point, fax the union a copy of the lists.

The parties are not usually able to change their positions at this point about what the bargaining unit description should be unless such a change is a result of the disclosure of the employee lists.[4]

The parties are expected to tell the officer their disputes concerning the inclusion or failure to include an employee ("challenges") or their agreed upon additions or deletions to the lists as the officer works through it. Your union might, for example, challenge the inclusion of an employee on the employer's list if that employee was in a managerial position. Or it might challenge the exclusion of a worker the union believed was an "employee" but whom the employer had excluded as an independent contractor — a non-employee.

Once it is completed, all the parties receive copies of the lists as revised or challenged. The officer submits copies with his or her report to the Board.

MEMBERSHIP EVIDENCE

The officer then deals with the membership evidence filed by the union. In most cases, this will lead to identifying the "count," that is, the percentage of support or the "appearance of the count" (that is, the potential results of the application, depending on how the issues still being disputed are resolved).

At this point, the employer is given access to the content of the union's A-4 Declaration, including the description of any "irregularities" disclosed in it. (See Chapter 10 for a discussion of this form.)

PREPARATION FOR THE SETTLEMENT DISCUSSIONS

You must go into these discussions with documents and arguments that will support your application. These discussions with the Waiver Officer or later, if necessary, at the pre-hearing meeting are important and you must be prepared for disputes. Once you have reached an agreement, you can't change your mind later. Make sure you have thought out the consequences in advance.[5]

The documents you must have include:

• your copies of the signed cards you filed with the Board ("membership evidence");

• your lists of employees to compare with the employer's lists of employees, which will be provided to you at the meeting. If, however, the employer agreed in his response to your bargaining unit description, you can get the employer's lists before the meeting by writing and asking for them;

- information that your witnesses might disclose (but not their names), for example, the organizers who signed people up and members who know about unfair labour practices if this has happened;

- your constitution, relevant minutes, and any other material you want the Labour Board to have if your union's status is in dispute.

Prior to any officer discussions, the union will know how many cards it has and who has signed them, but may not know for certain how many of those cards are "good," that is, how many correspond to the names of employees who will ultimately be found to have been employed in the bargaining unit as of the application filing date. The union won't know this until it sees the employer's lists and, even then, it may need to wait to see what is decided about who is in the bargaining unit.

On the other hand, the employer at this point has the records that show who will ultimately be found to have been employed at the date of the application, but he doesn't know what level of membership support the union has among those employees.

Sometimes, the employer adds names to the lists ("padding the list") in order to try to jeopardize the union's application. For example, he may list employees as being managerial when they aren't, he may list employees who have quit, or he may list family members. Sometimes he may omit names of workers who are suspected of being union supporters. You need to be alert when dealing with this issue.

BARGAINING UNIT

If the employer proposed a different bargaining unit from the one you applied for, you will have to prepare your argument to defend your proposal and oppose theirs. Another union or an employee may also raise a dispute about what the appropriate bargaining unit should be in the intervention which they file (see Chapters 8 and 11).

THE EMPLOYER'S EMPLOYEE LISTS

Review these lists carefully. If there are names missing or names on it that shouldn't be, then you should challenge the list. Check your own list of employees against the employer's list, and make notes about who you are disputing and why.

Tell the officer who you are challenging and why. Provide the officer with any evidence you may have or can get to support your challenge. For example, if employees are left off the list, ask them to provide you with their pay slips or anything else which will prove they are employed or working.

Since challenges can be withdrawn later, but new challenges cannot usually be made at any later hearing, you should include the names you are not sure about. Most challenges are usually resolved with the officer's assistance. If they are not, then they can be dealt with through an examination at a later date (see Chapter 14). Since examinations cause delays and delays can cost support and money, you should only insist on this procedure if it is crucial to your application.

Always have a calculator handy when you are looking at the list. Remember that your goal is to figure out the "magic number" of employees on the list — the total number of employees compared with the number of cards signed. Remember that more than 55 percent will get you automatic certification and between 35 percent and 55 percent will get you a representation vote.

Do not reveal this number to your employer — it will tell him the union's level of support and you don't want him to know this. The officer will know what this number is from his or her review of the cards and the lists. Make your challenges with this number in mind, but remember, you cannot challenge names that are off or on the list just to get to the magic number. You must have legitimate arguments about your challenges.

MEMBERSHIP SUPPORT

There are two areas that have to be dealt with under membership support: problems with your membership evidence and the count.

You will get information from the Labour Board before any discussions with the officers telling you if there are any problems with your membership evidence. These problems could include cards without dates or signatures, petitions, or charges that intimidation or misleading information was used during the card signing campaign.

These issues could be settled ahead of the meeting. For example, your union is only in a vote position and there is a petition from anti-union employees. Since the only thing a properly filed petition would get for the employees is a representation vote, and since you know you would get a vote anyway, you may just want to agree to hold one. If you know you are in an automatic certification position though, you may want to contest the petition as much as possible. These are strategic questions to be thinking about before any discussions.

"The count" is the process of deciding whether your union has enough membership support for automatic certification or whether you will be going to a vote. The officer counts your good cards and compares the total with the number of names on the employee list of the bargaining unit in order to determine what percentage of support you have. Good cards are properly signed and dated, and match the employees names on the employer's lists (Schedules A-B).

Remember, the cards are considered confidential information. The employer does not get to look at them, although the officer will tell the employer if there are problems with the cards and what those problems are. You can object to any company attempt to find out the name of a union member. Section 113 of the *Labour Relations Act* requires that no information about union membership be revealed unless the Labour Board consents. This rule is meant to protect union members from harassment and make it easier for them to decide in private whether they want a union.

WHAT HAPPENS AFTER THESE SETTLEMENT DISCUSSIONS?

If you are able to agree on everything, the parties sign the Form A-5 Application for Certification — Waiver of Hearing, and the Board will usually agree to cancel the scheduled oral hearing and issue a certificate based on the parties' agreement. Otherwise, the issues that remain in dispute will be dealt with at an oral hearing before the Board, and you will have to prepare for that.

INTERIM CERTIFICATION

Depending on the issues that remain in dispute after the waiver discussions, you may want to consider asking the Board at that point for interim certification. Interim certification can speed things up and keep your members excited and enthusiastic by getting bargaining rights immediately for the part of the unit which is not being disputed.

If a disagreement about which jobs are in your bargaining unit does not affect your right to be certified, section 6(2) of the *Labour Relations Act* allows the Labour Board to grant your union interim certification. Your union can then start bargaining with your employer. A dispute will not affect your ability to be certified if you would still have over 55 percent membership support even if the employer's bargaining unit description were accepted over yours. The disputed jobs are excluded from interim certification until the bargaining unit dispute is resolved, then a formal and final certificate is issued. In the meantime, the employer is not required to bargain with your union about the issues affecting the disputed jobs.

Here's an example of how to make this calculation: In a case where there are 100 employees in the bargaining unit you have applied for, and you have signed up 70 employees, even if 1 or 2, or even 10 employees are not included in the unit, you could still have 70 out of 90 employees, or 77.7 percent. Even if all 10 of the excluded employees signed cards, you would still have 60 out of 90 employees signed up, for a total of 66.6 percent support, or more than enough for an automatic certification.

The Board won't order interim certification unless it believes that effective bargaining can take place between the employer and the union concerning the undisputed jobs.[6] The Board has issued a certificate even when a third of the bargaining unit was in dispute.[7]

The request for interim certification can also be made at the oral certification hearing.

THE CERTIFICATION HEARING

If there are still objections raised to your application, or if the Board decides it wants to hear in person from the parties even though a Waiver of Hearing was signed, then the Labour Board hearing to consider your certification will go ahead as scheduled.

WHERE ARE MOST HEARINGS HELD?

Most hearings are held at the Labour Board offices in Toronto, although the Board can hold hearings in other parts of Ontario if required.

The Labour Board hearing rooms are somewhat like courts, but less formal. This does not mean that your application will not be given a serious hearing and consideration.

Sitting at the front of the room will be the vice-chair with the employee representative usually sitting to the vice-chair's right, and the employer representative to the vice-chair's left. Your union representative will usually sit on the same side as the employee's representative. (For more information on the Labour Board see Chapter 7.)

Interpreters are available if needed, but notify the Registrar at the Labour Board in advance of your hearing day so she can arrange this. The Registrar will also attempt to provide hearing impaired interpretation or hearing devices or any other aids for persons with disabilities if notified ahead of time.

Usually there is no transcript of the hearing, so it is best to choose someone in your group to take detailed notes of what happens. Each Board member also will keep careful notes of what happens, but these are private and are not given to the parties.

Sometimes management brings a court reporter to the hearing

to take down the evidence so that there is a formal transcript of the hearing. You can ask the Board to ensure that the employer makes the transcripts available to the union at cost if you need them for any reason. The Board will usually make it clear to everyone that their notes remain the "official" record of the hearings, not the transcript prepared by the court reporter.

WHO CAN COME TO A HEARING?

Labour Board hearings are public. Anyone who is interested may attend.

Your main organizers should certainly attend the hearing. If you know that there are going to be problems raised, such as anti-union petitions, make sure your witnesses who can talk about these things are also there.

THE DAY OF THE LABOUR BOARD
HEARING — WHAT TO EXPECT

Although the Board was set up originally as an informal alternative to the courts, many of the Board's practices look a lot like a court's. Everyone stands up when the Board members enter. They are referred to as the "Board" even though the panel is made up of three individual people. The person chairing the hearing is the vice-chair and is addressed in formal terms, such as "Madam Chair."

It is important to remember that the Board members are not judges, but individuals who hear and decide these cases. The employee representative is a person who has usually come from the labour movement and is supportive of labour's interests. The employer representative is there to provide management perspective and it is often in his or her interest to ask you tough questions, so just remember the source. The vice-chair is usually, but not always, a lawyer and is there in part to ensure that the proceedings are fair. Your union representative or lawyer can ask questions about anything at any time, or can object if something is happening that doesn't seem fair or appropriate.

SHOULD YOU HAVE LEGAL ASSISTANCE?

Usually all parties in a hearing bring an experienced lawyer or representative to the hearing. The employer will almost always have a lawyer or management consultant to assist him. Employees who are opposed to the union often get a lawyer as well, and unions who oppose your application for certification will almost certainly have their lawyer or union representative with them.

You may not need a lawyer if the issues are simple and some of your members who have expertise on the legal arguments can present your case. Pick one spokesperson who will present your case clearly.

But it is usually a good idea to have an experienced lawyer or union representative to act on your behalf and present your case at the hearing. Established unions provide experienced assistance through their representatives or their lawyers.(See Chapter 3 for help on getting legal assistance.)

IF YOU ARE UNREPRESENTED

If you or another committee member are representing your union at the hearing, remember that you can ask as many questions as you need to about the process. If you don't understand what is going on at any particular moment, politely interrupt, and ask the vice-chair on the Board panel to explain it to you.

Don't be intimidated. The members of the Board are each different people with different levels of experience; some may be quite helpful without prompting, while others need to be asked directly to explain the process. In order for the hearing to be fair, you are entitled to ask these questions, so don't be shy about it.

THE USUAL ORDER OF ISSUES AT THE HEARING

The Labour Board panel will consider each of the key questions that concern certification of your union and will hear evidence in support and against each issue. You need to be prepared to present evidence or argument about any of these issues if they are still in dispute.

- Does your union have trade union status?
- Are your union and your employer correctly named?
- Are there any objections about your application's timeliness?
- Is your bargaining unit appropriate?
- Is there a correct number of employees in your appropriate bargaining unit?
- Are there allegations of misconduct against your union?
- Have any petitions or objections been filed against your application?
- Were any reaffirmations signed voluntarily?
- Finally, the panel will disclose your union membership count.

PREPARING FOR THE HEARING

WITNESSES

Be well prepared! Make sure that you have gotten together all the evidence you will need before the hearing and that your witnesses have proof that they have been properly served with a summons. Talk to your witnesses beforehand and prepare notes about what they will say to help you ask them questions when they are testifying.

If your witnesses are nervous, practise asking and answering questions before the hearing, but emphasize to them the importance of telling the truth. Explain that you are practising asking the questions beforehand not to tell them what to say but to make them more comfortable with explaining the truth to the Board. A favourite trick of management lawyers is to ask a witness whether they were coached or told to say something by the union, so it is important for a witness to understand the preparation process.

If you are charging your employer with unfair labour practices, make sure to arrange ahead of time for your witnesses to attend.

WITNESSES — SERVING A SUMMONS

Witnesses cannot submit signed statements for your evidence in order to avoid testifying at the Labour Board. They must appear in person so that they can be cross-examined and the Labour Board can judge their credibility.

Even if you are very certain that your witnesses will come to the hearing, you should still serve them with a summons (sometimes called a "subpoena"). A summons to witness is a legal document issued by the Labour Board that orders the witness named in it to go to the hearing to give evidence and to bring to the hearing any required evidence. The Labour Board will give you a summons signed by the vice-chair. You will have to print or type in the names of the parties, the Labour Board File Number, and the correct name and address of the witness, as well as the date, place, and time of hearing. If you want the witness to bring documents, then state this in the summons as well.

Reasons for and ways of serving summons:

- Some people are afraid they'll get fired if they volunteer to testify — with a summons they are not "volunteering" any more and they can prove to the employer that they had to attend the hearing whether they wanted to or not. You should remember that it is illegal under the *Labour Relations Act* for the employer to threaten someone just because they want to testify at a Board hearing.[8] A summons helps reassure your witnesses.

- Sometimes even your best witnesses will just not show up at the hearing for whatever reason. If they don't attend, it is almost impossible to get the hearing adjourned if you have not summoned them. Make sure that the person who gave the summons to the witness is at the hearing to tell the Labour Board that he or she did this if your witness doesn't show up; then the Labour Board is more likely to adjourn the hearing so that the witness can be compelled to attend.[9]

- If you need to call a witness who is not a union supporter, but has valuable information just the same, a summons will make sure that he or she attends and gives evidence. For example, you may need to summons someone from the employer's office to bring records that will help you prove your case.

- Bring the original summons with you to the hearing in case you have to prove that it was served and what it looked like. If you or any of the other servers cannot come to the hearing, make sure you have an affidavit that states who you are, who you served the summons on, when and where, and attach a copy of the summons to it. Have this affidavit sworn by a lawyer or notary public and make sure it gets to the hearing.

- When you give the summons to the witness, or "serve" him or her, you should have the original summons with you to show if he or she asks, and you should give a copy of the original to the witness. Note the date and time you served it, so that you will remember if you have to prove this to the Labour Board.

- When you summons someone, you must pay them witness fees or "conduct money." If you do not give the witness this money in cash when you give him or her the summons, it will not be considered to be a valid summons by the Labour Board and the witness is allowed to refuse to come to the hearing.

- The Labour Board's current witness fees are:
  - $53.00 for each day of necessary attendance;
  - when the hearing is held in the city or town where the witness lives, $3.00 for each day of necessary attendance;
  - when the hearing is within 300 kilometres of where the witness lives, $0.24 a kilometre each way between his or her residence and the place of hearing;
  - when the hearing is more than 300 kilometres from where the witness lives, the minimum return air fare plus $0.24 a kilometre each way from his or residence to the

airport and from the airport to the place of hearing plus $75 for every overnight accommodation.

- Check with the Labour Board for current fees if you are not sure.

- If you end up needing a witness for more than one day, you will need to give the witness the witness fee for each day she or he is needed to attend the hearing.

PUTTING FORWARD YOUR EVIDENCE: CALLING YOUR WITNESSES

The Waiver Officer will have told you which issues remain in dispute before he or she reported to the Labour Board. Based on this information, you will have evidence prepared for these and will present witnesses who can testify with firsthand knowledge. You will need to prove your evidence (calling witnesses to testify or bring forward documents for the Board to consider) and present a final argument based on the evidence heard at the hearing. The vice-chair on the Labour Board panel will direct how your hearing is conducted. Take your cues from her or him.

Do not plan to call your Waiver Officer or the Labour Relations Officer to provide evidence. Labour Board employees cannot be made or compelled to testify at the hearing about things they did as employees, without the Board's consent. You cannot make these officers testify about things that happened in your discussions or meetings with her or him.[10]

Your union will put its evidence forward first by calling its witnesses to the stand.

Your union representative or lawyer (sometimes referred to as the union presenter) will ask questions of each of its witnesses in direct examination. Then the representative of management or other intervenors or objectors asks each union witness cross-examination questions. Finally, you can ask your witness questions in "re-examination" to clarify anything raised in cross-examination.

Management or any intervenors or objectors will then ask their witnesses questions in the same way. For example, management will call and directly examine each of their witnesses, then there will be cross-examination by the union and any intervenors and objectors and re-examination by management. The Labour Board members can ask questions at any time, but they often wait till everyone else has asked their questions.

When your opposition is finished calling its witnesses, then the union is allowed to call further witnesses and this is called "reply evidence." It is important to remember that reply evidence is usually very brief because it can only deal with new things raised by the other parties' evidence. Reply evidence cannot include or repeat evidence you have already presented, and it cannot be about issues that you should have proved in the first place, such as trade union status.

DIRECT EXAMINATION, CROSS-EXAMINATION, AND RE-EXAMINATION

DIRECT EXAMINATION OR "EXAMINATION IN CHIEF"

These are the questions you ask your witnesses in order to get the information you need to prove your case. These questions are usually short, simple, and "open-ended." Open-ended questions are questions that let a witness tell their story in their own way without the presenter suggesting words or answers to them. Some examples are: "What is your name?" "Where do you work?" "Tell us what happened?" "Tell us what happened next?"

Remember though, you cannot lead your own witnesses, and management cannot lead theirs. You can object if you think management's representative is leading or "putting words in the mouth of its own witnesses," and you can be sure that management's representative will object if you lead your witnesses.

In order to avoid asking leading questions of your own witnesses, try to steer clear of questions that can be answered with only a yes or a no. Don't let the question suggest the answer, let them give the evidence without prompting. A leading question is "Did you sign the petition because you were afraid you would lose your job?" A non-leading is "Why did you sign the petition?" The only exception to this rule is that you can ask leading questions if you know there is no dispute about the answer and you are trying to get to the matters in dispute promptly. For example, "I understand that you have been employed by the X Company as a dishwasher for ten years, is that correct?"

If either you or the company's representative object to a question because it is leading, the chair will decide whether or not to allow the question to be answered or not. If the question is found to be leading, it may have to be re-phrased. Even if no one objects to leading questions, the Labour Board may give the answer to the question less weight when it is considering the evidence because it had to be prompted from the witness.

CROSS-EXAMINATION

Under cross-examination, you ask the opposition witnesses questions that will lessen the effect their evidence may have on your case or put their evidence into dispute. The most common kind of a cross-examination question is the "leading question," such as, "Isn't it true that you told your employees they would lose their jobs if they joined the union?" and, "Wouldn't it be fair to say that the meeting you held in the lunchroom was designed to intimidate and scare the employees?"

Leading questions are supposed to make the witness answer with a simple yes or no, but it is unlikely that the witness will let it go at that, especially if the questions are very damaging to the opposition's case. Be prepared to listen to explanations that begin with "Yes, but...." or, "No, and the reason is...." Interrupt the witness and tell her or him that the question only requires a simple yes or no answer. Also, listen carefully for inconsistencies and changes in the witness's story. Sometimes the more explaining witnesses have to do under cross-examination, the more trouble they find themselves in. Follow up with more questions that challenge the story and show its inconsistencies.

If you believe a witness is not telling the truth, and you have another witness who will give different evidence or a document that says otherwise, tell the witness on the stand that you have a witness who will give different evidence, tell the witness what the different evidence will be, and ask the witness if she or he wants to change the answer to your previous question now that she or he is aware of this contradictory evidence.

For example:

Union Presenter:

"Isn't it true that you told the employee that they would lose their job if they signed a union card?"

Employer witness:

"No."

Union presenter:

"I have two witnesses who each will testify that on X date at the water cooler you approached them and said this. Do you want to change your answer?"

Often the witness, at this point, will either admit something or try to explain the incident differently. Either way, the Board can see the first answer may not have been entirely truthful.

Although it is important to be thorough, don't ask too many questions. Sometimes you will get an answer that hurts your case. And remember, don't ask a question you don't need the answer to and don't ask a question unless you're reasonably sure of the answer. These are good rules both for cross-examination and direct examination.

If your union's witness is on the stand and being harassed or insulted, your representative should not be afraid to interrupt the cross-examination with an objection. You make an objection simply by saying to the panel "Objection" or "I object." Then you will be given a chance to explain why you are making the objection, the other side then replies and you can respond again, if necessary. The panel will decide to either agree with or overrule your objection.

RE-EXAMINATION

Re-examination questions are like direct examination questions, open-ended and not leading.

Re-examination is limited to asking questions that allow a witness to clarify or explain any matters that were raised in cross-examination. If you forgot to ask a question in direct examination and the other side didn't raise the issue in their cross-examination, then you cannot ask it in re-examination.

A good technique for asking re-examination questions is to link your question to something management asked. Of course, the same rule as always applies, only ask the question if you are reasonably sure of what the answer will be. In this example, you would ask this question only if you were sure the answer would help.

Union Presenter:

"Management asked you in cross-examination about why you signed the petition and you said because you did not want the union — can you tell us why you thought you did not want the union?"

Management witness:

"I thought I didn't want the union because management had told me that I would lose my job if the union came in."

ORDER EXCLUDING WITNESSES

Sometimes the Labour Board will make an order "excluding witnesses" so that anyone who has yet to give evidence must stay out of the hearing room until they testify. This order is made when one party requests it, whether the other party wants it or not.

An exclusion order makes sure that witnesses do not listen to one another's evidence and, either on purpose or by simply being influenced, change what their evidence would be. This is important when credibility is an issue, that is, whether to believe management's witnesses or the union's witnesses.

When this order is made, you have the right to keep your lawyer or union representative as well as the advisor in the courtroom. If you are going to call the advisor as a witness, you would call her or him as your first witness.

Once witnesses testify, including yourself if you gave evidence, they can usually stay in the hearing room if they are not going to testify again in reply. However, they cannot talk about their evidence with the witnesses still waiting to be called, or with anyone else. Company lawyers often question union witnesses to see if they have violated this rule.

IF YOU HAVE TO GIVE EVIDENCE

You may have to give evidence for a number of reasons, including:

- if you observed anything about the creation or circulation of the petition that would show it was not voluntary;

- if you are named by the employer as an employee or as the organizer who, on behalf of the union, has intimidated or coerced some members into signing union cards. You would then have to come to the hearing and testify about what really happened;

- if your union's status is in dispute and you were involved in setting up the union.

If this happens, here are some tips about what to expect:

- Your lawyer or union representative will call you to the witness stand by saying to the Labour Board "Our first witness is _____ _____." You will then come forward, and the chair will indicate where you are to sit and ask you if you wish to swear on the Bible or to solemnly affirm that your evidence is the truth.

- Try to talk directly to the panel when you are answering questions. They will be judging whether or not to believe what you say.

- Tell the truth and answer questions directly. Even if your answers don't always appear to be helpful, it is the easiest way to convince the Board that all of your evidence is truthful.

- Always ask for a question to be repeated if you didn't quite catch it. It is better to be sure that you understand the question before answering it.

- Watch the panel members' pens carefully since they are writing down what you say. This also helps you pace your testimony by not talking too fast, a very common problem for witnesses who may be nervous or unfamiliar with the proceedings.

- You will be given a glass of water at the start of your evidence. Your throat gets very dry when you are a witness, so don't forget to ask for another glass of water if you need one.

- If your evidence is very long and you are in the witness stand more than a couple of hours, it is okay to ask for a 5 or 10 minute break. The Board takes a morning and afternoon break of 15 minutes, and they will often take it when the witness needs it, if you ask.

- The employer's lawyer will cross-examine you, which means he will ask you questions about the evidence you have given. Sometimes this is very uncomfortable because he might suggest you are not telling the truth. Just remember that he is not necessarily trying to get at the truth, but rather, to get you to say things that will help your employer's case.

- Most employers will be represented by a lawyer who has been taught that cross-examination is about attacking your credibility. Try to remember this when it gets uncomfortable, and remember that the Board members know this is what the lawyer is trying to do as well.

- When you are being asked questions by the employer's lawyer, listen to the questions carefully and answer as directly as you can. Try counting to three to yourself before answering the question. This will give your union representative or your lawyer time to object if the question is obnoxious or improper.

- Sometimes if the employer's lawyer doesn't like the answer you gave, he will ask the question over and over. It is okay to say that you have already answered it the best you can.

- You may be asked to look at and identify a document. That is, telling the Board that you wrote it, or sent it, or received it, or explain where you have seen it before. Take your time in answering so that you are accurate. You can also ask to read it before you answer. This will let you see what it says and refresh your memory about what it is.

- You may be given a document you have never seen before and be asked by the employer's lawyer to read it. Don't be shy about asking the Board for 10 minutes to read it, or even longer if it is a lengthy document. It is being shown to you so that you can answer questions, and you have to make sure that you have the time to read it carefully and to understand it. Often the Board will take a break so that you can read the document without them sitting there and staring at you. When you are asked questions about a document that you didn't write or haven't seen before, don't try to answer questions if you can only guess at the answers. Instead, just tell the Board that you don't know the answer, or that you don't understand what a particular sentence means, or you don't have any information on why something was written. Don't worry, the Board will know that you are being honest, and it will be the employer's responsibility to call a different witness to answer those questions.

- Your lawyer or union representative can object if the company tries to reveal through questioning you what the names of your union members are. The Labour Board will not allow this evidence to be heard at the hearing, unless it orders otherwise, to protect union members from harassment.[11]

- Often panel members will ask you questions at the end of your testimony. This is often to clarify something that got a bit muddled in the cross-examination. Listen carefully, because you can often clear up something that they didn't quite understand and that might be important to your evidence.

FORMAL OBJECTIONS DURING YOUR EVIDENCE

- Often employers try to delay the hearing by making objections. Your union representative or lawyer will be familiar with these tactics and they will answer them. It is often a shock to find out that the Board doesn't want to hear something that you have to say because of some technical rule of evidence. For example, you wanted to testify that a co-worker had told you that she had changed her mind about the union because the employer told her she better not support the union or she would lose her job. Even though you are sure this is the truth, the Board could decide that they don't want to hear this second-hand and will only hear it if the co-worker is called as a witness. This can be very frustrating for you as you sit on the witness stand.

- The Board may ask you as the witness to leave the room for a few moments when there is an objection. Don't worry, this is not a reflection on you. The Board sometimes just doesn't want a witness influenced by what is going to be said about the objection.

- If the Board rules that you can't answer a question, don't be worried or upset, even if you have the answer or think that the evidence is important. The union may be able to find another way to let you give the information to the Board by rephrasing the question, or it may call another witness to make sure the information gets heard and considered by the Board.

PREPARING EVIDENCE FOR YOUR HEARING

UNEXPECTED PROBLEMS AT THE HEARING

There are two common problems that may occur at your hearing.

• Your employer may say that you have not presented all the necessary evidence to support your application for certification. This can happen, for example, if you are a new union and need to prove your trade union status. You may have presented all your evidence about how the union was formed, and then your employer argues that you did not give evidence about how the union officers were elected or how your constitution was adopted by the members. The Labour Board can be flexible, and even if you said that you were finished, may let you call more witnesses to correct such a problem.

If you do not have the witness you need at the hearing, try asking for an adjournment. The Labour Board will not be happy about such a mistake though, and you may have some trouble in getting the adjournment. If necessary, remind the Labour Board that the rights under the *Labour Relations Act* are not supposed to be defeated by mere technicalities. The best plan is to play it safe and have your witnesses there.

• At the hearing, management may suddenly make an accusation or objection to your evidence that you have never heard of before. This should happen less with the new Labour Board rules that require each party to disclose in their documents *all* the facts and arguments that they are relying upon. But it may still happen. When it does, you can handle it in two ways:

— you can argue that, according to Labour Board Rules 14 and 16, management should have made this accusation or objection in its reply as it is required to do and should not be allowed to argue this point now. The Board should rule in your favour, then the accusation or objection is overruled.[12]

— if the Board allows the accusation or objection to be heard, request an adjournment to prepare your response and for permission to amend your application to include your new argument. You should be granted both requests without too much difficulty.

"MATERIAL FACT" RULE

What is a "material fact"? The Labour Board's new rules require that if you are going to rely on a "material fact" in support of your case, you have to include it in the statement of material facts that you file with your application for certification. If you have not stated this fact, or if the other side forgets to state a fact, evidence about the fact may not be allowed by the Labour Board at the hearing. The Labour Board has the power to adjourn the hearing to allow a party to amend its application or reply, but the later the party asks for an amendment, the less likely it is to get the amendment.[13]

In the past, the Labour Board has allowed parties to get adjournments provided the parties agreed to give the details or particulars they wanted to use to amend their application by a certain date. But now the rules for including material facts are even stronger, and the Labour Board is being very strict about not allowing evidence where no material facts have been included in the application and, therefore, restricting adjournments for this purpose.[14]

In addition, you will not be allowed to question a management witness with contrary facts that you intend to prove by questioning your own witness if you have not promptly notified the Labour Board of those material facts in your application or in subsequent correspondence with the Board.[15]

However, the Board did make an exception for an employee who failed to state all the material facts in his application, and allowed him an adjournment to try again.[16]

PROVING A "MATERIAL FACT"

A material fact might be that the employer held a "captive audience meeting" of all the employees on July 6, and told them that if they joined the union, the company would shut down. The evidence for this would be given to the Labour Board by questioning your witnesses who went to the meeting and heard what was said.

You can call this evidence into question if you named the people, the date and place where the conversation happened and what was said, either word for word or giving the gist of it, in your application. The description of this material fact must be enough so that the other side knows clearly what you are talking about.

DOCUMENTARY EVIDENCE

WITH YOUR APPLICATION

If you want to present any documentation as evidence at the hearing, you must identify these documents in your application and provide the Board at that time with *seven* copies of each document. If you want to show, for example, that the employer was distributing anti-union literature that frightened the employees by threatening their jobs, then you should include copies of this flyer if you have it.

Of course, you must file your membership evidence with your application. If you do not, it will not be admitted in evidence by the Labour Board. There are no exceptions to this because the Act says that the only evidence of membership that the Labour Board can look at is the evidence filed with the application.[17] (See Chapter 10 for more information concerning the Labour Board's rules regarding evidence in applications for certification.)[18]

IN EVIDENCE

Every document admitted in evidence gets an exhibit number from the Labour Board to identify it. Mark your copy of the exhibit with the exhibit number at the top of the first page. Have your notekeeper keep a list of the exhibits and their numbers so that you can easily talk about the document when it comes time to make your arguments, or if you want another witness to look at the document.

In order to put documents in evidence, you will have to call a witness to describe the document and how it was made. You do this by asking the witness if she or he can identify the document. You also ask the witness why she or he can identify the document, that is, how she or he came to know about it. Introducing any kind of letter is one example. The witness may either have written or received such a letter, may be able to identify the signature, and may also be able to explain how the letter fits into the flow of events in the certification process. By doing so, the witness has proved having some direct knowledge about the document, and so it is admissible.

If management disputes whether the union can put a document in evidence through a witness, you will have to argue why it should be "admitted in evidence" by showing how you have properly identified it through your witness.

When the company wants to put a document in evidence, you are allowed to ask to look at it before the witness testifies. Then you can decide if you want to object to the document being admitted in evidence.

The main reason to object to a document is because the witness has no knowledge about it. You will sometimes have to wait to hear what the witness has to say about the document before you will know this, and then you can make your objection. The usual way the Labour Board deals with these kinds of objections is to see if the party wanting the document in evidence will be calling someone with direct knowledge later in the hearing. If they will be, the document sometimes is admitted "subject to identification later," and sometimes it is not admitted until that witness is called.

PHOTOCOPIES AND ORIGINALS

The Labour Board may ask you to produce the original of any documents rather than a photocopy, which can be unclear or even altered.[19] Whenever possible, bring the original document with you to show the Labour Board if necessary. If the Labour Board wishes to keep the original document until it makes its decision, just ask that you have it returned when the Labour Board is through with it. Sometimes, as long as the Labour Board, the parties, and the witnesses have a chance to look at the original, the Labour Board will take a copy of the document for its records. Copies of documents are not usually returned.

If your only choice is to use a copy of the document, bring a witness who can testify to having seen the original document and who can testify that the copy is a "true copy" of the original.

If there are signatures on the document, the witness should also be able to testify that these are "true copies" of the signatures.

When you are going to put a document in evidence, you should bring further copies for each of the other parties, one for yourself, and one for the witness. The "witness copy" should never have anything extra written on it except the exhibit number. It should be a "clean copy" of the document. If there are extra notes written on it, the other side may object to the witness looking at it, since the notes may influence her or his testimony. The only exception to this is when notes have been written on the document by the witness or were on the document before the witness first saw it.

TECHNICAL RULES AND ADMISSIBILITY

You probably have heard of lawyers keeping evidence out of a hearing on a "technicality." The technicality is usually a rule about evidence that was originally developed by the courts to make sure that they only heard the best evidence and that the most accurate evidence was heard or "admitted."

Although the Labour Board is not bound by those technical rules, it can follow them if it feels it is necessary for a fair hearing.[20] If you think that your evidence is going to be kept out because of one of these technical rules, you should object and argue that the Labour Board should accept the evidence in order to allow the workers to exercise their rights under the *Labour Relations Act.*

You can also argue that the Labour Board can hear the evidence, subject to whatever "weight" or relevance they may believe it has. This means that the Labour Board listens to the evidence but can decide later that it was not as persuasive or credible or important as other evidence it heard. At least, though, you will have gotten the Labour Board to hear your case and you will be able to make arguments in closing about why the evidence should be accepted by the Labour Board.

HEARSAY EVIDENCE

The most important rule of evidence is the one against hearsay. Hearsay evidence is evidence given by a witness who has no personal knowledge about the matter, but is only repeating what someone else told him or her about the matter. An example of hearsay would be when a witness says: "Mary Brown told me that the manager told her that anyone who signs a union card will be fired."

The only people who can testify as to what was actually said in this conversation would be Mary Brown, the manager, or somebody who was there when the words were said and overheard them. That kind of testimony would be direct evidence of the conversation between Mary Brown and the manager.

It is possible for this statement by your witness to be submitted in evidence, but not to show what the manager said to Mary Brown. It would go in evidence to show what Mary Brown said to the witness. This statement could also be used to show what the witness believed to be true, but not whether the conversation between Mary Brown and the manager was really true. What the witness believed and what action the witness took as a result of the belief will be allowed by the Board. For example: "I believed my co-worker Mary that I would be fired and so as result of my conversation with Mary I signed the petition."

The Labour Board will often let this kind of evidence in, but only to show what was said to the witness and what the witness believed. If you want to show what was really said by the manager, you will have to call Mary Brown, the manager, or someone who actually heard the conversation. This is an area where the union often runs into problems, because none of those people wants to testify. This is an example of when you would have to summons someone to testify if you wanted that evidence submitted.

FINAL ARGUMENTS

After all the evidence has been heard, both your union and your employer will be given the chance to make final arguments or submissions, that is, they can summarize what they believe the Board should conclude about the evidence. Don't be upset if you think that the important parts of your evidence got lost or confused during the employer's cross-examination and that no one said anything when you left the witness stand. This happens all the time. In summarizing, your union representative or lawyer will ask the Board to take special note of the important parts of your evidence and will also summarize the evidence in favour of the union and explain or dispute any evidence against the union. For example, if management witnesses were evasive or contradicted themselves, the panel will be asked to disregard their evidence.

At this time, you also make your legal arguments and bring any cases that support your position to the attention of the Labour Board. You should bring enough copies of cases for the members of the panel and for the other parties. Paragraphs in Labour Board decisions are numbered, so refer to these and the page numbers.

The employer's representative will also present legal arguments and your presenter must be prepared to explain why the cases the company relies upon are different from the ones your union wants to rely upon, and why the Board should not follow the company's cases.

THE BOARD'S DECISION

Quite often the Board will give an "oral decision" for straightfor- ward cases. An oral decision is reached by the panel members who, after the hearing, leave the room for a period of time and then return to tell the parties what they have decided. If, however, the evidence and arguments were complex or controversial, it is more likely that the Board members will "reserve" their decision because they need time to think about all the evidence and submissions. A written decision will be issued some time after the hearing.

If your case was on a fast-track schedule, the written decision will be issued within two days from the date of your hearing. If it wasn't fast-tracked, the decision will take longer. The Board's reasons for its decision may be included with the decision, or the Board may say that the reasons are to follow. If there are no reasons and the Board has not written that they are to follow, you are entitled to ask the Board to give written reasons to you.

Don't worry if the Board can't give you an oral decision at the hearing. Often the panel must go away and re-read all the evidence and then meet to discuss the case.

◆

CHAPTER THIRTEEN

ORGANIZING PROTECTIONS AND FIGHTING UNFAIR LABOUR PRACTICES

UNIONS AND EMPLOYEES have the right to organize with certain positive protections and free of unfair labour practices. Many employers try to stop an organizing drive in its early stages by taking actions that interfere with employees' rights to organize a union. Such "unfair labour practices" are illegal under the *Labour Relations Act,* which gives employees and unions many organizing protections against improper employer conduct. Listed here are summaries of key legal points. (Unfair practices used to influence employees to vote against a union in a representation vote are dealt with separately under Chapter 15. Appendix F reviews decisions that deal with unfair firings during a campaign.)

The protections under the *Labour Relations Act* state that:

- if the Board decides that because of the employer's violations of the Act the employees wishes about union representation cannot be known, the Board may certify the union even if it does not meet the membership requirements;[1]

- union organizers have the right to talk to employees about joining a union outside of the entrances and exits of the workplace. If union activity disrupts the employer's business, the Board may restrict this right;[2]

- employers must not interfere with the formation of a trade union;[3]

- employers must not fire or lay off someone because of union activity, include as a term of employment that a person refrain from union activity, or threaten an employee in any way in order to force that person to stop union activity;[4]

- employers must not use intimidation or force to prevent or stop someone from joining a union;[5]

- employers must not fire or lay off, threaten, discriminate against or intimidate someone because she or he may testify in a Board proceeding;[6]

- from the time the employer receives notice of the application for certification until the Board makes its final decision, the employer may not alter the wage rates or other terms of employment without the consent of the union.[7]

EXPEDITED OR FAST-TRACKED HEARINGS

[New] If an employee files a complaint for having been disciplined, fired or discriminated against at any time during the organizing campaign — from when it started to when the union submitted its application for certification — the complaint will be dealt with at a fast-track hearing if the union asks for an expedited hearing under section 92.2 (Form A-61). The Labour Board will start an investigation into the complaint within 15 days after the request has been given to the Labour Board and to the employer and give a declaration within two days after its completed.[8]

The Labour Board may also hear other complaints related to the issue.[9] For example, if an employee was fired for trying to organize a union, and there was another complaint with the Board that the employer was harassing other union supporters, the Labour Board could hear both complaints at the same hearing.

Unions can also use fast-track hearings to apply for an interim order to address their complaints. Under section 92.2, the union can ask the Labour Board to make a quick ruling on a complaint before the main hearing takes place. It might be possible, for example, to have a fired employee reinstated until the matter is finally decided by the Labour Board.

COMPLAINTS OF CHANGE
IN WORKING CONDITIONS

Unless the union agrees to a change in working conditions, such as a decrease in employees' salaries, section 81(2) of the *Labour Relations Act* makes it illegal to change working conditions, from the time the employer receives notice of the application for certification until the Labour Board makes its final decision. This is known as the "freeze" period.

Not every change made in the freeze period is a violation of the Act. To determine which changes are improper the Board will look at the conditions that existed before the freeze to see what the employees could reasonably expect their working conditions to be with the particular employer.

In one case, an employer's alteration of a five-year-old policy about payment of commissions was found to violate the freeze.[10]

In another case, an employer's failure to give employees the annual increase they had received over the previous 11 years was found not to violate the freeze. This was because the employer faced budget restraints and the Board found it reasonable for the employees to expect no increase.[11]

If your employer ignores the law and changes working conditions anyway, your union can apply to the Board under section 91 of the Act to have a Labour Relations Officer investigate the complaint. The officer may decide to compensate employees if there were loss of earnings and reinstate earlier working conditions. The union can also ask to be automatically certified because, in effect, the employer influenced the outcome of a representation vote.

COMPLAINTS OF UNFAIR LABOUR PRACTICES

You or your co-workers can file an unfair labour practice against your employer if he is harassing or discriminating against you for union activity, or if he threatens a loss of jobs if you join a union.[12] The Labour Board can make the employer stop harassing you or re-hire and compensate you for lost wages if you have been fired.[13]

The most common unfair labour practice is the firing of an employee for union activity, especially if that employee is a union organizer. This can have a chilling effect on an organizing campaign and can frighten other employees into silencing their views on unionization. The Labour Board is very critical of this kind of action. (See Appendix F for a review of Board decisions.)

The procedure to follow is the same for any employee who is fired — whether or not she or he is a union organizer. The employee should speak to an organizing committee member immediately, write down notes about what happened and what the employer did, and find out if there were any other people around who heard or saw what happened and who could be witnesses if the fired employee goes to the Labour Board. In addition, the employee should prepare an Incident Report to document the unfair practice (see Chapter 5).

It is important that the employee find out the reasons for being fired and try to find proof that will discredit the employer's accusations. For example, if the employer says he fired the employee because she or he is incompetent, find another worker who will testify that the employee does her or his job well or just as well as other workers. It is even more important to prove that the employee was fired for participating in the union.[14]

The employer must prove to the Board that the firing had nothing to do with the union activity. In deciding this, the Labour Board takes into consideration any factors that point to the employer's anti-union feelings.[15] For example:

- Is there a pattern of anti-union activity in that employer's company?

- How much did the employer know about the union activity?

- How was the employee fired?
- Which witnesses are believable? If different employer witnesses give different stories, or if important employer witnesses do not appear at the Labour Board to tell their story,
  the Labour Board may decide against the employer.[16]
- Was the timing of the discharge or lay-off suspicious? If the
  employer fires someone the same day that he learns of the
  union's application, the Board may infer that the employer
  had an anti-union motive.[17]

FACTORS THE LABOUR BOARD CONSIDERS

The following cases demonstrate that the closer the time of the
discharge is to the period of union activity, the easier it is to win
your case. You will likely notice as you read this section and the
cases referred to in it that the Labour Board decisions are not
always consistent. This is because each decision is decided by a
different panel of Board members, all of whom bring to their decision-making their own experiences, perceptions, and knowledge.

A PATTERN OF ANTI-UNION ACTIVITY

If a person was fired during an organizing campaign and at the
same time the employer had been saying that people's jobs would
be at risk if they supported the union, this may point to the firing
being illegal because it was part of an anti-union campaign. The
employer must then show that the firing has nothing to do with
union activity. But the pattern of anti-union activity must be at or
around the time of discharge to be convincing to the Labour
Board.[18]

TIMING

In the *Beaver Lumber*[19] case, the Board looked at the timing of the
employer's actions as one factor in deciding whether or not he had
improperly fired workers.
    Beaver Lumber had five different stores; the union's application

249

for certification affected only one, the Parkdale store.

The company implemented a night crew to stock shelves in all of their stores in January of 1991. The organizing campaign at the Parkdale store began in April 1991 and involved night crew workers; the employer was aware of this from the start. A company memo dated June 11, warned employees that company premises and time should not be used for union solicitation. A subsequent letter said that the employer did not think the employees needed a third party to represent their concerns.

At the end of June, the five night crew workers at the Parkdale store were among 25 employees terminated across the chain.

The Labour Board decided that the discharges were not free of anti-union sentiments. The timing was very important. As organizing activity increased, so did the employer's responses, such as writing the memo and the letter. Furthermore, the employer's decision to terminate was inconsistent with its earlier approach to cutting costs. As well, there was other work available for which the grievors were qualified. The Board agreed to certify the union.

In the *Call-A-Cab* case,[20] even though the employer said it laid off 11 of its 22 drivers for actual business reasons, the Labour Board found there was an anti-union motive because all 11 drivers had signed union cards.

In the *Thermogenics Inc.* case,[21] six employees were laid off while membership cards were being signed. Most of the six employees were union supporters. The Board found that the lay-offs were improper, even though the employer had valid business reasons for downsizing. However, the Board doubted that the lay-offs, as they were done, were free of anti-union sentiment. The most persuasive factor was timing. The employer decided to consider lay-offs at the same time as the rise in union campaigning.

The Board also found that there were other options to the lay-offs. Work sharing had just been implemented and could have been extended.

A case in which a broader view was taken of the time span between union activity and a discharge is *G. Tamblyn Ltd.*[22] The Labour Board reinstated an employee when it found that there was a link between the worker's union activity and his discharge, even though there was a 10-week lag between the date he was seen at a union meeting and the date of the discharge. The union pointed out that union activity was still strong at the time of the discharge, since a contract had not yet been signed. As well, the union argued that the worker's services had been required during the 10-week period, and this explained why the employer did not fire him earlier.

THE EMPLOYER'S KNOWLEDGE OF UNION ACTIVITY

It is important to show not only some connection between the fired worker and the union but also the employer's knowledge of the connection. If the worker was an active union member, and you can prove that the employer knew this, your case is easier. However, the secrecy of organizing campaigns may make it difficult to prove that the company knew that the worker was in the union.

In *Thermogenics Inc.,*[23] though the extent of management's knowledge about who the union organizers were was unclear, the Board found that there were anti-union feelings because it was a major coincidence that those picked for lay-off were the major actors in the union campaign.

These cases show the importance both of gathering evidence that points to the employer's knowledge of the worker's union involvement and of keeping careful records of all union activities and incidents at the workplace.

Lack of such evidence defeated the union's side in the case of *Custom Converters Printers Ltd.* The Labour Board held that discharge for inventory shortages was valid even though the worker had written a letter to his fellow employees urging them to unionize. The Labour Board found that he "had engaged in no visible activities that would have linked him to the letter he wrote."[24] The worker was unable to produce witnesses, bankbooks, membership cards, or minutes to prove the existence of the union.

HOW THE EMPLOYEE WAS DISCHARGED

The Labour Board examines whether the manner of discharging the worker was different from that normally used by the employer. If an employee was discharged for something that normally brought only a verbal warning, the Labour Board could conclude that she or he was discharged for union activity.[25]

Remember that before your union is certified, an employer is not under an obligation to prove that the firing was for "just cause," as long as he shows that the firing was not related to the worker's union activity. For example, an employer could discharge a worker for a minor act of insubordination. While an arbitrator interpreting a collective agreement might not find such an act deserves a penalty as severe as discharge, the Labour Board does not look into the validity of the action, as long as the insubordination was the real reason and the only reason for the firing.

However, if the reason for discharge was frivolous or insubstantial, the Labour Board may suspect that the employer is not being entirely straightforward with the Board. In another example,[26] the employer fired a worker even though the employer knew he was part of the organizing campaign. The Board found there was no breach of the Act because the only reason for firing the employee was his poor performance and not his involvement in the union.

In another case, the Labour Board found that, although the grievor's work was unsatisfactory, this fact did not excuse the employer. The Board also found that the employee had been fired in an arbitrary manner. But it dismissed the case because it found no evidence that the dismissal was caused by the grievor's union activity.[27]

If a company claims that it laid off an employee who supported the union "because of a downturn in business," it is difficult to combat that excuse. Statistics showing that the company is not actually in a slump are very valuable in such cases. Your local newspaper's business section may well provide these figures.

Try to find evidence that other employees were hired to do the grievor's work. However, if you can show, as in *Call-A-Cab Limited*,[28] that the only people laid off were people who signed cards, that would counter the employer's claim it was only for business reasons.

In the *Corporation of the City of London*[29] case the grievor was reinstated because the employer could not provide a credible explanation for hiring other employees after the grievor was laid off.[30] The Labour Board found that the lay-off could well have been partly motivated by the grievor's advocacy of rights for temporary employees.

However, in the case of *Superior Glove Works Ltd.*, the Labour Board refused to interfere with certain lay-offs made in the midst of an organizing campaign, even though the company was openly opposed to the union. The Labour Board found that the company decided to lay off workers before it learned of the union campaign.[31]

THE CREDIBILITY OF WITNESSES

The union should impress the Labour Board with the frankness and sincerity of its witnesses. Some discharge cases have been lost because witnesses exaggerated something and were caught by the company lawyers.

A discharged worker should be prepared for testifying. If his or her past record is not good, the employee should admit it. The union can then point out that the work record was not the reason for the worker's discharge.

In *Wm. J. Davidson Electric Inc.*,[32] the Board found credibility problems with all of the witnesses in this discharge case. However it decided to accept the grievor's evidence over the employer's because the employer failed to call a witness who knew about key allegations of the unfair labour practice. The Board drew the inference that this witness's evidence would have been unfavourable to the employer.

An example of the consequences of lack of candour is found in the *Barrie Examiner* case,[33] where the employer witness would not admit how vigorously he had opposed the union. The Labour

Board stated:

Probably one of the most effective ways in which an employee can satisfy the new onus under Section 79 (now section 91) is for it to tell its story through its witnesses in a frank and honest manner. Conversely, lack of candour, even in respect of only one part of the testimony, is likely to raise doubts as to the genuineness of the reasons provided by the Respondent.[34]

You should make sure that all people who witnessed the events in question are brought forward to testify. For example, in *Repla Limited*,[35] the employer's witnesses contradicted each other and the employer didn't call a witness who could have clarified the evidence. The Labour Board held it against the company and found that part of the reason for firing the employee was motivated by anti-union reasons.

CHARGING THE EMPLOYER WITH AN UNFAIR LABOUR PRACTICE

The important factor here is time. You don't want to delay your complaint.

If you still have enough support for automatic certification despite an unfair labour practice, you may not want to create any delays by complaining to the Labour Board.

On the other hand, if you have less support, you may want to ask the Labour Board to find that the employer's unfair tactics mean you should be automatically certified, even if you don't have enough signed membership cards.[36]

However, if a worker has been fired you will want to fill out a complaint in order to have her or him reinstated as soon as possible.

The new amendments to the Act have tried to correct many of the delay problems. They allow you to ask for interim relief [37] and an expedited hearing.[38]

If you choose to file a complaint, you can file in one of three ways:

1. Make an application for consent to prosecute under section 103 of the Act. This process is expensive and is rarely done. It is more often done as a symbolic gesture.

2. Include the complaint as part of your certification application. For example, your union may want to raise charges that your employer intimidated some members and now they do not want to join the union. In addition, you must show that your employer's interference was so intense that other employees are unlikely to vote freely even in the secrecy of a voting booth.

   In your application, your union can ask the Labour Board for a section 9.2 certification or at least a vote. Certification will be granted if the Labour Board finds that the employer indeed violated the Act and that because of what he did, the true wishes of the employees are not likely to be known.[39] The Board has held that discharges, lay-offs, and harassment of known union organizers fulfill these requirements.[40] If certification is granted under section 9.2, the Act no longer requires the union to prove that it has adequate membership support for collective bargaining.

3. File a separate complaint under section 91 of the Act saying that the employer has not followed the Act. In the same complaint, you can ask for an expedited hearing under section 92.2 if there is a complaint about an employee being terminated or discriminated against while you were organizing. You can also ask for an interim order.

MAKING A COMPLAINT UNDER SECTION 91

Most section 91 complaints deal with someone being fired for union activity or with an employer changing the working conditions so that employees will vote against a union. Section 91 is a general section that allows the Labour Board to decide whether or not an employer, union, or employee has not followed a provision of the Act, and allows the Board to make an order to correct the situation. If you make a section 91 complaint, you have to tell the

Labour Board which unfair labour practice section has been violated.

A section 91 complaint is filed on a Form A-35 and should be submitted to the Labour Board as soon as possible after the incident happened.[41] If you wait too long, the Labour Board may dismiss your complaint because of delay.[42] (See Appendix E for a sample Form A-35.)

In the "Statement of Material Facts" section, list the names of people who violated the Act, describe how they violated the Act, and when and where these violations took place. You have to list all the details about the events in your complaint. This is very important; if you leave out an important detail the Labour Board might not let you introduce it at the hearing.[43]

If you do forget to include a detail, you can ask the Labour Board before or at the hearing to let you amend your complaint.[44] It's up to the Labour Board to decide whether or not to let you do that.[45] Attach any documents you want to rely on. If the Labour Board thinks there might be other important documents it wants, it will ask for them.

The Labour Board is also allowed to extend the time period if you give a good reason why you were late.[46] However, the Labour Board is being tough on enforcing its rules, so it is best to be as complete as possible when you first file.

ESTIMATE HOW LONG THE CASE WILL BE

The Labour Board will also want you to estimate how long the case will be and how many witnesses you think you will need to speak to the Labour Board. This gives the Labour Board a better idea of how many days it needs to schedule. Include this information with Form A-35.

If you want an expedited hearing, the Labour Board will only let you file your complaint after you have delivered a copy of it to your employer.

APPLYING FOR AN INTERIM ORDER

Sometimes a situation will be so urgent that you will want the Labour Board to make an interim order under section 92.1 before it hears the actual complaint. For example, if someone has been fired for trying to organize a union, you may want to bring an interim application to ask for her or his job back instead of waiting for the full hearing on the unfair labour practice. This will put the worker back to work as soon as possible. But file as soon as possible.

Any undue delay in bringing the application will undermine the union's argument that urgent interim relief is required. It will also make it difficult for the Board to quickly intervene and may increase the harm that the employer may suffer if he has to undo the disputed action, even on an interim basis.[47]

An interim order is temporary and is not based on a finding of a violation. The Labour Board looks at the process of "interim justice as an endeavour in problem-solving, rather than fault-finding."[48] The aim is to emphasize protecting the ability of employees to freely express their wishes on unionization. This is done by balancing the harm to the parties and minimizing the harm at an early stage of the organizing campaign. Reinstating a fired worker is an example of how confidence in the process could be restored.

The Labour Board can issue an order based on certified declarations and on written arguments without holding an oral hearing. In your application, your union must submit these certified declarations from employees (witnesses) who have firsthand knowledge about the unfair labour practice. A declaration must contain all facts the employee knows and must state that it was prepared by the employee and that it is accurate. The employee then signs it. These declarations will tell the Labour Board in advance what the employees intend to say at the hearing and might help the Board decide the issue without having the witnesses come and tell their story in person.

Remember that the Labour Board only wants the employees to write about their direct knowledge of the events. If a declaration has a lot of hearsay in it — reporting what someone else said rather than reporting firsthand knowledge — the Labour Board will likely pay no attention to it.[49]

The Labour Board also wants your union to include in its submission all the reasons it should win an interim order. For example, including cases similar to yours in which the Labour Board ruled in the union's favour. You must also establish that, without proving that the facts are true, you have an arguable case as presented in the application. In an unlawful discharge case, your union must establish that the discharge violated the *Labour Relations Act*. Your union must also show that the harm that would occur to the union if the interim order was not granted would be greater than the harm that would occur to the employer if it were granted. The most persuasive type of harm in an organizing campaign is harm that would interfere with the employees' ability to freely express their wishes on unionization.[50] See Appendix F for further information on Board decisions on interim orders.

ADJOURNMENTS

The Labour Board does not like to adjourn hearing dates, so be ready to go ahead with your case. If you are not ready to go ahead, the Labour Board may dismiss your complaint. Also, the new amendments say that the Labour Board will hear the case one day after another from Monday to Thursday until the case is finished. You must make sure that you can go to the Labour Board on all those dates.

BURDEN OF PROOF

If your unfair labour practice complaint alleges an employee has been unfairly dealt with at work, the employer has the burden of proving that his actions had nothing to do with anti-union feeling.[51]

Often the employer will come forward at the hearing and say that he never knew anything about the union campaign, so he couldn't have penalized anyone for union activity. (Keep notes on anything that will show that management knew about the campaign.)

To prove that, an employer must demonstrate that his actions had nothing at all to do with the employee being a part of or active in the union,[52] and that the reasons were not tainted by anti-union feelings. If anti-union feeling was present in the mind of the employer, it does not matter if it was only a small part of the reason for the action.[53]

REMEDIES

A remedy is anything the Labour Board has the power to make the employer do if it finds the employer has committed an unfair labour practice. Unlike the courts, the Labour Board has the power to order many different types of remedies.[54]

As an expert tribunal, the Board must ensure that its remedies are sensitive to the real forces at play beneath the legal issues. The Board still has a way to go, however, in carrying out its mandate of developing effective remedies.[56]

The Board recognizes that once social relations in a workplace have been disturbed by the employer's conduct, it is difficult to restore the workplace to the way it was before. Labour relations remedies are ordered as a rough substitute for what should have happened if the employer had not acted improperly to interfere with the organizing drive.[56] The Board can do whatever is necessary to put the union and the affected employee back in the position they would have been in if the unfair labour practice had not occurred.

At the same time, the Labour Board believes that a creative use of its wide powers will go a long way to repairing the damage caused by unfair practices.[57] The Board has said remedies must be developed to ensure that "delay does not in itself decide a case."[58]

In one case the employer closed down its company to avoid the union. The Labour Board made the employer pay the union for all its organizing and legal costs.[59] The Labour Board may also make the employer post signs in the workplace saying that he violated the Act,[60] and make him provide copies of the decision to each employee.[61] The Board has also required an employer to mail copies of such notices to all employees in the bargaining unit.[62]

REINSTATEMENT AND COMPENSATION

If employees are ordered to be reinstated, then usually the Board orders that they be given full back pay that should equal their normal take-home pay. This works as follows:

- the employer will deduct normal amounts, such as taxes, from the gross pay,[63]

- the Labour Board expects the fired workers will try to find another job while they are off work. This is called "mitigating" damages,[64]

- the employer will then have to pay the difference between what they used to get paid with what they earned at their new job,

- if the employees make an effort to find a new job but cannot, the Labour Board will usually say they have tried to mitigate their damages and will tell the employer to give them all the money that they lost.

NON-COMPLIANCE WITH LABOUR BOARD ORDER

Non-compliance is when the employer is ordered to do something, but he does not do it. The union can file a copy of the decision in the Ontario Court, General Division any time after it is made.[65] If the employer does not do what the Labour Board ordered him to do, the union can then enforce the order just as if that court had made the decision.

WORKERS AND UNIONS CAN ALSO BE PROSECUTED

Although we have mainly talked about how employers can commit an unfair labour practice, it is possible for unions or individual members to violate the Act as well. It is an unfair labour practice, for example, for a union to threaten employees with job loss if they won't vote for the union or if they vote for another union. A union cannot try to stop workers from exercising their rights under the Act.[66]

Nor can a union discriminate against any of the employees it represents or treat them unfairly or in bad faith.[67] If the union mistreats an employee, the employee can file a complaint under section 69, showing it was more than just simple mistreatment but, in fact, the employee was deliberately singled out to be treated badly or the union just did not care at all about that employee.[68]

Most charges brought against a union under section 69 are not successful. This section normally applies if a union fails to take up a grievance for an employee after a union is certified.[69] However, if you believe your union is not treating you fairly during an organizing drive, you might try to talk to the union first and if necessary use any complaint procedure in your union's constitution. If you are fired or disciplined for union activity before certification, you as an individual can apply to the Labour Board to be reinstated.

> FIRST THE EMPLOYER TOLD THE WORKERS IF THERE'S A UNION WE'RE GOING TO MOVE TO MEXICO. THEN THE EMPLOYER WAS COACHING PEOPLE ON HOW TO ASK FOR THEIR UNION CARD BACK. WE GOT A COURT ORDER STOPPING THEM FROM DOING THAT.
>
> MY FAVOURITE LEAFLET IS WHEN THE EMPLOYER DOES SOMETHING STUPID AND YOU FILE AN UNFAIR LABOUR PRACTICE AT THE LABOUR BOARD IN THE MORNING AND IN THE AFTERNOON YOU HAND OUT A LEAFLET SAYING WE'VE TAKEN THE BOSS TO THE LABOUR BOARD.

♦

CHAPTER FOURTEEN

EXAMINATIONS

THE LABOUR BOARD can ask a Labour Relations Officer to do a special investigation, called an "examination," to find out facts about a certain topic to help the Board decide an issue.[1] Normally, such examinations are used when the employer and union cannot agree if a particular job should be part of the bargaining unit, or if a job should be excluded because it includes managerial or confidential duties.

The officer conducts an informal mini-hearing to find out what the job duties and responsibilities are. While the officer collects the information, it is the Labour Board that makes the decision about the job based on the officer's report. The report is referred to as the "Report of the Examination" or more informally as the "LRO's Report."

An examination may also be used if there are disagreements about the employer's list of employees.

If you are involved in an examination, you should review an updated copy of the Board's Practice Note 4.

WHO REQUESTS AN EXAMINATION?

The Labour Board normally requests the examination, but so can the employer or union.

HOW IS THE EXAMINATION CONDUCTED?

The Labour Board Registrar will write to the parties and tell them the name of the appointed officer. The officer will set up a time for everyone to meet and try to give the parties at least one week's notice. Examinations[2] are usually held at the workplace during working hours.[3]

Where there is more than one person in a disputed job, you should discuss with the employer whether a particular employee can be agreed upon as the representative of the job. If you can't agree, the officer will issue an Interim Report after the first employee is examined. Then the parties have to show why it is necessary to examine additional employees to make their point.[4]

At the examination, the officer will ask the employee many questions to find out what duties are involved in the job. The officer usually has a list of questions prepared beforehand. The union and the employer can then ask other questions if they want,[5] and can also call other witnesses to ask them questions if it is useful.

Witnesses are permitted to consult with their representatives at the hearing before answering a question.[6]

How Long Does an Examination Take?

The examination can take a short time or several hours, depending on the type of position being reviewed. The examinations may take place over several months if a lot of witnesses have to be called or if the employer and the union have a lot of questions.

What Happens When the Examination Is Finished?

When the officer has completed the examination, she or he will promptly write up a report of the examination and give a copy to each party.

How Do You Respond To The Officer's Report?

The LRO Report sets out the evidence heard at the examination in a question and answer format. It does not contain any summary or analysis of the examination by the officer. So you must provide the Board with written comments that point out the key evidence and the conclusions that want the Board to draw from this evidence.

Otherwise, the Board may miss key evidence when looking at possibly hundreds of pages of evidence.

To do this you must file a complete statement of those representations with the Board.[7] If you also want an oral hearing, you must request this in your representations giving reasons why an oral hearing is necessary. The Labour Board decides whether it will hold an oral hearing or not.

If there are no written representations or if no one asks the Labour Board for an oral hearing, the Board can decide the case on the information it has.[8]

You can only argue based on what is in the officer's report. You cannot argue about the accuracy of the report unless your objection is because:

- statements in the report are not the same as the evidence given at the time of the examination

- you wanted to give evidence at the time of the examination, but the officer said she or he would not listen to it

- new evidence has come up which you could not have known about at the time of the examination

CAN THE UNION ASK FOR FURTHER EXAMINATIONS?

The officer will ask if everyone is satisfied at the end of examination and then report back to the Board. If the union says it is satisfied, the Board probably will not let the union ask more questions at a later date.[9]

EXAMINATION TIPS

KNOW THE JOB BEFOREHAND

If you are the person representing the union group, you should talk to the people in the job in question before the examination so you have a good idea about what they do. You should check to see if there are any documents, such as job descriptions that show how the employer or others saw the job prior to the application for certification application.

MAKE YOUR OWN NOTES

Because you will only receive transcripts of the examination after it is over, you should make your own notes during questioning so that you can prepare questions for the employees when you get a turn to cross-examine them.

YOU DON'T NEED A LAWYER

Usually an experienced union representative can handle an examination on her own. If you think some witnesses will be very difficult to deal with, you may want a lawyer to help.

CROSS-EXAMINATION AND RE-EXAMINATION

PREPARING EXAMINEES

The workers being questioned are called the "examinees." If it is possible, you should prepare the examinees beforehand. You should explain the union's position so they know why the employer may ask certain questions. If you think the employees will exaggerate in front of the employer, it may be a good idea to bring other co-workers from the same area along to listen. That way the employees being examined may be more accurate if they know that co-workers who really know what they do will be listening.

ANTI-UNION EXAMINEES

Employees whom the employer calls for examination may be against the union. The employer may call supervisors, for example, to talk about what they think employees do and whose answers may make the employees' work sound different than what the employees believe they do.

KNOW YOUR TOPIC

The best preparation for an examination is to review the law and facts that the Labour Board considers important on a particular issue. For bargaining unit issues review Chapter 8. For employee status issues, review Chapter 10.

EXCLUSION OF MANAGERIAL/CONFIDENTIAL EMPLOYEES

Sometimes the employer will try to keep someone out of the bargaining unit by saying that employee is part of management or has a job that involves confidential labour relations duties. To decide on questions to help you determine an employee's status, see "Management and Confidential Jobs Check List" in Chapter 5 and "Excluding Managerial and Confidential Employees" in Chapter 8.

If the employer tries to show some evidence to the officer and won't let the union see it, you should complain. You should insist that either you see the information or it is not used.

OTHER EXAMINATIONS ON BARGAINING UNITS

The Labour Board may also conduct examinations on other bargaining unit questions, such as whether or not to combine two plants into one unit or sales and office staff in to one unit. See Chapter 8 on bargaining units.

◆

CHAPTER FIFTEEN

THE REPRESENTATION VOTE

IF YOUR UNION is able to sign up more than 55 percent of the workers eligible to be in the bargaining unit, you will likely get automatic certification.[1] If you have the support of 40 percent to 55 percent of the workers in the bargaining unit, the Labour Board will order a "representation vote."[2] This vote determines if the workers are to be represented by your union. If more than 50 percent vote in favour, the Board will certify your union.[3]

Workers vote by a secret ballot supervised by a Labour Relations Officer. Neither the employer nor the union will know who voted for or against the union.

This chapter will deal with normal representation votes, pre-hearing representation votes, eligibility for voting, rules about campaigning, the vote itself, and what you can do if your employer's unfair tactics cause you to lose the vote.

PRE-HEARING REPRESENTATION VOTE

A union can ask for a pre-hearing representation vote in its application for certification if it has signed membership cards for at least 35 percent of employees in the bargaining unit.[4] Votes that take place before a hearing are set up more quickly than regular representation votes, which occur after a hearing.

A pre-hearing vote may also be useful if you think that there will be big seasonal lay-offs in the near future, which may lower the number of people who will be able to vote for the union if the vote does not occur for quite a while.

You should be careful before deciding to ask for a pre-hearing representation vote. If you lose the vote, the Labour Board won't let your union change its mind and then say that it does not want the pre-hearing vote to count. Your union's only choice would be to withdraw its application, and then it could be barred from re-applying for six months.

Any dispute about whether the membership cards are genuine or whether the bargaining unit is appropriate must be brought to the Labour Board's attention before the pre-hearing vote. These issues will not be dealt with by the Board until after the pre-hearing vote takes place,[5] and the votes will not be counted until the Labour Board rules on the issues.[6]

> SOME WHO VOTED 'NO' TOLD US THAT SECRETLY THEY WERE HOPING THE UNION WOULD WIN BUT THEY WERE AFRAID.
>
> THERE WERE VOTES IN SIX LOCATIONS, THE LABOUR RELATIONS OFFICER HAD TO BRING THE BOXES DOWN TO THE BOARD FOR THE COUNT. WE HAD TO WAIT WITH OUR ARCH ENEMY THE PERSONNEL GUY SITTING THERE WITH A GRIN ON HIS FACE, SURE THEY'D WON. WHEN THE ANNOUNCEMENT CAME, WE'D WON! I WAS ALL GEARED UP FOR DEFEAT AND IT WAS A VICTORY!
>
> I KNOW IF WE'RE GOING TO WIN. LIKE A TRAPPER WALKING THROUGH THE BUSH: AHH I SEE THE BEAVER DAMS, THE BARK'S THICKER THIS YEAR... YOU HAVE THAT SENSE WHEN YOU'RE GOING TO WIN. YOU NEED AT LEAST 60 PER CENT TO WIN A VOTE, WE'VE HAD 70 PER CENT AND LOST.

VOTE TIPS

WHO IS ELIGIBLE TO VOTE?

GENERAL RULE

The question of who is eligible to vote is very important. Without enough eligible supporters you will lose the representation vote.

The general rule for a regular representation vote is that employees can vote if they are employees both on the date the vote is ordered by the Labour Board and on the date of the vote.[7] For a pre-hearing representation vote, the date used to assess eligibility of workers is the application date for the union's application and not the date on which the vote was ordered if the vote is ordered as a result of the waiver process.[8]

If an employee quits, is fired for cause, or is transferred or laid off between the Labour Board's vote order and the date of the vote, she or he will not be eligible to participate in a representation vote. By the same rule, an employee who transfers into the unit between these dates also cannot vote.

This rule is unfair to unions because it allows an employer to transfer out employees who may be union supporters. If you can show the Labour Board that the only reason the employer transferred employees was to try to stop the union, the Labour Board can allow these people to vote.[9]

30-DAY RULE

To determine if employees are eligible to vote, even though they may not be working on the actual application date, the Labour Board applies the 30-day rule. This means that if the employees have worked sometime within 30 days before the application date, and will work sometime within 30 days after the application date, they will be eligible to vote.[10]

Similarly, workers who are ill, on holiday, on workers' compensation benefits, or on pregnancy leave can vote if the rule applies to them. They must vote on the same day as the other employees.[11]

LAID OFF EMPLOYEES

If you are on "definite lay-off" for a specific period of time, you may be able to vote. If you are on an "indefinite lay-off," which means that the employer does not know if you will ever be called back to work, you are not considered an employee and you cannot vote.[12] However, if you can show that your employer has put workers on indefinite lay-offs simply because he does not want the union and not for a real economic reason, the Labour Board may order that those workers can still vote.

Your union can also complain of unfair labour practices or of a lockout if you can demonstrate that your employer:

- did not lay-off in order of seniority,

- re-hires employees right after the vote, or

- has employees doing a lot of overtime just before the vote while others are laid off.

YOU NEED A REPRESENTATIVE NUMBER OF WORKERS

The Labour Board only allows a vote at a time when the bargaining unit consists of a representative sample of the employees who work in the unit.[13]

NO EMPLOYEES

Some employers try to say that there are no workers in the unit when it's voting time. They can do this by shutting down their operation and opening up under a new name. If this happens, the Labour Board may conduct an investigation. If it finds that the employer did this to avoid the union, the Labour Board can order a vote.[14]

LAY-OFFS

The Labour Board has ruled that even if an employer lays off many employees before the vote, the remaining employees are "representative" and the vote is held. If the union can show that the other lay-offs were only done to avoid the union vote, the union can ask the Labour Board to delay the vote until the other employees are back at work.

BUILD-UP

A build-up is the opposite of a lay-off. It occurs when a large and representative number of employees are not at work on the voting day, but it is likely that a lot of employees will be hired shortly after the voting day, say, within six months.

A build-up must occur for reasons that are in the employer's control. Factors such as an anticipated increase in market sales are not allowed.

If a build-up is anticipated, the employer usually asks the Labour Board to order that the vote be delayed until the other employees start working and can vote. In deciding, the Labour Board balances the right of present workers to unionize with the right of future workers to have a say in whether to bargain collectively.[15]

If the Board orders a delay in the vote, it usually tells the employer to report regularly to the Board until more than 50 percent of the total projected workers are at work.

An employer may try to delay the vote by saying it is going to build-up its workforce, but instead uses the time to intimidate workers. If you can show that the build-up argument is being used to stop the union, and the Labour Board agrees with you, it can order the vote right away[16] or, in some cases, certify you without a vote.

EMPLOYEES ON VACATION

You should try to avoid having a vote when a lot of your supporters will likely be on vacation. The Labour Board will not delay the vote until they come back from holidays.

CAN YOU POSTPONE THE VOTE?

Once scheduled, the Labour Board does not usually postpone a vote. If you complain that employees can't vote freely because of the employer's tactics, the Labour Board can close the ballot box and not count the votes ("sealing the ballot box") until it holds a hearing about your complaints.[17]

CAMPAIGN TO WIN THE VOTE

You probably have a majority of workers signed up. Now your job is to keep these people as union supporters and gain more union votes.

The Labour Board no longer imposes a 72 hour silent period before every vote, which created more problems than it solved in the past, so you can campaign up until the day of the vote.

LEAFLETS

Union leaflets can be very important. If the employer has been saying bad things about the union, a leaflet can answer an employee's concerns. The Labour Board will not try to stop you from handing out leaflets unless the leaflet:

- tries to unfairly force employees to vote one way or the other;

- makes the workers think the vote won't be secret and everyone will know who they voted for;

- makes it sound like the Labour Board is working for one side or the other as opposed to being neutral;

- makes it hard for workers to think about alternatives.

UNFAIR VOTE PRACTICES

Union supporters and the employer are free to engage in electioneering before and on the day of the vote, as long as their activities are not intimidating, coercive, or destructive of the employees' freedom to vote as they wish.

The Labour Board will investigate matters if a party complains that the campaigning of the other party did not allow the voters to exercise their free choice.[18] The Board may set aside the vote and order a further one if a party can show that the improper conduct deprived employees of the ability to vote freely.[19] The Board decides this based on what the likely effect of the employer's conduct is on what the Board describes as the average employee.

The Board has refused employer's requests to find that immigrants are more likely to be intimidated and therefore voted for the union out of fear.[20]

(See the section on "Complaining about the Vote" below for when and how to complain.)

EMPLOYER COMMUNICATIONS

Employers may try to find out who's organizing the campaign and may try to intimidate them before the vote. The employer is allowed to make public speeches and send letters, but if they threaten employees or tell them that they will be fired or hurt if they join a union, your union can make an "unfair labour practice"[21] complaint to the Labour Board. This is discussed in greater detail in Chapter 13.

VOTING PROCEDURE

THE VOTING LIST

Before the voting day, the employer and the union meet with a Labour Relations Officer to make up a voting list. This list is different from the employer's employee lists that are used to determine whether a vote even needs to be ordered. This list is composed of all the employees in the decided upon bargaining unit who were employees on the date the vote was ordered.

Make sure you check this list very carefully. Sometimes the employer will put people on this list who do not belong there, like people in management. If you see this, you should complain right away to the officer. If you agree to the voting list, you can't change your agreement later on except in extraordinary circumstances.[22]

PREPARING FOR VOTING DAY

The Labour Board will print notices of the representation vote and the ballots in English and French only. If there are employees who speak different languages, the Labour Board leaves it up to the union and the employer to explain the vote to those employees.[23] Rather than relying on the employer's explanations, the union should provide an explanation and an accurate translation of the documents for the employees as soon as possible.

Before voting day, you should ask that the "Returning Officer" (the person from the Labour Board who watches over the vote and initials the ballots) use a stamp. That way you can make sure that everything is done properly.

SCRUTINEERS

All the parties involved in a vote are allowed one scrutineer each. These people watch the voting procedures to make sure nothing illegal takes place. The Labour Board will not pick the scrutineers, so be alert for some employer's tricks. Sometimes an employer will make a boss a scrutineer to scare the employees. In such a case, the vote may be found to be invalid if the Board decides that a scrutineer intimidated a voter.[24]

THE DAY OF THE VOTE

The union scrutineer and other union members should get to the polling station early to check for things that do not look right. For example, they can make sure that there is a private place to mark the ballot and that the line up for the vote is not in front of the office of a boss.

The Board has cautioned unions not to let supporters near the voting area as someone might make a charge of threatening or intimidating conduct.[25]

The scrutineers should watch the votes very carefully and should not leave the voting area until the vote is over.

SEGREGATED BALLOTS AND SEALED BALLOT BOXES

When there are challenges or disputes to the list or bargaining unit in a pre-hearing vote, the challenged ballots will be segregated and the ballot boxes sealed pending further direction of the Labour Board.[26]

If there is a complaint about the representation vote, the officer may also seal the ballot box pending the resolution of the charges.

AFTER THE VOTE

After the vote, the Returning Officer makes a report (setting out the results of the vote), which must be given or sent to the parties and be posted in the workplace by the employer.[27] She may also ask a scrutineer to make a report, too. By law, the union scrutineer does not have to sign anything but may be asked to sign the Returning Officer's report. If there have been any problems with the vote, the union scrutineer should not sign. If the union scrutineer does sign, the Board is likely to dismiss any later complaint and the union will then have to show very good reasons (for example, its scrutineers could not have seen or observed the problem at the time of the vote) to have the vote discounted.[28]

WILL THE EMPLOYER KNOW HOW PEOPLE VOTED?

The Labour Board has a firm rule that employees' votes are secret.[29]

SPOILED BALLOTS

Sometimes people may not mark an X in the appropriate box. This does not mean that the vote is automatically discounted. If the ballot clearly shows what the employee wanted, then it is usually counted by the officer and the scrutineers.[30] A ballot must clearly be destroyed or defaced for it to be considered a spoiled ballot and not counted.

COMPLAINING ABOUT THE VOTE

Complaints about election voting practices — before the vote or during the vote — must be made orally to the Labour Relations Officer as soon as you are aware of them and before the counting of the vote.

If you find any problems with the Returning Officer's report or you felt that during the voting your employer tried to intimidate workers, report these to the Labour Board as well and as soon as possible.

Your complaints must be in writing and submitted no later than seven days after the date the report was first posted.[31] The Board will only listen to a later complaint if the problem turned up after this seven-day period or if the complaint could not reasonably have been filed before that time.

IF YOU LOSE THE VOTE

If you lose the vote because the employer's unfair tactics made a free vote impossible, you can ask for a hearing to determine if you can be certified anyway or ask if the Labour Board will order a new vote. (For more details on how to do this see Chapter 13.)

If you believe you have enough support for an automatic certification, you may want to re-apply. Try to save your application. However, the Labour Board usually makes a union which loses a vote wait six months before allowing it to apply again.

If there wasn't a vote, you can apply again as soon as you have corrected the problem. This might happen if some cards were not signed in the right way. You can get these employees to re-sign and you can use the membership cards from the first application as long as they were not signed too far in the past. If they were signed over six months prior to the application, the Board may not count them as a current expression of the employees' wishes without some evidence that the employees continue to wish to be represented by the union.

THE SUPERVISOR SCARED A LOT OF PEOPLE ON THE
KITCHEN AND HOUSEKEEPING SIDE. TOLD THEM 'THE
UNION'S GOING TO TAKE AWAY YOUR JOB, THEY'LL BRING
IN UNION PEOPLE TO DO IT AND YOU'LL BE OUT THE
DOOR.' THEY BELIEVED HER.

WE'VE GOT A PROBLEM WITH THE EMPLOYER'S LISTS AT
THE BOARD. THEY INCLUDED DEAD PEOPLE'S NAMES,
THE SAME NAMES REVERSED, AND PLAYERS FROM THE
TORONTO MAPLE LEAFS!

WE CONTINUE TO PUT OUT LEAFLETS EVERY NOW AND
THEN IN PLANTS WE HAVEN'T BEEN ABLE TO ORGANIZE.
JUST TO REMIND THE BOSS WE HAVEN'T GONE AWAY. JUST
TO LET THE WORKERS KNOW WE HAVEN'T FORGOTTEN.

♦

CHAPTER SIXTEEN

NEGOTIATING YOUR
FIRST CONTRACT

AS SOON AS THE Labour Board approves your application and certifies your group, you have the right to "bargain collectively" with your employer. If you've gone the "voluntary recognition" route, then you have the right to bargain as soon your union and your employer have signed the special agreement that the law requires.[1]

This chapter:

- explains what a collective agreement is
- describes what's in a collective agreement
- outlines how to get ready for bargaining
- makes suggestions about strategy
- describes the bargaining process
- summarizes useful tactics
- outlines how to apply for "first agreement arbitration"

Within 60 days of being certified, the union *must* send the employer written notice that it wants to bargain. If the union doesn't send this notice, the Labour Board can take away the certificate or order a representation vote to see if employees still want a union.[2] Be sure to keep a copy of your notice as proof that you've sent it. If you're bargaining under the *Hospital Labour Disputes Arbitration Act,* give your employer notice to bargain immediately. If your union has to go to arbitration, the earliest date a wage increase can take effect is the date you gave your notice.[3]

The employer by law must meet with union representatives and bargain in good faith.[4] Bargaining "in good faith" means that the employer has to sit down and really try to work out a collective agreement with the union, whether he likes the idea or not.

WHAT IS A COLLECTIVE AGREEMENT?

Having a union means you can bargain and sign a collective agreement with the employer, an agreement that both you and the employer have to stick to, by law.

A collective agreement is a legal, written contract that is negotiated between the employer and the union representing a group of employees.[5]

The collective agreement sets out the terms and conditions of work.

It is made up of a series of sections, called *articles,* and numbered paragraphs, called *clauses.*

The words used in collective agreements often sound very legalistic. Some contracts are full of words like "aforementioned," "notwithstanding," and "save and except," which can make it difficult to follow the meaning.

Little words, too, mean a lot. For example, there's a big difference between saying an employer "shall" give paid time off to attend funerals, and saying the employer "may" give the time off. If your contract says "may" then management can decide whether or not you get time off. If the contract says "shall," your paid time off is guaranteed.

Collective agreements describe two kinds of issues: those that are about money and those that aren't. Those that aren't include things that have an indirect cost or where the exact cost is hard to predict, such as paid bereavement leave. Money items are called "monetary issues." The rest are called "non-monetary issues."

Examples of monetary issues are: wages, overtime pay, paid holidays and vacations, paid sick leave, medical and dental benefits, pension plans, shift premiums, and clothing allowances and staffing ratios.

Examples of non-monetary issues are: rules for promotions and transfers, provisions for hours of work, seniority rules, rules forbidding sexual harassment and discrimination, rules for lay-offs, procedures for settling grievances, an outline of management's rights, and provisions for labour-management committees.

Employers frequently emphasize that non-monetary issues can have some cost implications. For example, sexual harassment guidelines and procedures may require an employer to spend money in order to develop the procedures and training programs to cover the cost of employees being off work to attend the program.

SAMPLE CLAUSES IN A COLLECTIVE AGREEMENT

NON-MONETARY

Article 7
Harassment
7.01 Every employee has a right to be free from harassment because of the their gender, race, colour, religion, national origin, political affiliation or activity, marital status, family relationship, sexual orientation, disability, activity in the union, age, or other similar grounds and from any reprisal or threat of reprisal for the rejection of such behaviour.

MONETARY

Article 9
Premium Pay Provisions
9.01 Each employee shall be paid at the rate of time and one-half for time worked in excess of 8 hours per day or 40 hours in a weekly pay period.

WHAT'S IN A COLLECTIVE AGREEMENT?

The items in a collective agreement must be *at least as good* as the rights you have under laws such as the *Employment Standards Act,* the *Human Rights Code,* and the *Occupational Health and Safety Act.*[6]

There are some things that the *Labour Relations Act* states must be a part of every collective agreement:

1. THE "WITHOUT JUST CAUSE CLAUSE" [NEW]

The employer can't fire or discipline an employee "without just cause." You don't have to bargain with your employer to get this "just cause" section in your first contract. By law it's a given in every union contract.[7] In fact, it applies as soon as you get your union certificate.

You probably will have to bargain about how this provision is going to apply to probationary employees. The law says that the employer and the union may negotiate different rules about firing new employees who are on probation.[8]

2. EXCLUSIVE BARGAINING AGENT

Every collective agreement must state that the union is the only organization or person who can bargain for the employees who belong to the bargaining unit.[9]

3. NO STRIKE OR LOCKOUT

The union can't strike and the employer can't stop employees from coming to work (a "lockout") during the time period that the agreement covers.[10]

4. FINAL AND BINDING ARBITRATION [NEW]

If the employer and the union have a dispute about the collective agreement or a grievance that they cannot resolve themselves, they must go to an arbitrator who will hear both sides and make a final decision.[11]

5. CONSULTATION PROVISION [NEW]

If you or your employer want to adapt a clause about consultation to your particular workplace, then one of you must put in a request in writing after you've given notice to bargain, or you can give the notice in writing after bargaining has begun.[12]

The "consultation provision" says that the employer and the union have to meet at least once every two months to discuss workplace issues. This process is sometimes called a "labour-management committee."

This regular meeting will give you a chance to seek information and to bring certain kinds of problems, ones that aren't covered in the collective agreement, up for discussion.

If your committee doesn't (or is unable to) negotiate your own provision in the collective agreement, then your agreement operates as if it automatically includes the following article:[13]

On the request of either party, the parties shall meet at least once every two months until this agreement is terminated for the purpose of discussing issues relating to the workplace which affect the parties or any employee bound by this agreement.

You should give notice to your employer that you want a consultation provision written into your agreement. Then if your employer refuses to meet with you regularly, you will be able to use your grievance procedure to force him to meet.

7. Union Dues

If the union asks, the contract must include a clause that says the employer must deduct union dues from employees' pay cheques, and forward the money to the union.[14]

You should ask for this item because it's the easiest way to collect union dues. At income tax time the employer lists how much has been collected in dues money on your T-4 slip for your tax return.

8. Recognition Clause

Another point to keep in mind once you're certified is that you can lose your geographic bargaining rights at the bargaining table if you don't pay careful attention to how the recognition clause of your collective agreement is written. A recognition clause usually says that the employer recognizes the union as the bargaining representative and often repeats the language of the certificate. But if you include a narrower geographic description in your collective agreement than what you have in the certificate, the collective agreement will be what counts. Don't give away your hard won rights at the bargaining table!

There are two changes you may consider in the wording of your Labour Board certificate. One is to extend the geographic municipality to include another location if the employer moves or expands. The other is to include more jobs in the union. For example if "senior mechanics" were originally excluded, you might try to bargain to include them.

TIME AND TIME AGAIN IT'S NOT THE PEOPLE WHO HAVE LED THE WORKERS INTO THE UNION THAT GET ELECTED ON THE BARGAINING COMMITTEE, BUT RATHER THE WHITE WORKERS. THERE'S A FALSE PERCEPTION THAT THE WHITE WORKERS WILL GET MORE RESPECT, RATHER THAN THAT YOU SHOULD ELECT A BARGAINING COMMITTEE WHO'LL FIGHT FOR YOU, WHO'LL STAND UP FOR YOUR RIGHTS, AND THAT'S HOW YOU EARN RESPECT.

IT TOOK A HORRIBLE FIGHT TO GET CLERICAL WORKERS ON THE NEGOTIATING TEAM. THE PRESIDENT WANTED TO LOAD THE TEAM WITH TECHNICIANS, EVEN THOUGH MOST OF US ARE CLERKS.

THE ADVERSARIAL STYLE ISN'T THE ONLY WAY, ESPECIALLY FOR SMALL LOCALS. WHEN WE ORGANIZED EVERYBODY LEARNED HOW TO BE A NEGOTIATOR, LEARNED HOW TO BE A SHOP STEWARD, AND UNDERSTOOD EVERY CLAUSE IN THE AGREEMENT, WHY IT WAS THERE.

GETTING READY TO BARGAIN

The lead negotiator for the union co-ordinates the union side of the bargaining process. Often that person is a paid full-time union representative, a professional whose job it is to help the bargaining committee work out the best bargaining strategy.

Successful bargaining builds on your organizing drive. Choosing the bargaining committee is one of the first steps in getting ready to bargain with the employer. A committee to bargain for 20 members will be smaller than one to bargain for 500. Unions choose committee members in a variety of ways. They may be elected or be appointed.

UNION BARGAINING COMMITTEE MEMBERSHIP

Committee members should be willing and able to give time and energy to the task. Usually the committee includes some people who have been active in the efforts to organize the workplace. Some people on the committee should have bargaining type experience — in the community, in clubs, or at work — and everyone should be committed to working through workplace problems.

Most people have experiences that are related to bargaining, which is very much a matter of judgment. Mothers negotiate and balance the demands of family and work every day. Many disabled people have experiences as activists in advocacy organizations that negotiate with agencies and governments. The same is true for people active in the environmental movement, gay and lesbian organizations, tenant associations, and for members of visible minority groups that lobby for change.

The people on the committee should reflect the membership. Try to see that different jobs, departments, and groups are represented. This way the committee will know what different parts of the membership need and how decisions will affect each group.

Members of the committee also have to understand the interests of the membership as a whole. During bargaining the committee seldom has the time to consult point by point with the members. The committee has to make decisions that, in their judgment, the membership will accept.

In traditional bargaining, everyone on the bargaining commit-tee needs stamina to stay at the bargaining table for long periods of time, sometimes far into the early morning hours in the final sessions. This is the most common approach to bargaining.

Some unions call all-night bargaining the "macho" way of bargaining, so they've developed a different way to negotiate with some volunteer boards and boards of directors of co-operatives. They bargain only during regular working hours, or with set time limits in the evening so that women with children can participate more easily. They also use a consensual method, where each issue is discussed by both sides until they reach an agreement. This kind of bargaining has worked well for some day-care unions whose members work for non-profit employers.

UNION BARGAINING COMMITTEE'S TASKS

The lead negotiator speaks for the union at the bargaining table, and keeps track of the paper as both sides exchange proposals and information.

The lead negotiator will keep a detailed record of issues agreed upon and issues in dispute, a normal practice as you go along in bargaining. This information is also required if the union decides later to apply for first contract arbitration. Sometimes both parties will record and sign "agreed" items as they are resolved.

People on the committee divide the work. One person will keep an official written record of what goes on, but others on the committee may help with back-up notes, especially when there's confusion or disagreement. Someone who has good writing skills may prepare draft newsletters for the committee's approval. Someone who's good with charts might design ways to present information to management, and so on.

During planning sessions, and during bargaining with the employer, the committee should always try to work by consensus, rather than by taking votes. People should be willing to talk with one another until they've reached an agreement. That's not always as easy as it sounds. There's often pressure by the employer or even a government officer to get a decision from the lead negotiator, without much time for democratic discussion. The suggestions made in Chapter 5 for building unity in your organizing committee can be used with your bargaining committee too.

The committee follows the practice of *solidarity* when the employer is in the room. That means they present a united front to the employer and normally only one person speaks on the union's behalf. The committee should try to work out exactly when another committee member will make a special point. If other committee members find they disagree with the actual presentation of a union position, there should be an understanding that these members can ask for a special caucus of the union committee so that they can talk it through with other members of the committee.

Some bargaining committees put together a bargaining kit for each member of the committee. The kit might include a copy of the *Labour Relations Act,* the *Employment Standards Act,* and the *Ontario Human Rights Code* for reference.

The kit can be a loose-leaf binder in which members keep copies of proposals and counter-proposals. They note the date and time on each piece of paper they give to management or get from management. They note the items where there's agreement, and where there's disagreement. It's a good way to keep track of what's going on.

FINDING OUT WHAT YOUR MEMBERS WANT

The committee's first job is to find out what the members want, draft a list of proposals, and take these proposals to a membership meeting for discussion, possibly amendment, and then approval. The employer may also prepare a set of proposals.

This is a key time for the new union. The members will be watching the process carefully. It's a time to listen and build support. If you've joined an existing union, the union representative will help you put together your proposals.

Some unions send their members a survey or questionnaire as soon as the union applies for certification. Sometimes the new union leaders send a bargaining questionnaire that lists issues and asks the members to mark the most important ones. Or the union leaders ask the members to write in with ideas. Members can meet in small groups and decide what to answer, or they can write back on their own. Some new unions hold meetings in each department to discuss their first proposals.

Don't be discouraged if you send out surveys and don't get many written answers back. The rate of return for written surveys is usually low, but questionnaires are a good way of finding out what your most concerned members want, and those that don't answer know that you've made an effort to consult them. Make sure the questionnaire advises people that they can reply in another language if necessary.

It's a good idea for members of the bargaining committee to talk with their co-workers, to find out what they want *and* what they expect to get. The two things may be very different, and it's important to know both.

Some parent unions have a set of basics that they want included in each of their local contracts, such as particular wording for anti-harassment clauses and lay-off provisions. Some have a model contract that can be adapted to local needs. The union representative will give your committee these basics to include in your list of proposals to management.

WORDING THE PROPOSALS

When you are preparing your list of proposals, keep two general principles about collective agreement wording in mind.

THE MORE GENERAL THE PRINCIPLE IN THE CONTRACT, THE MORE YOU CAN DO WITH THE CONTRACT IN PRACTICE

If you make a very detailed proposal about something, you may find that you have no room to move during bargaining. And, if you do get very specific and detailed wording in the contract, you may find that you're boxed in when you have a problem to fix.

Workplaces and employers differ. Unions may deliberately negotiate very specific wording to deal with particular issues. The point is to be conscious of the implications of each approach.

EACH CLAUSE AFFECTS THE OTHERS IN THE CONTRACT

You may think you have won something in one clause, only to find management using your arguments against you when you're discussing another clause.

Take an example where the union proposes to reduce the probationary period for a job from six months to three months. Management argues that it takes six months to learn the skills of the job, and the union responds that three months is plenty. Then, when the time comes to discuss wage rates for the job, management can argue that the job isn't worth much, after all the union has argued it takes only three months to learn it. Watch for these contradictions in the employer's position. Save them for an argument to support one of your proposals.

MEMBERSHIP MEETING: PROPOSALS

The committee should put together the list of proposals to take to a special membership meeting. At this meeting the union president, chief steward, or the lead negotiator reads out or summarizes the proposals and explains each one.

This is a very important meeting. The members should be able to ask questions and discuss and debate the proposals. The elected officers of the union should have a formal process for members to use in order to propose additions and changes.

This meeting is also an opportunity to explain some of the issues that every agreement covers but that many people don't understand, such as seniority, union leave, union security, and the description of the bargaining unit. The meeting should be well-planned and well-chaired so that all topics are covered.

After the discussion, the person chairing the meeting conducts a vote to approve the final list of proposals. When the union presents the list of proposals to management, you know, and management knows, that your members are behind the proposals and are ready to back up the bargaining committee.

DEVELOPING A BARGAINING STRATEGY

The *goals* the union sets for itself will include the key proposals, as well as things like building community support or educating the members about a key issue.

The committee needs to work out a bargaining strategy that creates the greatest chance possible for reaching the union's bargaining goals. The committee also has to make choices about which bargaining proposals are most important to the union.

Asking one another questions is one way to work out a plan.

• How strongly do the members support each proposal?

• How can you build support for key proposals?

• What strategies can you use to involve your membership?

• How can you use public opinion to increase your bargaining power?

• What organizations and what people in other unions and in the community might help?

• What pressure might influence the employer? How can you affect that?

• If your employer is part of a government or is funded by government, what political forums might you use?

• How might you inform customers, clients, residents, patients about your issues?

BACKGROUND INFORMATION

You have to persuade your employer that each of the union's proposals are sensible and possible. To do this the committee has to present convincing arguments. The bargaining committee should collect information to back up the proposals. Some examples of useful information are:

• newspaper clippings of statements from community leaders, business people, and politicians

• information on the recent trends in the economy, clippings

from the business section of the newspaper
• rates of pay and working conditions in similar workplaces
• settlements other unions have made
• your employer's budget and financial statements

Sometimes you will need statistics about your members, such as the number who work at video display terminals, the number with young children, the number who need safety boots, a summary of accidents, or whatever might illustrate and strengthen the case you want to make.

Think ahead and collect information before the employer asks for it at the bargaining table.

The committee can ask experts for advice on issues like pensions, health and safety, and so on. The parent union may have staff who can advise you, or you can contact academics or other people with special knowledge.

If you serve the public you may want to gather information and put together arguments that show the relationship between your proposals and the quality of service at your workplace. An example is not reporting to work when you're ill if you're working closely with vulnerable people, such as small children or the elderly. It's better for *them and you* if you get paid time off when you're sick.

You have a right to ask for certain information from your employer. Put your proposal for data on job classifications, benefit costs, and so on, in writing to the employer in advance. Think ahead. For example, if you're proposing paid parental leave, ask for information on the number of employees who took parental leave in previous years. Bring this information with you to have on hand if the employer argues it will cost too much.

WHY DO UNIONS ASK FOR SO MUCH AT THE START?

You will have a long list of proposals when you bargain for your first contract because every item must be bargained for, even the wording for some of the issues that the law requires be in every agreement.

Why do unions usually ask for more than they expect to receive? Why ask for high wage increases? Why do employers offer so little?

One reason for presenting some exaggerated bargaining demands is that they create space for movement. Large demands create a situation where the sides exchange information, and during that process gather more information that helps confirm, or gives reason to adjust, opening strategy and tactics.

Another reason is that it's not accepted practice to add demands once bargaining has begun. Making a large general demand means you have more room to fit in changes or additions later.

A long list of demands also gives you a chance to bring up things you know are unrealistic in the present, but possible in future bargaining. It gives the employer a clear message that employees are talking about these issues and that they know what they need and deserve.

The disadvantage of a long list is that it may cause long delays in getting a settlement. Sometimes you may want to draw out your negotiations. Sometimes you will be anxious for a quick settlement. You have to adjust your approach to the circumstances.

The employer might also pick the least important proposals from a very long list, agree to them, and pretend that this is a major new position.

Keep in mind that asking for far more than you can get may mean that the community reacts against you, or that your members really expect you to deliver more than you possibly can. Their expectations may be so high that if the final settlement falls short, they may reject the agreement. This won't happen if you have a good system of informing and listening to your members throughout the bargaining process.

CHOOSING ARGUMENTS

The committee has to figure out how to present the best arguments in the strongest possible way. Look at all the choices you have. Do an inventory of all your resources, and discuss what you might do to convince all of the people on the employer's side to agree.

In conventional bargaining, the lead negotiator is the only person who ever speaks. An alternative is to share the task. The committee can let different people speak by identifying members who can best present each argument. It may be more effective for management to hear the case from someone who can talk from personal experience. Or, you could combine these approaches, assign one person the responsibility for the main line of argument and have others supplement her or his remarks at points in the discussion agreed upon beforehand.

Use your imagination. Outline different arguments. Think each option through, two or three steps ahead. Think about how the employer might respond. Together, choose the argument that seems most likely to work at the bargaining table.

When making these kinds of choices don't make the mistake of saying, "The employer will do *this* if we do *that*." Thinking that way can lead to problems if your prediction is wrong. You can be knocked off balance if your predictions fall through.

It's better to make a list of several possible outcomes of each action. Then make a judgment about the likelihood of each happening. You can make these judgments in rough percentages. If there's a 40 percent chance of an outcome that would hurt you, is the action worth the risk? If there's a 10 percent chance that the action will lead to what you want, is it worth the effort? What are the consequences of trying and failing, or, on the other hand, of doing nothing?

You may have to make a move with only a low possibility of success because there is no better alternative. If you're conscious of the risks and possible outcomes you're less likely to be surprised and more likely to be prepared when the time comes to respond, whatever happens.

SOLIDARITY

Solidarity is the foundation of every good settlement, the centre of every union strategy. Talk through every issue as a group beforehand. Take caucus breaks. Go for a walk together. Find other ways to keep up your spirits.

Never let the employer divide the bargaining committee. Divide and conquer is one of the oldest battle tactics in the world — don't fall for it!

Observe the people on the other side of the table. Watch their body language. Let your lead negotiator know, by note or during a caucus meeting, when you hear something from the employer that isn't quite right.

The management negotiator may favour one person on your team over others, or their negotiator may single out someone on your side, and attack them. Stay cool, keep calm, let your main negotiator lead. You'll have to weather some hot debates, but that doesn't mean you have to take insults and persistent, offensive remarks. Consider a well-timed early leave-taking from that kind of bargaining session.

Along the way there will be setbacks, frustrations, times when you may feel you've lost control of the situation. Don't panic. Be realistic in evaluating and criticizing your progress. Make changes if necessary. A good plan is a plan with room for adjustment.

MEMBERSHIP SUPPORT

The support of the membership is key to how much power the bargaining committee has to influence the employer.

To bargain well you need a way to communicate with the membership. Committee members should check with co-workers between bargaining sessions. This direct regular contact is ideal but not always possible.

Another good way to keep in touch, especially if you have a large local union, is to use the union stewards as a link between the bargaining committee and the membership. The committee keeps the stewards informed about the negotiations, and the stewards talk to their co-workers and report back to the committee.

If your local has monthly membership meetings you should report as a matter of course on what's happening at the bargaining table. Even if nothing is happening, that's news that management is being stubborn!

The employer will certainly ask the supervisors what employees are saying about bargaining issues. Some employers try out an idea or new proposal for bargaining by asking the supervisor to test the employees' reactions. If you keep in touch with the members during bargaining, they'll know what's going on at the table, you'll know what's going on back at work, and the employer will get the message you want to send.

Workshops, leaflets, panel discussions, films, and meetings about particular proposals can keep the members and the bargaining committee well-informed and well-prepared.

NEGOTIATIONS: THE BARGAINING PROCESS

EARLY STAGES

Sometimes each side has forwarded a set of proposals to the other side before the first meeting. Each side may read their list of proposals out loud while the other side watches, listens, and takes notes. Or, a spokesperson for each side may begin by outlining what the union wants to accomplish in the workplace, then giving an overview of the proposals, with a clear message about priority areas.

In conventional bargaining the lead negotiator for each side makes a vigorous opening speech, and the other side responds with great surprise. This kind of drama helps you find out which proposals are most important to the other side, which are clearly open to amendment, and which can be dropped later on. Others prefer a less dramatic approach. Your bargaining committee should discuss what kind of bargaining process will work best for you.

Bargaining rarely begins with one side or the other presenting a take-it-or-leave-it position, although that *has* been known to happen. At the beginning it's common for each to present demands that are at odds with each other.

There is always a period of "exploration and probing," where each side asks questions and clarifies the proposals and arguments of the other. Both sides seek information, give information, and try to persuade. Each side tries to convince the other that their position is fair and reasonable. When management argues against proposals, it may give clues that show where a compromise might be reached later.

It's wise to deal with non-monetary proposals first — rights, working conditions — and deal with the monetary issues later. Once bargaining over monetary issues begins, the non-monetary issues may be pushed aside. If you can't come to a resolution about a couple of really tough non-monetary issues, such as "no contracting out of bargaining unit work," you can include them in or "carry" them into the session on monetary issues and revisit them near the end.

SIGNALLING

How do you change your position without locking yourself in? Giving verbal signals is a bargaining technique that can protect you and help you change your position when necessary. By using signals, negotiators point the discussion in the direction they want it to go, and then wait for an answering gesture. Getting to know how to send and interpret signals takes experience. Here are some key signals to know.

Passing up an item for the present may show that it can be settled later, depending on the outcome of other items. The lead negotiator can say, "We'll pass this up for now."

Silence may signal a potential concession.

The degree of *emphasis* a negotiator uses may show a change of attitude towards a proposal.

Avoid saying "Never" to several employer positions. Leave the way open for some modification. When you do say "No, never," you want it to be taken seriously.

PACKAGE APPROACH

Many negotiations are done using the package approach. This means that you discuss each issue, note its initial acceptance or rejection, and then move on to the next item. You don't take anything "off the table," you just set items aside, one by one, leaving every issue open until the whole package is ready to be presented as a basis for settlement. This is one of the reasons why committee members usually don't talk about details of each bargaining session back at the workplace. Until the very end of negotiations each acceptance or rejection is only temporary.

Usually both sides decide on the minor items fairly quickly, until only a few are left. Then they negotiate hard on the more difficult issues.

Not everyone bargains this way. In some places, negotiators prefer to "sign off" each article as soon as both sides agree. They say that this shows the members progress as bargaining proceeds. This method is more commonly used where unions and employers negotiate by consensus.

Other unions sign-off items one by one as a way to avoid last minute disagreements. Some don't sign-off items, but slowly reduce the number of proposals in the package through withdrawing selected items.

MORE ON TACTICS

There are no magic tactics. Success in bargaining means being able to understand the special circumstances you face every time you go to the table. It means having the confidence to make common sense decisions. Here are some points to consider.

CALL FOR A CAUCUS

A caucus is a confidential meeting of the bargaining committee, one that takes place privately, away from management.

Take scheduled and unscheduled breaks away from the bargaining table so that the committee can discuss proposals and new developments before responding to management. Find the right balance; you're not going to solve every workplace problem in this forum.

Call a caucus whenever there's a hint of disagreement among members of the union committee. Talk it out.

At the end of each day the union committee should take time to meet and go over what's happened and plan the next session.

DON'T UNDERESTIMATE THE EMPLOYER

The employer may be very well-prepared and experienced. Don't overestimate your position or what you're up against. Prepare thoroughly. The employer may have a lawyer helping behind the scenes or even helping at the bargaining table.

DON'T TALK TOO MUCH

You learn by listening. If you talk all the time your employer will learn all about you and your trade-offs will be very limited. Once you make your point, stop talking. When necessary, ask your employer to explain his problem with the proposal. Say you'll come back with new wording that answers any legitimate concerns.

TABLING

When you're not willing to make a concession, you can suggest that a proposal be tabled or set aside temporarily by saying, "We're 'holding' on this one for now." You can bring the item up for more discussion later.

DON'T GIVE AWAY POINTS EASILY

Place a high value on each issue and item you have to give up. Don't concede too early. Make only small concessions after careful consideration.

DON'T JUMP TO CONCLUSIONS

Don't debate. Listen to the employer's position. Question methodically and test your assumptions. Get all of the facts on the table.

USE FALL-BACKS

Fall-backs, the compromises you know you can make, are the safety valves in your position. Don't move past your fall-backs unless you've had a full discussion in a caucus. Be prepared to take the time to reach agreement within your committee before you make big moves at the table.

TIME

Make time work for you. Decide whether you want to draw out the process or whether it's better for you to move things along as quickly as possible. If you decide to compress the process, set deadlines on your proposals and counter-proposals. Set time limits to meetings. Limit debate by tabling selected items. Don't let management draw you off track. Most negotiators leave decisions on major items until late in the negotiations.

SHOWING YOUR STRENGTH

There's always a time when sound arguments and persuasion just aren't enough to get the employer to concede or to agree on an issue. At this stage, negotiating committees often become more aggressive.

You may decide to use "power" tactics to emphasize how reasonable your position is and also how strongly the membership supports this position.

A union's most powerful weapon is the strike, or threat of a strike. Management's equivalent is the lockout where the employer doesn't let employees enter the workplace. In order to legally go on strike (or in the employer's case, legally lockout the employees), the employer and the union must follow the steps outlined in the law. This includes applying for conciliation, and meeting with a Conciliation Officer who will issue a report saying whether or not he or she advises that a conciliation board be appointed. Usually, the advice is that a conciliation board not be appointed. Both unions and management commonly call this a "no board" report.[15]

The date on the labour minister's "no board" letter begins a

16-day countdown to the date when the union and employer can legally strike or lockout. During these 16 days a government mediator may try to get both sides talking again.

[New] In Ontario, employers know that the union can now apply to the Minister of Labour for first agreement arbitration 30 days after they are in a position to legally strike, which is usually two weeks after the "no-board" report.[16]

In places where unions can use the first contract arbitration route, time is on the union's side if the employer doesn't want to hand over the decisions about the first contract to a third party for arbitration.

This change in the law means that, in Ontario, unions can guarantee their new bargaining units that they'll be able to have a first collective agreement, even if the employer has not been cooperative during the bargaining process.

Even with the prospect of first agreement arbitration, you still need to be able to show your employer that your bargaining committee has the full support of the members of your union.

The bargaining committee should work with the stewards to decide on the best ways to apply pressure on the employer.

Unions can remind employers about their members' power by holding special well-publicized education meetings, wearing union buttons, or setting up information pickets, where union members hand out leaflets about the issues to the public. Some individual members may decide not to work overtime. If possible, provide information to consumers and clients explaining the union's position and its relation to good service.

AT THE POINT OF SETTLEMENT

Good negotiators unfold their side's final settlement position gradually, step by step. Often that position is one that has evolved during the process, both for the union and for the employer. When the positions of both sides are close to each other, the committees know that it's time to secure a settlement.

Both sides usually put the greatest pressure on each other just before they reach a settlement. Usually at this point there are only a few crucial issues left.

PROCEED WITH CAUTION

This is a time of great stress. Take the greatest of care when a settlement is close. This is a time when you can make errors in judgment due to stress, exhaustion, frustration, or being elated at the possibility of reaching a good settlement.

BARGAIN SMARTLY

If you hang on for just one proposal left at the end, and you lose it, that's that. A smart negotiating committee has three items outstanding at the end. Aim to win two of the three. And winning one is better than winning nothing.

GET A CLEAR UNDERSTANDING

Make sure you have a clear agreement on all of the details. Test your assumptions about the meaning of each clause in the settlement by going over a final draft of the memorandum of agreement with the employer's representatives. Sort out any disagreements on wording there and then — not later after the contract's been accepted and you no longer have any bargaining power.

SETTLE RESPONSIBLY

It's the committee's responsibility to make sure the settlement is one the members will support. Never sign unless you're confident that the members will approve. Communicating with the membership throughout the process, keeping in touch with the workplace, means you'll be able to predict success accurately.

APPROVAL

The terms of the settlement are usually set out in a document called a "memorandum of agreement." The union negotiating committee takes the document to a meeting of the membership for approval or ratification. The employer's negotiating committee also has to get approval, unless the person with authority to sign for the employer has been one of the people at the table.

FIRST CONTRACT ARBITRATION

WHAT IS ARBITRATION FOR A FIRST CONTRACT?

If your union can't come to an agreement with your employer, you can automatically apply for first contract arbitration. This is a process by which a third party, the board of arbitration, steps in and makes a decision on what the first collective agreement should say.

The first contract board of arbitration looks identical to a board of arbitration that hears grievances regarding violation of collective agreements. It is made up of a representative appointed by the union, a representative appointed by the employer, and a neutral chair person agreed to by both parties.[17]

When one party applies for first contract arbitration, both the union and the employer must give to the Labour Board a copy of a collective agreement that it would be willing to settle for.[18] The board of arbitration then reviews these proposals and makes a decision on all matters in dispute. This first contract will be in effect for two years.[19]

Don't easily give up on trying to bargain an agreement. With arbitration you risk ending up with a "bare minimum contract."

HOW TO GET A FIRST CONTRACT USING ARBITRATION

Both the union and the employer have the right to request a first contract board of arbitration. They can do this by one of two routes: making a request to the minister of labour, or making a request to the Labour Board. To use the Labour Board route, you must show that bargaining has been unsuccessful because of the serious misbehaviour of the employer. (In the employer's case, he must show that bargaining has failed because of the union's actions.)

If you don't have an agreement, you can ask the minister of labour to appoint a board 30 days after the parties are in a legal position to strike.[20]

If you don't have an agreement you can ask the Labour Board

to appoint an arbitration board any time after the "no board report," if you can prove to the Board that:[21]

- the employer has been refusing to recognize the union as the bargaining agent for the employees
- the employer has been making unreasonable demands in negotiations
- the employer has been dragging out the negotiations for an unreasonable time [22]

(If the employer applies to the Labour Board, he must prove that the union has made unreasonable demands or that it is dragging out the negotiations unreasonably.)[23]

The Labour Board has been generally willing to allow first contract arbitration if one of the parties is not making reasonable efforts to reach an agreement on a contract. For example, in one case the employer submitted an unusually large number of proposals at negotiations, and the Labour Board found that the employer was not making reasonable efforts to reach a collective agreement.[24]

FINAL OFFER SELECTION

Another option under first contract arbitration is final offer selection. In this process, the union and the employer each submit their separate versions of a collective agreement "they could live with" and an arbitrator chooses one or the other. This is a very risky option and one that most unions try to avoid.[25]

WHAT HAPPENS WHEN YOU APPLY

Each party has to advise the other of their nominee to the arbitration board within 10 days after the request for arbitration. They must agree on the person who will act as the chair within five days after the nominees are appointed.[26]

Once you or your employer apply for arbitration, any strike or lockout must stop.[27] The employer has to take all employees back to work under an agreement worked out with the union, or, if there isn't an agreement, the employer must take employees back in order of seniority.[28] The employer must take everyone back to work on the same terms as they were working before the union sent the employer the notice to bargain the first contract.[29]

YOUR FIRST CONTRACT!

As soon as your contract is approved, print copies, preferably in a pocket-sized version so that it's easy to carry. Distribute a copy to each person in the bargaining unit. If you have members who do not speak English, arrange for translations. Set up meetings for stewards to explain how to enforce the contract, and have information available for all members on how to file a grievance. Stewards should always have a copy of the contract handy at work, for easy reference. If your stewards and members understand the contract and how to use it, then their confidence will help set the tone for the union's relationship with supervisors and managers. Even though it's a contract between the employer and the union, many workers and supervisors, too, refer to the collective agreement as "the union book." With it, comes respect, because with a union you're working together from a position of strength.

> NEGOTIATING? IT'S AN ENDURANCE TEST. YOU HAVE TO SHOW THE BOSS YOU'RE WILLING TO SIT THERE UNTIL THE COWS COME HOME. HOW ELSE IS HE GOING TO KNOW YOU MEAN BUSINESS?
>
> AT FIRST I WAS VERY DEFENSIVE, I DIDN'T KNOW HOW TO CHAIR A MEETING, I WAS VERY OPINIONATED. I ASKED ONE OF THE OTHER WOMEN, TELL ME WHAT I DID WRONG. I REALLY LISTENED. I'M DOING BETTER NOW.
>
> I LOVED EVERYTHING ABOUT BARGAINING. EVEN THE LATE NIGHTS. WE GOT WHAT WE WANTED. IT WAS EXHILARATING.

APPENDIX A

DEPENDENT AND INDEPENDENT CONTRACTORS

SECTION 1(1) of the Ontario *Labour Relations Act* provides that dependent contractors are considered "employees" for the purposes of forming a union.[1] Independent contractors or self-employed persons are not considered to be employees and can't use the Act's protections to organize. Dependent contractors are persons who are so dependent on an employer that they should have collective bargaining rights.

THE ACT'S GUIDELINES

The Act has given us some guidelines on how to distinguish between a dependent and an independent contractor. Section 1(1) says that a dependent contractor:

• need not have an employment contract with his or her employer but has an obligation to work for the employer

• may work with either his or her tools, material, and equipment or those of the employer

• gets paid by the employer in a way that makes him or her economically dependent on the employer

The key factors the Board will look at are:

• whether the persons are economically dependent on the employer

• whether the persons are obliged to perform duties as an employee would[2]

• who owns the business

Even with these guidelines, it is often difficult to distinguish a dependent contractor from an independent contractor. So we are setting out here some of the Board's findings.

ECONOMIC DEPENDENCE AND CONTROL

Taxi-cab drivers, for example, have been found to be dependent contractors and are therefore employees who may form a union. See the recent case of *Diamond Taxi Cab Association (Toronto) Limited*,[3] which found that the control exercised by the cab owner was necessary because it was the cab owner's business and not the cab driver's.

Even though the cab drivers own their own vehicle, do not get paid directly by the cab company, and may pick up passengers off the street as well as getting them from the cab company, the reality is that these cab drivers are controlled in many ways by the cab company and are therefore so dependent upon the cab company that they are considered to be employees.

For example, the vehicle driven by a cab driver must be painted in the cab company's colours, the cab driver may be disciplined for breaking the cab company's rules and, most important, the cab driver relies upon the cab company for the majority of her or his fares and therefore for the majority of her or his income.

POSSIBILITY OF PROFIT AND RISK OF FAILURE

Similarly, persons who work occasionally for another person, for example carpenters doing contract work for a carpentry company, may be considered to be the dependent contractors.

This was considered in the case of *Supreme Carpentry Inc.*[4] Even though the carpenters in this case supplied their own tools, the carpentry company determined where the carpentry work would be done, how long the work should take, controlled the price paid to the carpenters, and relied on these particular carpenters to do the work. Also of importance was the fact that the carpenters earned a specific amount of money from the carpentry company for work performed and did not really have the possibility of making a profit or suffering a loss.

HELPERS

You can still be a dependent contractor even if you employ a helper to assist you in the work you do. This is reviewed in the case of *Alpha Wood Mouldings Company*.[5] The Labour Board ruled that piece work crews hired to do carpentry on houses in a carpentry business were found to be dependent contractors of the employer even though they hired a helper to assist them in doing their work.

♦

MODEL CONSTITUTION

This sample constitution is provided as a reference for model clauses. Your constitution does not have to include all of these clauses.

ARTICLE 1

TITLE OF ORGANIZATION

This organization shall be a national trade union known as the _____ Union. It will be referred to throughout this constitution as the "National Union."

ARTICLE 2

AIMS

The aims of this organization are:

1. To regulate relations between employees and employers, including, but not limited to, the right to bargain collectively on behalf of the employees in any company under the jurisdiction of the National Union.

2. To establish through collective bargaining a high standard of wages, shorter working hours, and improved working conditions.

3. To unite in this National Union all workers, regardless of sex, race, disability, religion, political belief, nationality, colour, age, marital status, or sexual orientation. The National Union will not discriminate on any grounds protected by the *Human Rights Code* or the *Canadian Charter of Rights and Freedoms*.

4. To promote legislation which benefits its members and Canadian workers generally, and to oppose legislation which is harmful to those interests.

5. To promote the study, defence, and development of the economic, social, and moral interests of its members.

6. To encourage the organization of the unorganized and to promote internal union democracy.

7. To strive for equal pay for work of equal value, with particular reference to raising the rates of the most poorly paid workers and reducing differences in pay rates.

ARTICLE 3

MEMBERSHIP

1. The National Union will include, but not be limited to, workers engaged in the _____ (name of industry or types of work).

   [Leave your area as wide as possible so that you don't have to amend your constitution if you decide to expand. It is usually best to concentrate in one field, however, for purposes of negotiations and membership unity.]

2. Membership of the National Union will be open to all workers, regardless of sex, race, religion, creed, national or ethnic origin, ancestry, colour, age, marital or family status, sexual orientation, mental or physical disability, or any other similar attribute. However, workers who have the right to hire and fire within a workplace for which the National Union is (or may become) the bargaining agent or who are considered managerial or confidential employees under the labour legislation will not be allowed membership or continued membership.

3. The National Union will not discriminate against anyone on any of the grounds prohibited by the *Human Rights Code* or the *Canadian Charter of Rights and Freedoms.*

ARTICLE 4

EXECUTIVE OFFICERS

1. The executive officers of the National Union consist of a President, Vice-President, and Secretary-Treasurer.

2. During their time in office, the officers have all of the powers set out below. Between conventions, they have the power to act on all matters.

3. Nominations and elections of the executive officers will take place annually at a National Convention. Elections will be by secret vote. All members in good standing of the National Union shall be eligible for election as officers.

4. DUTIES

   a. President — The President of the National Union will be responsible to the executive and the membership for the administration of the affairs of the National Union. He or she will be the executive head of the National Union and will chair the meetings of the National Executive Board and preside at conventions. He or she will enforce the laws of the National Union according to this constitution.

   b. Vice-President — The Vice-President of the National Union will assume the duties and authority of the President in his or her absence. He or she will assist the President whenever it is required.

   c. Secretary-Treasurer — The Secretary-Treasurer will be responsible for the National Union's bookkeeping. He or she will maintain complete records of minutes of all meetings of the National Executive Board and of the conventions of the National Union. He or she will maintain all records, documents, and correspondence of the National Union. He or she will issue financial reports at all meetings of the National Executive Board and at the national convention.

5. If the President's position becomes vacant, the Vice-President will automatically fill that position until the next national convention.

    If the Vice-President's or Secretary-Treasurer's position becomes vacant, the National Executive Board will have the authority to fill the vacancy with one of its members.

6. There will be a National Executive Board that will consist of the members of the National Executive and (number) members who are nominated and elected at the national convention.

    The National Executive Board will meet at least twice between conventions to consider all business of the National Union. The National Executive Board will have the entire management of the National Union between conventions and will be held responsible for its efficient management.

Article 5

Salaried Staff

1. The President will have the right to hire staff with the approval of the National Executive Board. Where possible, full-time staff will be hired from the membership. All paid staff of the National Union will work under the direction of the President.

2. Staff members will be paid a weekly salary that will not be in excess of the weekly earnings of the most highly paid worker in the industry. Staff will be granted expenses covering travel, hotels and meals in accordance with rates set by the National Executive Board. The National Executive Board will also decide the salaries and expenses of organizers and administrative and technical staff members.

3. Paid staff will not have the right to vote at the national convention or at meetings unless they are also elected officials of the National Union.

4. The Executive position(s) of [e.g., President and Vice-

President] are full-time paid staff positions in the National Union.

ARTICLE 6

FINANCES

1. All major financial transactions of the National Union will be made by cheque.

2. All cheques issued by, and all legal documents concerning the National Union will require the signature of any two of the Executive Officers. The signing officers will be bonded and the National Executive Board will determine the amount of the bond.

3. A chartered accountant who is not an employee of the National Union will audit the accounts. The auditor will be chosen by the National Executive Board subject to the approval of the national convention. The auditor may not be dismissed except with the approval of the national convention. An audit will be done annually and a report of the audit will be sent to each Local Union within thirty days of completion.

ARTICLE 7

REVENUE

1. Members and non-members in the bargaining unit covered by a collective agreement will pay union dues of one hour basic pay per month.

2. Ten percent of the union dues collected will be deposited in the strike fund.

3. The strike fund may be used only for the purposes of supporting a strike or lockout.

4. When a member becomes unemployed, he or she will retain full membership rights for ninety days from his or her last

payment. Members unemployed for more than ninety days and members employed outside of the bargaining unit may maintain membership rights by paying union dues each month. Membership will lapse if the union dues are more than three months in arrears.

ARTICLE 8

CONVENTIONS

1. The National Union will convene in regular convention once every _____. The convention will be the ultimate government of all Local Unions. The National Executive Board will have administrative authority of the union when not in convention.

2. The national officers will have the power to call a special convention when they deem it in the best interests of the union. At least four months notice will be given to all members or Local Unions of any convention at the National Union. The National Executive Board will decide a place for holding any convention and will make the necessary arrangements for the holding of such meetings.

3. RESOLUTIONS

   Any Local Union or member will have the right to submit resolutions to any convention. The Secretary-Treasurer of the National Union must receive these resolutions at least thirty days prior to the convention. Emergency resolutions may be presented at any time, provided that a majority of the delegates at the convention accept them. Resolutions submitted by an individual member must be signed by that member and include his or her Local number.

   At least fifteen days prior to the holding of the convention, the National Executive Board will send delegates a copy of the resolutions that have been submitted.

4. REPRESENTATION

   Any member in good standing at the National Union will

be eligible to be elected as a delegate to any convention. The number of delegates from each Local is determined on the following basis:

two delegates for up to the first one hundred members; and one delegate for each additional hundred members or majority fraction of one hundred.

All National Executive Board members will be considered delegates but will not be considered part of each Local's delegate allotment.

The names of all delegates elected to any convention will be submitted to the Secretary-Treasurer of the National Union at least sixty days prior to the holding of the convention. If a delegate is unable to attend due to an emergency, an alternate may be elected and his or her name submitted up to the day before the convention.

A fee may be levied for each Local delegate attending the convention. The fee will not be more than twenty dollars per delegate and will be paid by the Local Union concerned.

5. A simple majority of the registered delegates to a convention will constitute a quorum for the transaction of business.

6. CONVENTION COMMITTEES

   a. The majority of committee members will constitute a quorum for the transaction of business of that committee.

   b. There will be a committee known as the Resolutions and Constitution Committee. Each Local Union will be entitled to one member on this committee.

   c. Other committees may be formed by the National Executive Board or the convention.

7. AMENDMENTS

Amendments to the constitution may be made by majority vote at the annual convention.

8. COMPLAINTS

1. Any member of the National Union will have the right to bring a complaint against any other member, officer or full-time representative of the National Union. Complaints may be brought for violation of this constitution, for not acting in the best interests of the members of the National Union, or for any act which brings the National Union into disrepute. Complaints laid by a member against another member or officer of the same Local will proceed according to the Complaints section of·the Local's by-laws, subject to the provisions of this constitution. The procedure for complaining about members from other Locals, national officers, and national representatives is set out in the following paragraphs.

2. A complaint must be signed by no fewer than five members and must have the approval of the members of the Local Union from which it is submitted. The executive of the Local Union will forward the complaint to the Secretary-Treasurer along with a full explanation of the complaint being submitted. If a complaint is laid against the Secretary-Treasurer of the National Union, it will be forwarded to the President of the National Union.

3. When the National Executive Board receives any complaint, it will meet as soon as possible in order to decide whether or not the complaint merits holding a hearing as set out below.

4. A Hearing Board will be set up for the purpose of hearing evidence. The Hearing Board will be composed of five members of the National Union as follows:

   a. one person to be appointed by the person complaining;

   b. one person to be appointed by the person complained against;

    c. one person to be appointed by the Local Union to which the person complained against belongs; and

    d. two people to be appointed by the National Executive Board, one who will act as Chairperson, and another who will act as Secretary.

5. Each hearing will take place in the city of the person complained against.

6. Once the National Executive Board orders a hearing, the hearing will take place within three weeks. The decision to order a hearing will be sent to the person complaining, the person complained against, and to the Local Unions involved. If anyone fails to attend a scheduled meeting, the hearing will not be delayed for that reason alone unless the Hearing Board decides otherwise.

9. RULINGS OF THE HEARING BOARD

    a. The Hearing Board shall hear any evidence which it believes necessary to ensure a fair and proper hearing, including the calling and hearing of witnesses. The costs and expenses of any witnesses to be heard are the responsibility of the party calling them.

    b. After hearing all of the evidence, the Hearing Board will meet to decide the matter. It will report its findings to the affected parties and the Local National Union within fifteen calendar days.

    c. A Hearing Board will not be held liable in any court of law because of error in its judgment in arriving at a decision. No decision issued by the Hearing Board will be reviewable by any court of law so long as it was made honestly and impartially and in accordance with the procedures outlined here.

    d. If the complaint is proved, the Hearing Board will have

the authority to impose a penalty, including the right to fine, suspend, or expel from membership.

e. If a member wishes to appeal a decision of the Hearing Board, he or she must submit a letter requesting an appeal to the National Executive Board within thirty days of receipt of the decision.

f. If an appeal is launched, no penalty will be enforced until that appeal procedure has been completed.

g. The National Executive Board will constitute the Appeal Board. The Appeal Board will elect a Chairperson. If a National Executive Board member is being tried, he or she will not be part of the Appeal Board.

h. The Appeal Board will hear all the relevant evidence. It will give a decision within 30 days of the hearing. This decision will be immediately enforced. Any party disputing the decision of the Appeal Board will have the right to present their case at the next convention. The decision of the convention is final and binding on the parties in the dispute.

i. No member will resort to any court of law until all of the trial procedures outlined here have been complied with. Any member violating this clause may be expelled.

ARTICLE 9

RIGHT TO RECALL

1. Any officer or full-time representative of the National Union may be recalled at any time by a petition. If the petition is signed by at least 25 percent of the members working within the jurisdiction of the officer (i.e., within the region in the case of a regional representative, or all of the members in the case of an executive officer), the National Executive Board will follow the steps outlined below.

2. If the National Executive Board decides that the number of petitioners is 25 percent of the affected members, it will print ballots and circulate them to the affected members within thirty days of making the decision. A majority of votes cast will be necessary to recall the officer.

ARTICLE 10

STRIKES AND LOCKOUTS

1. A certified bargaining unit will go on strike only with the approval of the membership in the unit. Voting will be by secret ballot and a majority of the votes cast must be in favour of a strike for it to take place. The National Executive, in consultation with the Local Union concerned, will determine the amount of strike benefits. The National Executive will have the right to set rules regarding the support of strikes and lockouts.

ARTICLE 11

GRANTING OF CHARTERS AND GOVERNING OF LOCALS

1. The President and the Secretary-Treasurer will have the authority to grant charters to any group of workers who wish to enter the National Union. Before granting such a charter, the President and Secretary-Treasurer will first make sure that the group is worthy of being affiliated with the National Union and that the group will abide by the constitution of the National Union. For the purpose of organizing, workers may be signed up as members of the National Union until such time as a new Local is chartered; once their Local is chartered, these members will be automatically transferred into it.

2. If a charter is granted, the National Executive Board must be notified immediately.

3. All books, papers, funds, and other assets of any Local

Union will be the property of the Local, except under the following circumstances:

   a. the charter is revoked because there are fewer than five members in the Local Union; or

   b. the charter is suspended, pending the results of a referendum.

4. Two or more Local Unions may be combined into one if the majority of the members of the Local Unions concerned request it and the National Executive Board approves.

ARTICLE 12

LOCAL UNION BY-LAWS

1. The by-laws of each Local Union will contain the provisions set out in this article. They may contain other provisions, as long as they do not conflict with this constitution and have been approved by both the Local Union and the National Executive Board.

2. Each newly chartered Local Union will fill out the spaces provided in these by-laws by majority decision of its members present at a Local Union meeting. Section 6 of this article, "Election of Officers," will not apply to a newly chartered Local Union. Officers of new Locals will be elected by the members present at the first Local meeting called for that purpose.

   1. Title

   This Local Union will be known as the _____ Union, Local _____(number).

   2. Aims

   The aims of this Local Union will be the same as those of the National Union as set out in article 2 of the National Union constitution.

3. Jurisdiction

The jurisdiction of this Local Union will be the same as that in a National Union unless the charter grant says otherwise.

4. Membership

Application for membership in the Local will be in writing. It may be accepted from the applicant by a Local officer or other designated person. By signing an application for membership, the applicant agrees to comply with the aims, principles, and policies of the National Union. Upon approval of an application, the applicant will be entitled to full membership status.

5. Officers

The officers of this Local Union will include, but not be limited to, the following: President, Vice-President, Recording and Corresponding Secretary, Secretary-Treasurer, and three Trustees.

6. Election of Officers

Nominations of Local officers will begin at a regular monthly meeting in the month of ____ and close at the end of the following month's meeting. Elections will be by ballot within one month of the closing of nominations.

7. Meetings

Meetings of this Local Union will be held once each month. Special meetings may be held at any time by a majority decision of this Local Union or by petition of (some percentage) of the Local members. _____ of members of the Local Union will constitute a quorum at any membership meeting.

8. Procedure

Procedures will be the same as those as set out in article 16 of the constitution of the National Union.

9. Dues

Monthly dues will be _____ for each member of the Local and are payable each month. Dues can only be changed by 2/3 of the vote at a membership meeting. Notice must be posted for at least fourteen days prior to the vote.

Members who belong to units that have not been certified do not have to pay union dues.

10. Signing Officers

The signing officers of this Local will be the President, the Vice-President, and the Secretary-Treasurer. All cheques must be signed by the Secretary-Treasurer and either one of the other two signing officers. The Secretary-Treasurer will be bonded and the amount of the bond agreed upon by the Local.

11. Discipline

Any member working in a certified bargaining unit who does not pay his or her dues, fines, assessments, or special assessments for a period of more than two months may, upon vote of the Local Union be suspended or expelled from membership. While under suspension, a member has none of the rights, benefits, or privileges provided by the National constitution or Local by-laws.

A member suspended under this section will be reinstated when he or she pays the amounts owing plus a reinstatement fee of $10.00.

12. Complaints

a. Any member of this Local Union will have the right to file a complaint against any member, including officers or representatives of the National Union according to the following regulations and article 9 of the constitution of the National Union. Charges laid by a member of this Local Union against another member or officer of this Local will proceed according to the following provisions.

b. The proposed complaint must be signed by at least five members. Their signatures must be witnessed. The proposed complaint then will be submitted to the Local Executive Board and a copy sent to the person complained against. The Local Executive Board will set a hearing to take place within ten calendar days of receipt of the proposed complaint. It will notify the person complaining and witnesses of the time and place of the hearing. After the hearing, the Local Executive Board will submit its findings and recommendations at the next general meeting of the Local membership for consideration. If a majority of the members present at the Local general meeting believe that the complaint should have a hearing, the Local Executive Board will set up a Hearing Board.

c. The Local Executive Board will set up a Hearing Board within ten calendar days following the Local general meeting. The Hearing Board will consist of five members of the Local Union:

> i. one member to be appointed by the person complaining;
>
> ii. one member to be appointed by the person complaining against;
>
> iii. two members whose names will be drawn from the Local Union members who have attended at least one of the last three of the Local general meetings;
>
> iv. and one member appointed by the Local Executive Board and who will serve as chair.

The Local Executive Board may supply the

Hearing Board with a Secretary who will have no voice or vote at the Hearing Board.

d. Failure by anyone to attend a scheduled meeting will not alone be sufficient to delay the hearing unless otherwise decided by the Hearing Board.

e. Each hearing will take place in the City of the person complained against.

f. The Local Hearing Board will follow the "Rulings of the Hearing Board" in article 9 of the National constitution.

13. Amendments

By-laws may be amended by two-thirds majority vote at any meeting. Notice of the motion of the amendment must be posted at least seven days prior to the vote. Any amendments to the by-laws will become effective only once they have been approved by the National Executive Board.

14. Finances

Any officer of the Local Union who has union money will deposit it in the name of the Local Union. A complete record of all money received and paid out will be kept. Unless otherwise authorized, all money paid out will be by cheque and will require the signatures of at least two authorized officers of the Local Union.

ARTICLE 13

LOCAL UNION AUTONOMY

1. Local autonomy will be encouraged. This will not interfere with the right of Locals to co-operate fully in joint strategies in collective bargaining.

2. All Locals have the right to retain their assets and records and apply to the National Executive Board to secede from the National Union to:

a. affiliate to another Canadian union, or

b. to become an independent body.

On receiving such a request, the National Executive Board will investigate and conduct a referendum by mail of the Local Union members. If the majority of eligible members vote in favour of succession, it will be granted.

ARTICLE 14

AFFILIATIONS

1. The National Union will affiliate with a central labour body or other organization if directed to do so by the majority of delegates at an annual convention or through a referendum vote. Affiliations will be withdrawn only if two-thirds of the delegates at an annual convention vote to withdraw.

ARTICLE 15

PROCEDURE

1. Only members in good standing will be eligible for election to any office. The person who receives the largest number of votes will be considered elected. If only one person is nominated for office that person will be considered elected by acclamation.

2. The President will have the right to vote in the case of election or secret ballot vote. Otherwise, the President will not have a right to vote except in the case of a tie vote when the President will cast the deciding vote.

3. Referendum votes.

   On National Union questions to be decided by referendum ballot, the Secretary-Treasurer will send ballots to all Local Unions. The Trustees of the Local Union will have the responsibility of conducting the referendum, counting the votes in their local union and forwarding the results to the National Secretary-Treasurer within seven days of the completion of the vote. A final count will be made by a tabulating committee selected by and from the National Executive Board. The result of all referendum votes will be circulated to all Local Unions within seven days of tabulation. To ensure that a large number of the members participate in the referendums, the National Executive Board will be responsible for giving adequate notice of the vote and providing information about the referendum issues.

4. Any National or Local officer who fails to attend three consecutive meetings without reasonable excuse will lose his or her position.

5. No Officer or representative of the National or Local Union will enter into any agreement which changes the terms of a labour agreement unless the membership of the Local approves the changes.

6. In an extended organizing campaign or when a Local cannot reasonably comply with the provisions of the Local by-laws, the National Executive Board may waive some of the Local by-laws. Any provisions waived under this clause may be brought back into force through a vote of the Local.

7. Except as otherwise provided for in this constitution, Bourinot's *Rules of Order* will govern the conduct of all conventions, National Executive Board Meetings, and Local Union meetings.

◆

CHANGING UNIONS OR FACING A COMPETING UNION

TIMING YOUR APPLICATION (ONTARIO)

WHEN A COLLECTIVE AGREEMENT IS IN FORCE

If a collective agreement is in force, you can apply to the Labour Board to change unions only in the "open period" of your agreement.

You are allowed to campaign and sign up members before the open period. If the incumbent union is management-dominated, remember that its collective agreement is void and you may apply at any time.[1]

LENGTH OF COLLECTIVE AGREEMENT	OPEN PERIOD
Three years or less:	The last two months of the collective agreement.
More than three years:	The last two months of the third year of the collective agreement and the last two months of each subsequent year.[2]

WHEN THE PRESENT UNION AND THE COMPANY ARE NEGOTIATING FOR A NEW AGREEMENT

An established union has one year from the time it is certified in which to get a first collective agreement. During that year you may not apply to replace the union.[3] If such a union and the company use the conciliation services of the government and this process takes more than a year, there is a further "conciliation bar" preventing the union from applying for a further period of time.

If the established union is negotiating a second or third collective agreement, the conciliation bar could last at least a year. To determine the exact length of the bar, read section 62(1) and (2) of the *Labour Relations Act.* You can find out whether a union is in conciliation by calling the Mediation Branch of the Ministry of Labour.

WHEN THE PRESENT UNION IS ON STRIKE

A union is barred from applying for certification if the established union is on strike until either the passing of six months after the strike or lockout begins or the passing of seven months after a "no-board" report (a report that indicates the end of the conciliation process),[4] whichever happens first. Members can be signed up, however, before the strike is six months old. It is only the application that has to go in afterwards.

Once the strike is settled with the signing of a new collective agreement,[5] a further bar is imposed until the agreement reaches the open period.

WHEN THE FIRST BID TO CHANGE UNIONS IS LOST

If you lose your first attempt to change unions because of an unfavourable vote, a technical problem in your application, or for any other reason, the Labour Board may bar additional applications for up to 10 months.[6] (See Chapter 10 for further details.)

REPRESENTATION VOTES

You may compete with another union for the votes of the workers in two situations — when you are trying to displace a company union or an unsatisfactory union, or when you are competing with another union to organize your workplace for the first time.

The Labour Board has special rules to deal with each situation.

- If you are trying to displace an existing union, a vote is usually ordered even if your union has more than 55 percent membership, unless the incumbent union has abandoned its bargaining rights.[7]

- If you are competing with another union for a first certificate and your union has more than 55 percent membership, a vote is usually ordered as long as the other union has signed up 35 percent or more of the workers.[8]

- An employer can't add a "no-union" option to the ballot when there is an existing union. This is because there are other procedures in the *Labour Relations Act* for terminating bargaining rights.[9].

- When two or more unions are competing for a first certificate, however, the Board allows a no-union option. After the first vote, the union with the lowest votes is struck from the ballot and a second vote takes place between the remaining unions.[10]

◆

SAMPLE APPLICATION FOR CERTIFICATION

Form A-1

LABOUR RELATIONS ACT
APPLICATION FOR CERTIFICATION
BEFORE THE ONTARIO LABOUR RELATIONS BOARD

Between:

ABC Union, Local 2

Applicant,

- and -

Building Maintenance, Inc.

Responding Party.

The Applicant applies to the Ontario Labour Relations Board for certification of the employees of the Responding Party in a unit described below.

The Applicant states:

1. (a) Name, address, telephone number, and facsimile number (if any) of the Applicant:

ABC Union, Local 2
1 Union Dr.
Toronto, Ontario
M6Z 2B2
Tel: (416) 876-2303
Fax: (416) 876-2304

(b) Name, address, telephone number, and facsimile number (if any) of a contact person for the Applicant:

```
Sue Yi, Union Representative
ABC Union, Local 2
1 Union Dr.
Toronto, Ontario
M6Z 2B2

Tel: (416) 876-2303
Fax: (416) 876-2304
```

(c) Name, address, telephone number, and facsimile number (if any) of the Responding Party and contact person:

```
Building Maintenance, Inc.
3 Mall Rd.
Toronto, Ontario
M4B 3L1

Attention:    Sean O'Reilly
              Director of Operations

Tel: (416) 743-9075
Fax: (416) 744-9076
```

2. General nature of the Responding Party's business:

```
Office Cleaning
```

3. Number of locations where affected employees work:

```
One location at:
1 Office Tower Place
Toronto, Ontario
```

4. Detailed description of the unit of employees of the Responding Party that the Applicant claims to be appropriate for collective bargaining, including the municipality or other geographic area affected:

"All employees of Building
Maintenance, Inc. employed at 1 Office
Tower Place in the City of Toronto
save and except supervisors and persons above the rank of supervisor."

5. Does the bargaining unit include architects, dentists, land surveyors, lawyers, or domestics employed in a private home? If so, please specify:

No.

6. Approximate number of employees in the unit described in paragraph 4:

32

7. The name, telephone number, and facsimile number (if any) of any trade union known to the applicant which claims to represent any employee(s) who may be affected by this application:

n/a

8. Does the Applicant also want a combination of bargaining units? [__] Yes

[X] No

If the answer is yes, a separate application for bargaining unit combination must be filed with this form.

9. Does the Applicant request that a pre-hearing representation vote be taken in this matter? [__] Yes

[X] No

10. Are you making a claim for certification under section 9.2?

Yes. In the event that the Union is
not entitled to automatic certification, it requests that the Board certify it without a vote pursuant to

section 9.2 of the Act because the
true wishes of the employees of the
Respondent respecting representation
by the Applicant Union are not likely
to be ascertained because the actions
of the Respondent Company and those
acting on behalf of the Respondent
Company as detailed in Schedule A
attached have contravened the
Act,including sections 65, 67, and 71.

11. In support of its application, the Applicant relies on the following material facts:

> See Schedule "A" attached

(Include all of the material facts on which you rely including the circumstances, what happened, where and when it happened, and the names of any persons said to have acted improperly. Please note that you will not be allowed to present evidence or make any representations about any material fact that was not set out in the application and filed promptly in the way required by the Board's Rules of Procedure, except with the permission of the Board.)

12. Other relevant statements (attach additional pages if necessary):

> We have filed an application under
> section 91 and an application for an
> Interim Order under section 92.1 and a
> Request for an Expedited Hearing under
> section 92.2 (2) all dated the same
> date as this application.

DATED   September 27, 1993

Signature for the Applicant
Sue Yi, Organizer
ABCU, Local 2

IMPORTANT NOTE

You must file no later than the date you file this application form:

(a)   Any membership evidence relating to the application;

(b)   A list of employees, in alphabetical order, corresponding with the membership evidence filed;

(c)   A declaration verifying the membership evidence filed in the form set by the board (form A-4).

If you do not file your application and other required documentation in the way required by the rules, the Board may not process your application and documents, and may decide the application without further notice to you.

The Board's rules of procedure describe how an application must be filed with the board, what information must be provided and the time limits that apply.

Please consult the Board's rules of procedure before completing this application. Copies of the Board's rules may be obtained from the Board's office located on the 4th floor at 400 University Avenue, Toronto, Ontario (Tel. (416) 326 7500).

Schedule "A"

STATEMENT OF MATERIAL FACTS

Put here material facts set out in Schedule B to the sample unfair labour practice complaint in Appendix E.

Form A-4

LABOUR RELATIONS ACT

DECLARATION VERIFYING MEMBERSHIP EVIDENCE BEFORE THE ONTARIO LABOUR RELATIONS BOARD

Between:

ABC Union, Local 2

Applicant,

- and -

Building Maintenance, Inc.

Responding Party.

I, _____Sue Yi_____ , the __Organizer__

(name)   (office)

of the Applicant declare that, to the best of my knowledge, information and belief:

1. The documents submitted in support of the application represent documentary evidence of membership on behalf of __14__ persons who were employees of the Responding Party in the bargaining unit that the Applicant claims to be appropriate for collective bargaining, on the date of the making of the application.

2. There were __32__ persons who were employees of the Responding Party in the bargaining unit that the Applicant claims to be appropriate for collective bargaining on the date of the making of the application.

DATED   **September 27, 1993**

_____

Sue Yi, ABCU, Local 2.

SAMPLE UNFAIR LABOUR PRACTICE COMPLAINT

Form A-35

LABOUR RELATIONS ACT
APPLICATION UNDER SECTION 91 OF THE ACT
BEFORE THE ONTARIO LABOUR RELATIONS BOARD

Between:

                    ABC Union, Local 2

                                                    Applicant,

          — and —

          Building Maintenance, Inc.

                                            Responding Party.

The Applicant states that the Responding Party has violated section(s)   **65, 67, 71**   of the *Labour Relations Act.* (You must claim that some section OTHER THAN SECTION 91 has been violated.)

The Applicant requests the following:

          See Schedule "A" attached

(Describe in detail what you wish the Board to order as a result of this application.)

The Applicant states:

1.   (a)   Name, address, telephone number, and facsimile number (if any) of the Applicant:

```
ABC Union, Local 2
1 Union Dr.
Toronto, Ontario
M6Z 2B2
Tel: (416) 876-2303
Fax: (416) 876-2304
```

(b)   Name, address, telephone number, and facsimile number (if any) of a contact person for the Applicant:

```
Sue Yi, Union Representative
ABC Union, Local 2
1 Union Dr.
Toronto, Ontario
M6Z 2B2
Tel: (416) 876-2303
Fax: (416) 876-2304
```

(c)   Name, address, telephone number, and facsimile number (if any) of the Responding Party:

```
Building Maintenance, Inc.
3 Mall Rd.
Toronto, Ontario
M4B 3L1

Attention:    Sean O'Reilly
              Director of Operations

Tel: (416) 743-9075
Fax: (416) 744-9076
```

2. (a)   Name, address, telephone number, and facsimile number (if any) of any other person(s) who may be affected by the application:

n/a

(b)   The person(s) named in paragraph 2(a) is (are) affected by the application for the following reason(s):

n/a

3. In support of its request, the Applicant relies on the following material facts:

> See Schedule "B" attached

(Include all of the material facts on which you rely including the circumstances, what happened, where and when it happened, and the names of any persons said to have acted improperly. Please note that you will not be allowed to present evidence or make any representations about any material fact that was not set out in the application and filed promptly in the way required by the Board's Rules of Procedure, except with the permission of the Board.)

4. The following sections of the Act relate to this application:

> 65, 67, 71, 91

5. Other relevant statements:

> A. The Applicant Union has filed on the same date as this Application a separate Application for Certification, a copy of which is attached as Schedule "C".

> B. In light of the facts set out in Schedule "B" attached, the Applicant Union requests that its Application for Certification be consolidated with this application and be heard on an expedited basis.

DATED   September 27, 1993.

_____

Signature for the Applicant
Sue Yi, Organizer
ABCU, Local 2

IMPORTANT NOTE

The Board's rules of procedure describe how an application must be filed with the board, what information must be provided and the time limits that apply.

An application may not be processed by the Board if it does not comply with the board's rules of procedure.

Please consult the Board's rules of procedure before completing this application. Copies of the Board's rules may be obtained from the Board's office located on the 4th floor at 400 University Avenue, Toronto, Ontario (Tel. (416) 326-7500).

Schedule "A"
REMEDIAL RELIEF REQUESTED

The Applicant Union requests the following interim relief:

1. A declaration that the Respondent Company has violated sections 65, 67, 71 of the Act.

2. An order requiring the Respondent Company to:

   a. immediately cease and desist from all anti-union activities or any activities which are designed to interfere with and frustrate the lawful rights of its employees at 1 Office Tower Place to organize into a union with the Applicant Union as their bargaining agent;

   b. maintain all existing employees doing their regular duties without fear of reprisal or harassment;

   c. immediately reinstate Cesar Lopes to his former position at 1 Office Tower Place with full compensation and seniority for any losses he has suffered from the date of his unlawful firing to date of rein-statement, and to continue to employ him doing the same duties that he carried out prior to his unlawful termination;

   d. immediately transfer Maria Perreira back to her regular duties as a cleaner at 1 Office Tower Place and continue to employ her in her prior job as a cleaner at 1 Office Tower Place;

e. i. post for 90 consecutive days a
        Notice from the Labour Board in the
        usual form which advises the employ-
        ees that the Respondent company has
        violated the *Labour Relations Act* by
        its conduct and that employees are
        lawfully entitled to organize a
        union and engage in union activities
        without fear of reprisals;

   ii. this notice should be signed by Sean
        O'Reilly, Catherine, Carla, and
        Nadia and be posted in conspicuous
        places in the workplace where it
        will come to the attention of all
        the employees. It should be trans-
        lated into all such languages as are
        necessary in order that the contents
        can be communicated to all
        employees;

f. reasonable steps shall be taken by the
    Respondent to ensure that the said
    Notices are not altered, defaced, or
    covered by any other materials; reason-
    able physical access to the premises
    shall be given by the respondent to a
    representative of the Applicant so that
    the Applicant can satisfy itself that
    this posting requirement is being com-
    plied with.

g. establish workplace conditions which
    will facilitate the exercise of the
    employee's rights to collective bargain-
    ing, including, in particular:

   i. to provide the Applicant Union with
       an employee list, with addresses and
       phone numbers to allow the Union to

communicate with the employees;

ii. to allow the Applicant Union the opportunity immediately to conduct a meeting of all the employees just before the start of the 5:30 p.m. shift in the same meeting room where the employees were unlawfully held as a captive audience of the Respondent Company to dispel the chill caused by the employer's intimidation tactics;

iii. to provide the Applicant Union with access to post Union material on any bulletin boards or places where employer notices are placed.

3. Such other orders as may be appropriate to rectify the Respondent Company's wrongful conduct.

Schedule "B"
STATEMENT OF MATERIAL FACTS

1. The Applicant, the ABC Union, Local 2, started an organizing drive to sign up the cleaning staff employed by the Respondent, Building Maintenance, Inc., at 1 Office Tower Place in the City of Toronto in the Province of Ontario.

2. There are approximately 32 employees employed to do office cleaning by the Respondent at this downtown office building. Most of the employees work at night from Monday to Friday from 5:30 p.m. to 10:30 p.m.

3. The main rank and file organizer of the Applicant Union was Cesar Lopes and he was assisted by Maria Perreira. Both Cesar Lopes and Maria Perreira were part of the cleaning staff at 1 Office Tower Place and they both started to get employees to sign union cards in the beginning of January 1993. Cesar Lopes was unlawfully fired on February 15, 1993, by the Respondent Company as a result of his efforts to sign up employees as union members. Maria Perreira was unlawfully penalized and transferred to 2 Carlson Square on February 17, 1993, because of her support for the union and her efforts to sign up employees as union members. By the time Cesar Lopes was fired and Maria Perreira transferred, they had been quite successful in signing up union members.

4. Maria Perreira worked for the Respondent Company for over 20 years. Because of her length of service, Maria Perreira was always given favourable shifts and assignments. Cesar Lopes had only been working for the

Respondent Company for approximately one
month before he became the rank and file
union organizer; Maria Perreira's involvement in the organizing campaign was therefore integral because of her position of
respect in the workplace.

5. On Friday, February 12, 1993, the Respondent
Company started to harass and intimidate the
employees whom they believed were involved
in the union. Although they attempted to
intimidate all the employees in the workplace, they singled out Cesar Lopes and
Maria Perreira for harassment.

6. On Friday, February 12, 1993, Maria Perreira
was approached by the Respondent Company's
supervisors, known only as Carla and Nadia.
Both of these supervisors exercise managerial functions in hiring and firing employees.
Maria Perreira was asked by the supervisors
if she had been asked by Cesar Lopes to sign
a union card. She denied having signed a
union card for fear of the consequences if
she admitted that she was involved in the
union's organizing campaign. Maria Perreira
had signed a union card and had indeed been
assisting Cesar Lopes in signing up members.

7. At 10:30 p.m., after the other employees had
left work, Maria Perreira and Cesar Lopes
were called into a meeting by their manager
Catherine and their supervisors, Nadia and
Carla. At the meeting, Catherine told Cesar
that he was a traitor for helping to get the
union in. Carla told Cesar to hand over the
union cards or he would be fired. Maria
Perreira responded that it was against the
law to make him give back the cards.

8. On Monday, February 15, 1993, Cesar Lopes,
upon his arrival at work was asked by Carla

if he brought with him the union cards. When he said that he had not, he was immediately fired by her.

9. On Tuesday, February 16, 1993, Catherine and Carla came up to Maria Perreira while she was working and told her that if she brought the union in here she would suffer. They told her that as of the next night, Wednesday, February 17, 1993, she was transferred unilaterally to another office building at 2 Carlson Square, where the Respondent Company had a contract to do office cleaning. There is no past practice of transferring employees in this fashion.

10. As a result of her transfer, Carla Perreira was not able to stand up for the rights of her fellow workers at the 1 Office Tower Place location or to continue assisting with the organizing. A cleaner at 2 Carlson Square was transferred to take over Maria Perreira's cleaning duties at 1 Office Tower Place.

11. On Tuesday, February 16, 1993, ABCU organizers Sue Yi and Paul Mendes leafleted inside the office building at 1 Office Tower Place by the entrance to the workplace. However, no one would take their leaflets and almost everyone refused to talk to them. One employee said to the organizer, Sue Yi, "Please, I don't want to get in trouble."

12. Maria Perreira continued to try and sign up non-members but was unsuccessful as the employees were too frightened. Because she was well-respected by her co-workers, they made telephone calls to her in which they were crying and upset about the situation at work.

13. On Wednesday, February 17, 1993, as the cleaners were signing in for the 5:30 p.m. shift, they were asked by the Respondent management to come to a meeting with Sean O'Reilly, the Respondent's director of operations, and Catherine, Carla, and Nadia. At that meeting Catherine said that if everyone signed a document that said they opposed the union, then no one would be transferred like Maria or lose her or his job.

14. On Thursday, February 18, 1993, Catherine and Nadia, going from floor to floor, approached all the employees and asked them to sign a petition against the union. It is believed that a large number of the employees signed a petition against the union in these intimidating circumstances.

15. The above-noted intimidation campaign by the Respondent Company had a devastating and chilling effect on the employees and the organizing campaign. After the intimidation campaign, the Applicant Union was unsuccessful in trying to get the employees to sign further union cards. The employees were very frightened that they would lose their jobs, be transferred or otherwise be penalized if they signed for the union or even talked to someone who is known to be associated with the union.

16. On or about February 1993, the Respondent Company gave to each employee at work two notices which are attached as Schedule "C" to this document. These notices are derogatory to the union, are misleading about the process and benefits of unionizing, and were further designed to improperly erode the rights of its employees to organize with the Applicant Union.

APPENDIX F

CASES ON UNFAIR FIRINGS
DURING A CAMPAIGN

This appendix focuses on cases dealing with firings, but much of the law and principles also apply to other improper employer actions, such as refusing a promotion or suspending an employee.

The Labour Board, in the case of *810048 Ontario Limited c.o.b. as Loeb Highland,*[1] set out the following useful review of the Board's approach to the discharge of a union organizer.

36. Moving on to the specific balance of harm in this case, the Board has frequently recorded the chilling effects of a discharge of a union organizer on an organizing campaign. For example, in *Valdi Inc.,* [1980] OLRB Rep. Aug. 1254, the Board said as follows:

> However, the impact of unfair labour practices are seldom confined to an economic impact. For example, the isolated dismissal of an employee in the midst of or at the outset of an organizing campaign is likely to have a significant "chilling effect" on other employees who witness the incident and understand its origin. The dismissal of a fellow employee for union activity conveys a strong warning to other employees and can bring a stop to an ongoing drive in its tracks. The mere reinstatement of the employee directly affected, with back-pay some time later, may do little to assure his or her fellow employees that the employer is prepared to live within the requirements of the statute and that effective remedies exist for those occasions where he will not.

37. Moreover, the Board has found on quite a number of occasions that the discharge of a union organizer during a union campaign may lead to a situation where the true wishes of employees can no longer be ascertained, despite the Board's ability to reinstate the organizer. In other words, the intimidatory effect is so powerful that employees can no longer express their real views on unionization, with the result that certification is granted without a test of employee wishes. For example, in *DI-AL Construction Limited,* [1983] OLRB Rep. Mar. 356, the Board said in this regard:

> A discharge is one of the most flagrant means by which an employer can hope to dissuade his employees from selecting a trade union as their bargaining agent. The respondent's action in discharging Mr. Holland because of his support for the union would have made clear to employees the depth of the respondent's opposition to the union and likely have created concerns among them that if they were also to support the union, it might jeopardize their own employment. In the face of the discharge I doubt that the employees would now be able to freely decide for or against trade union representation. This is particularly so given the small size of the bargaining unit and the respondent's earlier conduct. In these circumstances, I am satisfied that because of the respondent's unlawful conduct, the current true wishes of the employees are not likely to be ascertained in a representation vote.

38. Similarly, in *Zenith Wood Turners Inc.,* [1987] OLRB Rep. Nov. 1443, the Board was faced with a situation where a company had laid off a number of employees during an organizing campaign in violation of the *Labour Relations Act.* In this case, however, the company recalled the employees shortly thereafter and issued a letter indicating that employees were free to choose union representation

or not. The Board found that the damage had already been done, despite the recall and letter, and that employees were no longer able to express their true wishes with respect to union representation. The Board came to a similar conclusion in *Elbertsen Industries Limited,* [1984] OLRB Rep. Nov. 1564, despite the reinstatement of an employee laid off in violation of the Act, although there were other factors which resulted in that finding as well.

39. Why is the impact so severe when a union organizer is discharged? The Board has previously commented on the peculiar vulnerability of employees who depend on the employer for their livelihood. In *Pigott Motors (1961) Ltd.* (1962), 63 CLLC, Vol. 2, 16,264, the Board said:

> There are certain facts of labour-management relations which this Board has, as a result of its experience in such matters, been compelled to take cognizance. One of these facts is that there are still some employers who, through ignorance or design, so conduct themselves as to deny, abridge or interfere in the rights of their employees to join trade unions of their own choice and to bargain collectively with their employer. In view of the responsive nature of his relationship with his employer, and of his natural desire to want to appear to identify himself with the interests and wishes of his employer, an employee is obviously peculiarly vulnerable to influences, obvious or devious, which may operate to impair or destroy the free exercise of his rights under the Act.

In *Roytec Vinyl Co.,* [1990] OLRB Rep. June 727, the Board commented on this problem in another context:

> In the Board's experience, employees are often concerned that they may be subject to such reprisals by their employer for union activity. The Board's jurisprudence is replete with examples of employees who were discharged or penalized in some way, at

least in part, because of their support for unionization. For an employee who fears that joining a union
will lead to a discharge or other penalty, the result he
or she contemplates can be a loss of economic security, the loss of the social milieu of the workplace, a
concomitant loss of self-esteem, identity or social
standing, the uncertainty of finding another job and
the possibility of a slide onto social benefits. Of
course, in most cases such a bleak picture will not
come to pass; nevertheless, the mere possibility of any
of these consequences may exert a powerful influence
on an employee contemplating collective bargaining,
a regime frequently not welcomed by employers.

For similar reasons, a discharge has been referred to in
arbitral jurisprudence as the "capital punishment" of
labour relations.

REVIEW OF DECISIONS ON
REQUESTS FOR INTERIM ORDERS

810048 ONTARIO LIMITED

The case of *810048 Ontario Limited*[2] gives us an example of how
the Labour Board looks at a request for an interim order reinstating
a rank and file union organizer who the union said had been discharged unlawfully during an organizing campaign. It was admitted that the organizer had lied to company officials to protect
another worker accused of stealing a can of soda pop. The Board
said it would look to see whether the union had an arguable case
and would balance the interests of the union and employees on the
one side and the employer on the other.

In this case, the union filed three applications:

- an application under section 91 of the *Labour Relations Act*
  alleging that the company had violated sections 65, 67,
  71, 81, and 82 of the Act;

- an application under section 92.2 for an expedited hearing of the main application (the union's hearing date was two weeks later and three weeks after the discharge);
- an application for an interim order under section 92.1, requesting reinstatement and compensation for the worker pending the hearing of the main application.

PROCEDURES FOR THE INTERIM ORDER APPLICATION

Both parties submitted written declarations of evidence by witnesses as well as written arguments. Although not required, the Board scheduled a hearing several days later to hear oral arguments in favour of and against the interim order. The panel hearing the case issued a unanimous interim order several days later reinstating the rank-and-file union organizer. The panel subsequently issued written reasons for the decision.[3]

CERTIFIED DECLARATIONS MUST CONTAIN FIRSTHAND EVIDENCE

The Board was critical of the declarations filed by the parties because they contained a lot of hearsay. Rules 86 and 89 require that declarations filed on interim order applications contain only the evidence of persons having firsthand knowledge of the facts.

While the Board stated that it had the power to make exceptions to that requirement under Rule 22, it heard nothing which indicated it should do so. Therefore, it refused to act on any evidence in the written declarations which was second hand or hearsay.[4]

The Board also refused to consider any facts which the union counsel relied on at the oral hearing which were not contained in the application.[5]

UNION ALLEGATIONS AND EMPLOYER RESPONSE

The union agreed that the employee had lied to the employer but argued the employer had tried to entrap him to find an excuse to fire him. Prior to his discharge, the fired worker had been actively signing up fellow workers to join the union. He had been questioned by the store owner and manager about why he wanted the union and told to stop organizing on company premises. Although denied by the employer, the union alleged that the store owner threatened that if the union got in, the store would be closed.

ARGUABLE CASE

The union's complaint alleged that a union organizer was fired by the company as a reprisal for his union activities, to interfere with those activities, and to influence other employees against joining the union. The Board found that there was little doubt that, if proven, there was an arguable breach of sections 65, 67, and 71 of the *Labour Relations Act*.

HARM TO THE UNION

The Labour Board acknowledged that the reinstatement order would have some temporary negative effect on the managerial authority of the company and its theft policy. However, the Board found that the interim reinstatement would only be in effect until the main application was decided, which was scheduled to be heard two weeks later, and it was unlikely that the offence the union organizer had been charged with would be repeated within that time.

The Labour Board found that the harm from granting the order was less than the harm which may flow from not granting it: "having regard to the critical momentum of an organizing campaign and the corrosive effects of delay, even a number of days may make a substantial difference in amplifying the chilling effect of the discharge of a union supporter."[6] It ordered the immediate reinstatement of the union organizer pending the final hearing.

INTERIM COMPENSATION

The Labour Board decided not to order any interim compensation to the worker for the wages he had lost while off work even though it acknowledged that the financial loss could have a chilling effect. The Board decided that the harm caused by a delay of several weeks until the main application was decided was not greater than the harm the employer might suffer.

This was because of the considerable difficulty the employer would face in getting the money back from the worker if the employer's discharge decision was upheld by the Board at the hearing on the main application. The Board also noted that it would likely award interest to the worker on any back wages awarded if the discharge was found to be improper.[7]

REYNOLDS-LEMMERZ INDUSTRIES DECISION

In this case,[8] the Canadian Auto Workers brought an application under section 91 of the *Labour Relations Act* alleging that the employer had violated sections 3, 65, 67, and 71 by distributing a letter to all employees with their pay cheque and posting it in the workplace during an organizing campaign. The CAW complained that the letter had intimidated the employees and interfered with their organizing drive. The letter referred to the loss of jobs in companies that are not competitive and pointed out that paying union wages would lead to the company being uncompetitive. The letter provided directions for employees on how they could resign from the union. The company argued that it was entitled to communicate with the employees and was only responding to their inquiries.

The Labour Board decided not to determine whether the allegations were true or not, but rather issued an interim order requiring the employer to remove the letter from any area in the workplace where it had been posted and further ordered the employer to stop counselling its workers to resign their membership with the union.

The Board stated the goal of its interim order was to preserve the right of the union to a meaningful remedy should the complaint be upheld on the main hearing while at the same time intruding as little as possible on the employer's interests. The Board referred to the *Loeb Highland* case,[9] which had just been issued and said its ruling was consistent with that decision.

HARM TO THE UNION

While the Board recognized that the order may have no remedying effect with respect to the actions already taken, it could serve to minimize the potential harm from the date of the order forward and therefore support the Board's ultimate remedies if they were necessary.[10] If it was proven that the allegations in the letter unduly influenced employees to not join the union, the Board found that it would be very difficult to place the union back in the position that it should have been had the unfair practice not taken place. By the time the complaint was heard, there would be no returning to the point in the organizing drive prior to the actions of the employer.

The order was found not to be too intrusive on the employer's interests since the employer was allowed to continue communicating with its employees except for one specific area.

MORRISON MEAT PACKERS LTD. CASE

In this case,[11] three union organizers were fired during an organizing campaign. The union filed its certification application on October 22, 1992, the day the organizers were fired. The union was certified approximately a month later. The section 91 application complaining about the unlawful firings was filed on October 27, 1992. The hearings on the section 91 application were still taking place when the union filed for an interim order on February 2, 1993.

The Board stated that interim relief is just that — interim. It is not a remedy for a violation of the Act since a finding on whether the employer violated the Act cannot be made until the main hearing is held. Instead, it is a means of minimizing the negative effects or potential serious harm that may result from the passage of time between the filing of the application and the full hearing.[12]

By the time the Board considered the interim order request, the union had been certified for over two and a half months. The Board found that the declarations did not disclose any evidence that the union had or would suffer any harm in its ongoing collective bargaining activities.

It accepted that the collective bargaining relationship between the union and employer was very fragile during the negotiation of the first collective agreement.

The Board concluded that the harm to the union was primarily financial in nature — that is, the lost compensation of the fired workers or "grievors" between the date of the application for the interim order and the date the application was decided, which was approximately three months later.[13]

The Board also stated that the application for the interim order should have been filed one month earlier than it was, on the date that the new provisions for interim orders became law, January 1, 1993. In any event, by the time the request was made, more than three months had elapsed since the firings. The Board concluded that this passage of time prevented the Board from intervening in a timely fashion, and increased the possibility of harm to the employer since it had hired three replacement employees who would have to be terminated if they temporarily reinstated the three workers. Furthermore, the harm might be permanent if those employees had found other permanent jobs in the meantime.

◆

APPENDIX G — ONTARIO LABOUR LAW BEFORE AND AFTER 1993 AMENDMENTS TO *LABOUR RELATIONS ACT*

ISSUE	BEFORE 1993 AMENDMENTS	AFTER 1993 AMENDMENTS
COVERAGE	Managerial and confidential employees excluded	Managers and confidential employees remain excluded
	Domestics, professionals and agricultural workers excluded from the right to organize	Domestics and professionals allowed to organize except for physicians, interns, and residents to whom the *Ontario Medical Association Dues Act, 1991*, applies
		Certain class of agricultural workers allowed to organize as prescribed by the regulations
	Security guards to be represented in a separate unit	Security guards may form own unit or be included in unit with other employees if no conflict of interest exists
ORGANIZATION AND PROTECTION OF UNION	Employers are prohibited form discharging, disciplining, or discriminating against employees for engaging in union activity, no procedure for expedited hearings in these cases	Expedited Labour Board hearing (15 days) in which the Labour Board must sit 4 consecutive days each week until hearing completed; oral or written decision must be issued within 2 days
	Where Act violated, the Labour Board provides remedies to make the parties whole, but it does not provide interim relief	Labour Board given general power to make orders before completion of hearing.
	Employer has no duty to provide list of employees to union during organizing and usually no access to employees during working hours to campaign	Union may organize on premises to which the public normally has access, but *only* at or near but outside the entrances and exits of the employees' workplace; still no duty to provide employee list to union
	Employees may present petitions opposing unions to the Labour Board during certification process; employees may revoke union membership	Membership support determined as of date of application, based on membership cards submitted by union; former petition process is abolished, except Labour Board may consider revocations of union membership filed with the Labour Board on or before the date of application for certification

Appendix G — Ontario Labour Law Before and After 1993 Amendments to *Labour Relations Act*

Issue	Before 1993 Amendments	After 1993 Amendments
Requirements for Certification	Union automatically certified if it has more than 55% to be eligible for representation vote, union must have 45% support	Union still automatically certified if it receives more than 55% to be eligible for representation vote, union now only requires 40% support
	Union automatically certified without majority support if "true wishes" of employees not likely to be determined due to employer's unfair labour practices and there exists "adequate membership" support for collective bargaining	The Labour Board must still be satisfied the "true wishes" of employees unlikely to be determined, but union would not be required to show it has "adequate support" for collective bargaining
	Employees must pay at least $1.00 to join	Employees no longer required to pay $1.00 to join union
Defining the Bargaining Unit	Labour Board determines scope of appropriate bargaining unit considering various factors such as community of interest.	Further criteria for determining appropriate bargaining unit
	Part-time employees and full-time employees are to be in separate units, if either party requests it	Union has option of a combined full-time/part-time unit, or separate units if the union lacks 55% in a combined unit (does not apply to craft units or bargaining units in the construction industry)
		Labour Board may determine that separate units are appropriate if the union applying for certification, or another union, is already the bargaining agent for either the full-time or the part-time employees
	No power to consolidate bargaining units	Consolidation of bargaining units when same union holds bargaining rights, but Labour Board not to consolidate different operations of a manufacturing operation if employer proves that consolidation • would interfere unduly with the employer's ability to continue signifcantly different methods of operation or production at each of these places • would interfere unduly with the employer's ability to continue to operate those places as viable and independent businesses

APPENDIX G — ONTARIO LABOUR LAW BEFORE AND AFTER 1993 AMENDMENTS TO *LABOUR RELATIONS ACT*

ISSUE	BEFORE 1993 AMENDMENTS	AFTER 1993 AMENDMENTS
DUTY TO BARGAIN	Labour Board only has jurisdiction to impose any terms of the collective agreement under the 1st agreement provisions of the Act No statutory duty to bargain during lifetime of collective agreement.	Where there is a violation of duty to bargain in good faith, Labour Board may impose terms of agreement where it decides that other remedies are not sufficient to counter effects of the contravention. In cases of permanent discontinuance of all or part of the business or lay-offs of more than 50 employees, there is a statutory duty to negotiate a labour adjustment and plan Provision for mandatory periodic consultation on workplace issues is to be included in every collective agreement
UNION REPRESENTATION RIGHTS	Employer precluded from altering terms and conditions of employment, and from discriminating against union supporters after certification, but before first agreements, but allowed to discharge or discipline employees for just cause "No strike" and "arbitration" clauses are the only mandatory provisions in the agreement	Discipline or discharge without just cause prohibited after certification and during term of collective agreement, except for negotiated clauses limiting this protection for probationary employees All collective agreements deemed to include clause providing: • mandatory just cause protection for discipline and discharge (except for negotiated exemptions for probationary employees) • arbitrators have the power to interpret all employment-related legislation
FIRST AGREEMENT ARBITRATION	Either party may apply to the Labour Board to direct the settlement of a first collective agreement by arbitration by the Labour Board Statutory criteria must be met in order to have access to arbitration (e.g., employer refusing to recognize the bargaining authority of the union)	Either party can apply to the Labour Board or minister of labour for automatic first contract arbitration after the parties have been in a legal strike/lockout position for 30 days First contract disputes to be resolved by private arbitration rather than by Labour Board

CHARTS COMPARING ONTARIO LABOUR LAW WITH OTHER CANADIAN JURISDICTIONS

The following three Charts highlight some of the key differences between Ontario's *Labour Relations Act* and its counterpart in other Canadian jurisdictions. To keep them brief, it was necessary to simplify the law. The actual legislation for each jurisdiction set out below should be reviewed before any action is taken.

1. Federal: *Canada Labour Code* (Part 1) (R.S.C. 1985, c.L-2, as amended). The term "Board" refers to the Canada Labour Relations Board.

2. Alberta: *Labour Relations Code* (S.A. 1988, c.L-1.2). The term "Board" refers to the Alberta Labour Relations Board.

3. B.C.: *Labour Relations Act* (S.B.C. 1992, c.82). The term "Board" refers to the B.C. Labour Relations Board.

4. Manitoba: *Labour Relations Act* (R.S.M. 1987 c.L-10, as amended). The term "Board" refers to the Manitoba Labour Board.

5. N.B.: *Industrial Relations Act* (R.S.N.B. 1973, c.1-4, as amended). The term "Board" refers to the Industrial Relations Board.

6. Newfoundland: *Labour Relations Act* (R.S.N. 1990, c.L-1, as amended). The term "Board" refers to the Newfoundland Labour Relations Board.

7. Nova Scotia: *Trade Union Act* (R.S.N.S. 1989, c.475). The term "Board" refers to the Nova Scotia Labour Relations Board.

8. Ontario: *Labour Relations Act* (R.S.O. 1990, c.L.2, as amend-
    ed). The term "Board" refers to the Ontario Labour Relations
    Board.

9. P.E.I.: *Labour Act* (R.S.P.E.I. 1988, c.L-1, as amended). The
    term "Board" refers to the P.E.I. Labour Relations Board.

10. Quebec: *Labour Code* (R.S.Q., c.C-27)

11. Saskatchewan: *Trade Union Act* (R.S.S. 1978, c.T-17, as
    amended). The term "Board" refers to the Saskatchewan
    Labour Relations Board.

The phrase "not specifically mentioned" is used if there was not
any reference in the Act or regulations to the topic. You should
consult the particular Board's policies, practices, and decisions in
case they deal with the topic.

These Charts do not deal with the special organizing rules for
many public sector workers. These workers are in some cases
covered by separate laws in each jurisdiction. Public sector employees should consult these specific laws for the rules that apply to
them.

Chart A — Representation Vote and Certification

Chart B — Timeliness of Application

Chart C — Bargaining Unit

CHART A — REPRESENTATION VOTE AND CERTIFICATION

JURISDICTION	REPRESENTATION VOTE	PRE-HEARING REPRESENTATION VOTE	CERTIFICATION WITH VOTE	CERTIFICATION WITHOUT VOTE	INITIATION FEE	TERMINAL DATE	EXPEDITED HEARING
ONTARIO	Board must direct vote if at least 40%, but not more than 55% of the employees in the bargaining unit are members of the union: s.8(2) Board may direct a vote if more than 55% are members of the union: s.8(3)	If not less than 35% are members, the Board may direct a pre-hearing representation vote if the union requests one: s.9	Certified if union wins majority of the votes: s.9.1(1)	If more than 55% are members of the union and the Board does not direct a vote, the Board must certify the union: s.9.1(2) If the employer contravenes the Act, the Board may certify the union: s.9.2	No fee	8-10 days after date of application for certification	Expedited hearings granted for complaints under s.91 alleging certain unfair labour practices during the union's organizing activities up to the disposition of its application for certification: s.92.2(91), (2)
FEDERAL	If between 35% and 50% are members, the Board will direct vote: s.29(2) If less than 35% of eligible employees vote, the vote is void: s.31(2)	Not specifically mentioned	Certified if union wins majority votes: ss.28, 31(3)	If Board satisfied majority of employees support union: s.28	$5.00 payable within the 6-month period proceeding the date of filing the application for certification: CLRB Regs., 1978 s.27(2)	Generally membership is assessed as of the application date, but the Board has discretion to change the date if it deems it appropriate: s.28(c)	Not specifically mentioned

CHART A — REPRESENTATION VOTE AND CERTIFICATION

JURISDICTION	REPRESENTATION VOTE	PRE-HEARING REPRESENTATION VOTE	CERTIFICATION WITH VOTE	CERTIFICATION WITHOUT VOTE	INITIATION FEE	TERMINAL DATE	EXPEDITED HEARING
ALBERTA	If at least 40% of the employees support the union, then the Board will order a vote: s.31, 32	Not specifically mentioned	Certified if union wins majority votes: s.16(2), 32(1), 37	Not specifically mentioned	At least $2.00 payable within the 90 days preceding the application: s.31	Support determined as of date of application. ss.31,32(2)	Not specifically mentioned, however, an application for certification must be processed as quickly as possible. When an application is received, a hearing date is almost immediately set: LRB Information Bulletin #4, Location and Conduct of Board Hearings
BRITISH COLUMBIA	If not less than 45% and not more than 55% are members, the Board shall order a vote: s.24(2)	Not specifically mentioned	Certified if union wins majority votes: s.25	If not less than 55% of employees are members at date of application, the Board shall certify the union: s.23(1)	At least $1.00: set out in *Phillips Cables Ltd.* (1977), BCLR No.52/77	Support determined as of date of application: s.18(1).	Board is required to expedite certification applications: LRB Practice Guideline No. AD3-2

CHART A — REPRESENTATION VOTE AND CERTIFICATION

JURISDICTION	REPRESENTATION VOTE	PRE-HEARING REPRESENTATION VOTE	CERTIFICATION WITH VOTE	CERTIFICATION WITHOUT VOTE	INITIATION FEE	TERMINAL DATE	EXPEDITED HEARING
MANITOBA	If between 40% and 65% are members, the Board must direct a vote: s.40(1) Application rejected if less than 40%: s.40(1)	Not specifically mentioned	Certified if union supported by majority of those who cast a ballot: s.40(3)	If more than 65% of support at date of application, the Board will certify the union: s.40(1) If employer commits unfair labour practice, Board may certify union: s.41	No minimum fee mentioned, but employee must be informed of any if applicable: s.45	Support determined as of the date of application: s.40(1)	Not specifically mentioned
NEW BRUNSWICK	If between 40% and 60% are members in good standing, Board may direct a vote: s.14(2) Board may hold additional votes to determine employees' wishes: s.126(2)	Pre-hearing representation vote may be allowed if not less than 40% in unit are members: s.15	Certified if more than 50% of ballots of all eligible voters are cast in favour of union, or more than 60% in unit are members in good standing. Employees absent from work during voting hours and who do not cast their ballot are not counted as eligible: s.14(3),4	If more than 50% are members in good standing as of date of application may be certified without vote: s.14(1), (5) Board may certify where employees' rights have been violated so that the true wishes of the employees are unlikely to be ascertained: s.106(8)(g)	At least $1.00: s.16(3)	Board to determine terminal date (may extend beyond date of application): s.126(e)	Not specifically mentioned

CHART A — REPRESENTATION VOTE AND CERTIFICATION

JURISDICTION	REPRESENTATION VOTE	PRE-HEARING REPRESENTATION VOTE	CERTIFICATION WITH VOTE	CERTIFICATION WITHOUT VOTE	INITIATION FEE	TERMINAL DATE	EXPEDITED HEARING
NEWFOUNDLAND	If between 40% and 50% are members, Board may direct vote: s.47(3) Board may take vote as it seems expedient: ss.46,47(1)	Not specifically mentioned	Certified after vote if unit wins majority or, at least 70% of unit has voted, and, majority of those voting support the union: s.38(2)	Certified if majority in unit are members as of date of application: s.38(2)	At least $2.00 payable within the period commencing on the 1st day of the 3rd month preceding the calendar month in which the application was made and ending upon the date of the application: LRB Rules of Procedures s.46(1), Nfld. Reg. 270/90	Date of application is the operative date for determining union support: s.47(5)	Not specifically mentioned
NOVA SCOTIA	If union claims membership to be 40% or more, Board shall conduct a vote. If less than 40%, Board will dismiss application: s.25(1), (7)	Board will take pre-hearing vote on every application unless it is impossible or inappropriate to do so: s.1 Policy Statement of the LRB issued June 1975	Certified if wins majority votes: s.25(8) If employer contravenes Act resulting in vote not reflecting employees' true wishes, Board may certify if at least 40% of unit are members: s.25(9)	Certified without vote where documentary evidence shows more than 50% support, the employer does not contest, and there are no interventions or petitions. s.4 Policy Statement of LRB issued June 1975	Not specifically mentioned	Membership determined as of date of application: ss.23, 25(7)	Not specifically mentioned

CHART A — REPRESENTATION VOTE AND CERTIFICATION

JURISDICTION	REPRESENTATION VOTE	PRE-HEARING REPRESENTATION VOTE	CERTIFICATION WITH VOTE	CERTIFICATION WITHOUT VOTE	INITIATION FEE	TERMINAL DATE	EXPEDITED HEARING
PRINCE EDWARD ISLAND	Board will take vote whenever it seems necessary: s.13(3)	Pre-hearing representation vote may be allowed: s.14	Certified if wins majority vote: s.13(4), (8)	Not specifically mentioned	At least $2.00 payable within the 3 months preceding the filing of the application: Revised Regs. of P.E.I. c.L-1 s.3(4)	To be fixed by Chief Executive Officer: Revised Regs. of P.E.I. c.L-1 s.4(1)	Not specifically mentioned
QUEBEC	Labour Commissioner decides whether union is representative, and may hold vote to investigate membership: s.32; if between 35% and 50% are members vote will be conducted: ss.21, 28(b)	Not specifically mentioned	Certified if obtains absolute majority of those having right to vote: ss.21, 28(b)	Certified if it is representative (majority support): ss.21, 28	At least $2.00 payable within the 12-month period preceding the filing of the application or the mailing of the petition or the assessment of the union as to representation: s.36.1	Support determined as of date of application: s.36.1	Not specifically mentioned

Chart A — Representation Vote and Certification

Jurisdiction	Representation Vote	Pre-Hearing Representation Vote	Certification with Vote	Certification without Vote	Initiation Fee	Terminal Date	Expedited Hearing
Saskatchewan	Board has discretion to order a vote: s.6(1); however the Board will order vote where: a) an order exists determining that another union represents the majority of the employees in the unit; and b) 25% or more of the employees in the unit have within 6 months preceding the date of application indicated that the applicant union is their choice as representative for purpose of collective bargaining Board may refuse to conduct vote if satisfied that another trade union represents clear majority of employees: s.6(20)	Not specifically mentioned	Certified without vote if Board is satisfied majority of those eligible to vote cast ballots, and union wins majority of votes: s.8	If satisfied that a trade union represents clear majority of employees: s.6(2)	Not specifically mentioned	Date of application is the operative date for determining support: s.10 as interpreted in *Beaver Lumber Company Ltd.*, [1978] 2 CLRB R.187(Sask.)	Not specifically mentioned

CHART B — TIMELINESS OF APPLICATION

JURISDICTION	NO CERTIFIED UNION, NO AGREEMENT	CERTIFIED UNION, BUT NO AGREEMENT	WHERE AGREEMENT ALREADY IN FORCE	WHERE APPLICATION REFUSED	WHERE STRIKE OR LOCKOUT IN EFFECT	EXCEPTIONS	OTHER
ONTARIO	At any time: s.1	12 months after date of certification: s.5(2)	a) *3 years or less* — within last 2 months of its operation. s.5(4) b) *More than 3 years* — during the 35th and 36th months of operation, during the last 2 months of each year that agreement continues to operate, or during the last 2 months of operation: s.5(5)	Board may bar an unsuccessful applicant for a period not exceeding 10 months: s.105(2)(i)	The earliest of: i) until 6 months after the commencement of the strike or lockout; ii) or until 7 months after the minister has released to the parties the report of the conciliation board or a notice that not advisable to appoint a conciliation board: s.62(3)	*Voluntarily recognized union, but no agreement after recognition* — where bargaining rights have not been terminated, 12 months after the voluntary recognition occurred: s.5(3)	*Agreement in force — automatic renewal for further term(s)* — during the last 2 months of each year of the further term(s), or the operating of the agreement: s.5(6)
FEDERAL	At any time: s.24(2)(a)	After expiration of 12 months from the date of certification, or with the consent of the Board at any earlier time: s.24(2)(b)	a) *3 years or less* — during the last 3 months of operation: s.24(2)(c) b) *More than 3 years* — during the 34th, 35th, and 36th months of operation, and thereafter during the last three months of each year that the agreement continues to operate after the 3rd year of operation, or after the commencement of the last 3 months of operation: s.24(2)(c)	No subsequent application from the same trade union for the same or substantially the same unit for 6 months unless the Board abridges that period: Canada Labour Relations Board Regulations, 1992, s.31	No certification application can be made during the first 6 months of a strike or lockout, except with consent of the Board: s.24(30)	Not specifically mentioned	Not specifically mentioned

CHART B — TIMELINESS OF APPLICATION

JURISDICTION	NO CERTIFIED UNION, NO AGREEMENT	CERTIFIED UNION, BUT NO AGREEMENT	WHERE AGREEMENT ALREADY IN FORCE	WHERE APPLICATION REFUSED	WHERE STRIKE OR LOCKOUT IN EFFECT	EXCEPTIONS	OTHER
ALBERTA	At any time: s.35(2)(a); however, no application can be made until at least 60 days after the applicant union has filed its constitution, by-laws, or other constitutional documents with the Board, unless the Board gives its consent: s.35(1)	Anytime after expiration of 10 months from the date of certification: s.35(2)(b)	a) *2 years or less* — anytime in the 2 months prior to the end of the terms of the agreement: s.35(2)(d) b) *More than 2 years* — in the 11th or 12th month of the 2nd or subsequent years of the terms, but at least 10 months prior to the end of the term, or in the 2 months prior to the end of the term: s.35(2)(e),(3)	Where refused or withdrawn — no subsequent applications that are the same or substantially the same for 90 days unless the Board gives its consent: s.55	No application may be made without the consent of the Board: s.35(1)	Not specifically mentioned	*Where certification revoked* — no application from the bargaining agent concerned for the same unit for 6 months from the date of revocation: s.52(2)
BRITISH COLUMBIA	At any time: s.18(1)	When: a) 6 months have elapsed since the date of certification of a trade union for the unit, or b) the Board has consented to an application before the expiry of the period of 6 months: s.18(2)	Only during the 7th and 8th months in each year of its term or any renewal or continuation thereof, but not within 22 months of a previous application decided by Board on its merits: s.19(1),(2)	No new application by the same applicant for a period determined by the Board (minimum 90 days if such a period is prescribed): s.30	No application during a strike or lockout without the consent of the Board: ss.18(3), 19(3)	a) A trade union that is a party to the collective agreement, but is not certified with respect to employees covered by it, may apply at any time b) A council of trade unions may apply at any time to be certified in place of those trade unions it represents: s.18(4)	*Where certification cancelled* — no application by another trade union for 10 months unless the Board abridges that period: s.33(10)

Jurisdiction	No Certified Union, No Agreement	Certified Union, but No Agreement	Where Agreement Already in Force	Where Application Refused	Where Strike or Lockout in Effect	Exceptions	Other
Manitoba	At any time: s.34(2)	After the expiry of 12 months from the date on which the incumbent bargaining agent was certified or from the date on which any court proceedings regarding the certification were terminated, whichever is later, or when certification is cancelled: s.35(1)	a) *Generally* — after 6 months from the date on which the agreement became effective and before the last 3 months of its term: s.35(2)(a), (b) b) *18 months or less* — during the 3 months immediately preceding the last 3 months of the term: s.35(2)(c) c) *More than 18 months* — during the 3 months immediately preceding any anniversary of the date on which the agreement became effective or during the 3 months immediately preceding the last 3 months of the terms: s.35(2)(d)	No application by the same applicant for the same unit, part of it, or any unit containing the same employee for at least 6 months, except as otherwise specified by the Board: Manitoba Labour Board Rules of Procedure s.8(14), (15)	After 6 months from the date of commencement of legal work stoppage and with the consent of the Board: s.35(5)	a) Where the parties to an agreement reach settlement within fewer than 30 days from the date of giving notice to bargain, on application, the Board may require either or both of them to show cause why an application by another union should no be permitted: s.36(1) b) In all cases, at any time with the consent of the Board: s.37	a) *Agreement in force 1 year and provides for successive 1 year terms* — during the 3 months previous to the 3 months immediately preceding any date on which the agreement may be terminated: s.35(2)(e) b) *1st Agreement in force* — if the terms and conditions have been settled by the Board, no application during the term of the agreement: s.35(4)

CHART B — TIMELINESS OF APPLICATION

JURISDICTION	NO CERTIFIED UNION, NO AGREEMENT	CERTIFIED UNION, BUT NO AGREEMENT	WHERE AGREEMENT ALREADY IN FORCE	WHERE APPLICATION REFUSED	WHERE STRIKE OR LOCKOUT IN EFFECT	EXCEPTIONS	OTHER
NEW BRUNSWICK	At any time: s.10(2)	12 months after date of certification of incumbent union or 12 months after termination of agreement in force at the time of certification: s.10(3)	a) *3 years or less* — within 2 last months of agreement: s.10(5) b) *More than 3 years* — during the 35th and 36th months of the agreement and during the last 2 months of any subsequent year of its operation: s.10(6)	The Board may prescribe a waiting period before a new application will be considered from the same applicants: s.20	Applications prohibited until 6 months have passed since strike or lockout began, or until 7 months after the minister's release of a conciliation board report or notice that not advisable to appoint board, whichever comes first: s.11(3)	a) In certain circumstances when a collective agreement is in force, the Board may give consent to an earlier application: ss.10(8),33(3) b) In all cases, an application is subject to delays related to conciliation, mediation, strike, or lockout: s.11	a) *Agreement in force for further terms* — during the last 2 months of each year of the further term or of the operation of the agreement: s.10(7) b) If employer or employee would suffer unreasonable damage or loss if application not entertained at a time other than that authorized, application may be made at any time: s.10(8)
NEWFOUNDLAND	At any time: s.36(2)	Certified, but no agreement or bargaining has commenced - 12 months after date of certification, unless the Board consents to an earlier application: s.36(3)	a) *2 years or less* — within 2 last months of its term: s.36(4) b) *More than 2 years* — in the 23rd and 24th months and during the last 2 months of each subsequent year of operation: s.36(4)	No subsequent application by the same applicant for the same or substantially the same unit for 6 months, unless the Board gives its consent. Labour Relations Board Rules of Procedure, 1990, s.17	Not specifically mentioned	Not specifically mentioned	Not specifically mentioned

CHART B — TIMELINESS OF APPLICATION

JURISDICTION	NO CERTIFIED UNION, NO AGREEMENT	CERTIFIED UNION, BUT NO AGREEMENT	WHERE AGREEMENT ALREADY IN FORCE	WHERE APPLICATION REFUSED	WHERE STRIKE OR LOCKOUT IN EFFECT	EXCEPTIONS	OTHER
NOVA SCOTIA	At any time: s.23(2)	12 months after date of certification, unless Board gives its consent to an earlier application: s.23(3)	a) *3 years or less* — within 3 last months of its operation: s.23(4) b) *More than 3 years* — during the 34th, 35th, and 36th months of the agreement; during the last 3 months of each year that the agreement continues to operate after the 3rd year; or during the last 3 months of operation: s.23(5)	The Board may prescribe a waiting period before a new application by the same applicant will be considered: s.25(16)	Not specifically mentioned	Not specifically mentioned	Not specifically mentioned
PRINCE EDWARD ISLAND	At any time: s.12(2)	10 months after certification; the Board may consent to an earlier application: s.12(3)	a) *2 year or less* — during the last 2 months of operation s.12(4) b) *More than 2 years* — during the 23rd and 24th months of the term; during the last 2 months of each subsequent year; or during the last 2 months of operation: s.12(5)	The Board may prescribe a waiting period before a new application may be made by the same applicant: s.13(7)	No application may be made without the consent of the Board: s.12(8)	*Trade Union and expired agreement* — when notice to bargain has been given, 10 months after the expiration of the agreement; the Board may consent to an earlier application: s.12(7)	*Agreement in force, automatic renewal for further terms* — during last 2 months of each year of further terms, or of operation of the agreement: s.12(6)

CHART B — TIMELINESS OF APPLICATION

JURISDICTION	NO CERTIFIED UNION, NO AGREEMENT	CERTIFIED UNION, BUT NO AGREEMENT	WHERE AGREEMENT ALREADY IN FORCE	WHERE APPLICATION REFUSED	WHERE STRIKE OR LOCKOUT IN EFFECT	EXCEPTIONS	OTHER
QUEBEC	At any time if there is no other application concerning all or some of the employees: s.22(a) 1st filing rule: the 1st filing of a petition for certification, regarding non-unionized employees, renders inadmissible any similar petition filed in the days following: s.27.1	6 months after the right to strike or lockout is acquired, where the dispute has not been submitted to arbitration and no legal strike or lockout is in progress: s.22(c)	From the 90th to the 60th day before the date of expiration, the agreement or its renewal or the expiration of an arbitration award replacing an agreement: s.22(d)	*Where refused or withdrawn* — no renewal of application for 3 months, unless the petition is not admissible because of the 1st filing rule or the withdrawal occurs following a merger of school or municipal corporation, an integration of personnel within an urban community, or the establishment of a transit commission: s.40	Not specifically mentioned	Not specifically mentioned	*Failure to file agreement with the office of the labour commissioner general* — an application for certification may be made by another association 60 days after the signing of a collective agreement or of any amendment thereto until such agreement admendment has been filed: s.72
SASKATCHEWAN	Not specifically mentioned	Not less than 30 days or more than 60 days before the anniversary date of certification: s.5(k)(ii)	Not less than 30 days or more than 60 days before the anniversary of the effective date of the agreement: ss.5(k)(I),33(5)	No subsequent application by the same applicant for the same or substantially the same unit before 6 months, unless the Board abridges that period: s.5(b)	Not specifically mentioned	Not specifically mentioned	Not specifically mentioned

Chart C — Bargaining Unit

Jurisdiction	Definition	Determination	Dependent Contractors	Professional Employees	Security Guards and Officers	Managerial and Confidential Employees	Supervisors	Domestic Workers
Ontario	"Bargaining unit" means a unit of employees appropriate for collective bargaining; s.1(1); must have more than one employee: s.6(1)	Board has power to alter the unit proposed by the union: s.6(1)	Included in definition of "employee": s.1(1); may form own unit or be included with other employees: s.6(4.2)	Architects, dentists, land surveyors, engineers, and lawyers may form own unit, or may be included in unit with other employees if majority agrees: s.6(4), (4.1), and (4.2)	May form their own unit; if no conflict of interest, they may be included in a unit with other employees: s.6(6)	Excluded: s.1(3)	Not specifically mentioned	Domestic workers may organize, not excluded
Federal	"Unit" means a group of 2 or more employees: s.3(1)	Board has power to determine unit, may include or exclude employees: ss.16(p), 27(1)m(2)	Definition of employee includes dependent contractors	Board may determine that professionals can form own unit, unless inappropriate: s.27(3) and (4)	Private constables cannot be included in a unit with other employees: s.27(6)	Excluded: s.3(1)	Board may certify units that include supervisory employees: s.27(5)	Not specifically mentioned
Alberta	Unit means any group of employees of an employer: s.1(1), (y)	Board may modify description of unit, may include or exclude employees: ss.33(1), 11(3)	Not specifically mentioned	Doctors, dentists, architects, professional engineers, and lawyers are excluded: s.1(i)	Not specifically mentioned.	Excluded: s.1(i);	Not specifically mentioned	Not specifically mentioned

Chart C — Bargaining Unit

Jurisdiction	Definition	Determination	Dependent Contractors	Professional Employees	Security Guards and Officers	Managerial and Confidential Employees	Supervisors	Domestic Workers
British Columbia	"Unit" means an employee or a group of employees: s.1(1)	Board determines appropriateness of unit, may include or exclude employees: s.22(1)	May form own unit or be included in an existing unit if Board deems appropriate: s.28(1)	May form own unit or be included with another unit upon application to Board: s.21;	Not specifically mentioned	Excluded: s.1	The Board may certify units that include supervisory employees: s.29	Not specifically mentioned
Manitoba	"Unit" means an employee or a group of employees: s.1	Board has power to alter the unit, include or exclude employees and add additional units: ss.39(2), 142(5)	Not specifically mentioned	May form own unit or be included in unit with other employees if majority of the professionals agree: s.39(3)	Not specifically mentioned	Excluded: s.1	Not specifically mentioned	Not specifically mentioned
New Brunswick	"Unit" means a group of employees: s.1(1); units of agricultural employees require at least 5 employees: s.1(5)	Board has power to alter unit: s.13(1)	Not specifically mentioned	May form own unit or be included with other employees: s.1(5)	Not specifically mentioned	Excluded: s.1(1)	Not specifically mentioned	Excluded: s.1·1)

CHART C — BARGAINING UNIT

JURISDICTION	DEFINITION	DETERMINATION	DEPENDENT CONTRACTORS	PROFESSIONAL EMPLOYEES	SECURITY GUARDS AND OFFICERS	MANAGERIAL AND CONFIDENTIAL EMPLOYEES	SUPERVISORS	DOMESTIC WORKERS
NEWFOUNDLAND	"Unit" means a group of 2 or more employees determined in accordance with Act for purpose of collective bargaining: s.2(x)	Board determines if unit appropriate, may include employees: s.38(1)	Included in definition of "employees": s.2(m)	Board may determine that a group of professionals is an appropriate unit and may include in it other persons whose work is closely related: s.40(1)	Not specifically mentioned	Excluded: s.2(m)	Excludes superintendents: s.1(m)	Not excluded, but "unit" requires 2 employees: s.2(x)
NOVA SCOTIA	"Unit" means a group of 2 or more employees: s.1(1)(x)	Board determines appropriateness of unit, and may include or exclude employees: s.25(4)	Not specifically mentioned	Excludes doctors, dentists, architects, engineers, and lawyers: s.2(2)(b)	Includes police constables or officers: s.2(1)(k)(i)	Managers excluded: s.29(2)(a)	Not specifically mentioned	Not specifically mentioned
PRINCE EDWARD ISLAND	"Unit" means a group of employees whether it is an employer unit or a plant unit, or a sub-division of either: s.7(1)(n)	Board may include or exclude employees to make unit appropriate or for other good reason: s.13(2)	Not specifically mentioned	Excludes architects, dentists, engineers, lawyers, doctors, and teachers: s.7(2)(a)	Includes police constables and security police: s.7(h)	Managers excluded: s.7(2)(b)	Not specifically mentioned	Not specifically mentioned

CHART C — BARGAINING UNIT

JURISDICTION	DEFINITION	DETERMINATION	DEPENDENT CONTRACTORS	PROFESSIONAL EMPLOYEES	SECURITY GUARDS AND OFFICERS	MANAGERIAL AND CONFIDENTIAL EMPLOYEES	SUPERVISORS	DOMESTIC WORKERS
QUEBEC	A single employee may form a unit, except farm employees, they may only form a unit if there are at least 3 of them ordinarily and continuously employed: s.21	Labour Commissioner has power to settle disputes about the unit, and may modify the proposed unit for this purpose: ss.28(d), 32, 39	Not specifically mentioned	Not specifically mentioned	Municipal constables can only be members of an association of employees that is comprised solely of municipal constables: s.4	Excludes managers and superintendents and a public servant whose position is of a confidential nature: s.1(L)	Excludes foremen: s.1(L)	Not specifically mentioned
SASKATCHEWAN	"Appropriate unit" means a unit of employees appropriate for collective bargaining: s.2(a)	Board has power to determine appropriate unit: s.5(a)	Not specifically mentioned	Not specifically mentioned	Not specifically mentioned	Excluded: s.2(f)	Not specifically mentioned	Not specifically mentioned

NOTES

INTRODUCTION

1. "The National Vector Poll for the Ontario Federation of Labour" (North York, Ontario: Vector Public Education Inc., June 1992), 11.

2. Sections 119 to 155.

CHAPTER ONE

1. "Jobless rate 'natural,' bank memo says," *The Toronto Star*, 28 June 1993, 1, quoting a memo from Daryl Merrett, a senior Bank of Canada official. Statistics Canada, *The Labour Force Survey* (Monthly). No. 71-001. Unadjusted figures for July 1993: 1,656,000 unemployed, seasonally adjusted unemployment rate of 11.6 per cent.

2. Statistics Canada and Ontario Ministry of Treasury and Economics, 1992. Internal document, Ontario Ministry of Citizenship.

3. Esther Reiter, *Making Fast Food, From the Frying Pan into the Fryer* (Montreal and Kingston: McGill-Queen's University Press, 1991), 14: "...If any worker can do the job then the cheapest workers can be used."

4. *Hard Times, New Times: Fighting for our Future — Report to the National Collective Bargaining and Political Action Convention* (Toronto: CAW/TCA Canada, May 1993), 74.

5. Pat Armstrong, "The Feminization of the Labour Force: Harmonizing Down in a Global Economy" (Toronto: Author's draft, 1993).

6. Canadian Union of Public Employees, "Restructuring: How unions are coping," *The Facts*, vol. 14, no. 1 (July 1993), 19.

7. John Anderson, *Total Quality Management: Should Unions Buy Into TQM?* (Don Mills, Ontario: Technology Adjustment Research Programme, Ontario Federation of Labour, 1993).

8. Statistics Canada, *Labour-Force Survey*. 1993 figure is year-to-date annual average, as of August 1993.

9. *The Saturday Star* (Toronto), 7 August 1993, 1, quoting David Rosenberg, an economist with the Bank of Nova Scotia.

10. Pat Armstrong,"The Feminization of the Labour Force: Harmonizing Down in a Global Economy," 5. Calculated from Statistics Canada, 1991 Census, *Labour Force Activity*, No. 93-324 (Ottawa: Ministry of Industry, Science and Technology, 1993), Table 2. In 1991, 60.5 per cent of men between the ages of 25 and 65 were employed mostly full-time for 49 to 52 weeks and so were 38.8 per cent of women in this age group.

11. Advertisement of Olsten Temporary Services featured in subway cars on the Toronto Transit Commission, October 1992. "How to Survive in a Changing Economy as Revealed by Gumby," Olsten Temporary Services full-page ad in *Fortune*, October 19, 1992, 102.

12. Report of the Commission of Inquiry Into Part-time Work, *Part-time Work in Canada* (Ottawa: Ministry of Supply and Services, 1983), 93-100. Julie White, *Women and Part-time Work* (Ottawa: The Canadian Advisory Council on the Status of Women, 1983.)

13. Only 21 per cent of workers employed part-year, and 27 per cent of workers employed part-time belong to unions. Julie White, *Sisters and Solidarity* (Toronto: Thompson Educational Publishering, Inc., 1993), 170. White reports that 44 per cent of workers in personnel-business services work part-time and part-year; 37 per cent of those in trade, and 32 per cent of those in education and health work part-time or part-year.

14. We are indebted to Pat Bird for sharing drafts of her manuscript ("Just Managing") on clerical and secretarial work with us. Our comments on clerical workers are based on her analysis.

15. Pat Armstrong and Hugh Armstrong, *The Double Ghetto: Canadian Women and Their Segregated Workplace*, 3rd edition. Toronto: McClelland & Stewart, 1994, Table 6, "Similar Leading Female Occupations, 1971-1991," 34.

16. Jean Rands, "Towards an Organization of Working Women," in *Women Unite!* (Toronto: Canadian Women's Educational Press, 1972).

17. Ray Jackson, "Electronic Surveillance," in Canadian Union of Public Employees, *The Facts*, vol.10, no.1, (January/February 1988). Jackson quotes from *The Electronic Supervisor* (Washington: United States Office of Technology Assessment, September 1987): "...between 30 and 35 per cent of

all U.S. clerical workers...are currently being monitored."

18. See Chapter 2, page 45.

19. Only 32 per cent of clerical employees are covered by a union contract. Julie White, *Sisters and Solidarity*, 172.

20. Wayne Roberts, *Where Angels Fear to Tread:Eileen Tallman and the Labour Movement* (Hamilton, Ontario: McMaster University Labour Studies, July 1981).

21. Ontario Federation of Labour (CLC) and Ontario Women's Directorate, *Sexual Harassment: Working it Out, Sexual Harassment in the Workplace: It has to STOP*. A training video and discussion workbook. A Change Agent Project (Toronto, 1993).

22. White, *Sisters and Solidarity*, 93. White reports that 56 per cent of public sector workers and 20 per cent of workers in the private sector have harassment clauses in their collective agreements, 96.

23. *Robichaud v. Canada (Treasury Board)*, [1987] 2 S.C.R. 84.

24. Logo courtesy of the Ontario Women's Directorate, Toronto.

25. Between 1979 and 1989, 58 per cent of new jobs in Canada were created in places with less than 20 employees, Statistics Canada, Small Business and Special Surveys Division, File no.141358. Courtesy of the Ontario Federation of Labour.

    Jack McArthur, "War didn't pull us out of Depression," in *The Toronto Star*, 23 August 1993, *Business Today*, E-1. McArthur points out that "As for the rise of smaller business...its increase in share is spectacular."

26. John O'Grady, "Beyond the *Wagner Act*: What Then?," in Daniel Drache, ed., *Getting On Track, Social Democratic Strategies for Ontario* (Ottawa: Canadian Centre for Policy Alternatives and Montreal: McGill-Queen's University Press, 1992),153-169. O'Grady explains why it's difficult to organize small workplaces and concludes that "when it comes to organizing and to collective bargaining, small is definitely not beautiful."

27. Rosemary Warskett, "Bank Worker Unionization and the Law," in Armstrong and Connelly, eds., *Feminism in Action, Studies in Political Economy* (Toronto: Canadian Scholars' Press, 1992.)

    Telephone conversation with Linda Gallant, Canadian Labour Congress, Moncton, New Brunswick, June 4, 1993.

28. Ontario Labour Relations Board, *Annual Report*, 1990-1991, 1991-1992 (Toronto, 1992), 53.

29. In the summer of 1992, the Ontario Ministry of Labour estimated that there were 11,280 "Housekeepers, Servants and Other Related Occupations" working in the province. Ontario Ministry of Labour, "Highlights, Labour Relations Act Reform" (Toronto, 1993).

30. White, *Sisters and Solidarity*, 7.

31. "Telework is a profound restructuring of work, as profound as the industrial revolution," Daryl Bean, Public Service Alliance of Canada, quoted in "Union goes to bat for home workers," *The Toronto Star*, 7 September 1993, B4.

32. "Pizza Pizza: First Homework Contract," in *TECHnotes, A technology bulletin for Ontario workers*, Ontario Federation of Labour — Technology Adjustment Research Programme, October 1993.

33. Pramila Aggarwal and Shelley Gordon, interview with author, Workers' Information and Action Centre, Toronto, March 29, 1993.

34. Twenty-six per cent as calculated by Leo Troy, "Is the U.S. Unique in the Decline of Private Sector Unionism?," *Journal of Labour Research*, vol. 11, no. 2 (Spring 1990), 125, cited in John O'Grady, "Beyond the *Wagner Act*? What then?"

35. Armine Yalnizyan, "From the Dew-line: The Experience of Canadian Garment Workers," in Linda Briskin and Patricia McDermott, eds., *Women Challenging Unions: Feminism, Democracy, and Militancy* (Toronto: University of Toronto Press, 1993).

36. Nineteen per cent of private sector employees were unionized in 1992. Ontario Ministry of Labour, *Fact Sheet*, "Union Density in Ontario by Sector and Major Industry," May 13, 1992. Public sector includes education and related services, health and welfare and related services, and federal, provincial and local administration, but does not include Canada Post, public utilities, and the like.

37. White, *Sisters and Solidarity*, 204-205.

38. *Meeting the Needs of Vulnerable Workers: Proposals for Improved Employment Legislation and Access to Collective Bargaining for Domestic Workers and Industrial Homeworkers* (Toronto: Ontario District Council of the International Ladies' Garment Workers' Union and INTERCEDE, February 1993.)

O'Grady, "Beyond the *Wagner Act*? What Then?"

Patricia McDermott, "Sectoral Bargaining and the Low Waged" (Paper prepared for the Ontario Ministry of Labour, May 1993).

Judy Fudge, "The Gendered Dimension of Labour Law: Why Women Need Inclusive Unionism and Broader-based Bargaining," in Briskin and McDermott, eds., *Women Challenging Unions: Feminism, Democracy, and Militancy.*

39. O'Grady, "Beyond the *Wagner Act*: What Then?" O'Grady says that "Only a successful shift in union strategy or a major change in the legislation governing unionization and collective bargaining can reverse the slide. If present trends in unionization and employment patterns continue, the rate of private sector unionization will be 16-17% by no later than the end of this decade."

40. Yalnizyan, "From the Dew-line: The Experience of Canadian Garment Workers."

41. Susan Ward, "Rising to the Challenge, Organizing White-collar Workers"(Unpublished paper, School of Industrial Relations, Queen's University, 1990), 27.

42. Fudge, "The Gendered Dimension of Labour Law: Why Women Need Inclusive Unionism and Broader-based Bargaining," 245.

43. Linda Briskin, "Union Women and Separate Organizing," and Ronnie Leah, "Black Women Speak Out: Racism and Unions" in Briskin and McDermott, eds., *Women Challenging Unions: Feminism, Democracy, and Militancy.*

44. Patricia McDermott, "The Eaton's Strike: We Wouldn't Have Missed It for the World!," in Briskin and McDermott, eds., *Women Challenging Unions: Feminism, Democracy, and Militancy.*

45. McDermott notes: "In his study of unionization in Canadian banks, Lowe (1981) concluded that the greatest obstacle to unionization was fear of management reprisal (p.889)."

46. McDermott, "The Eaton's Strike: We Wouldn't Have Missed It for the World," 28. Susan Ward's study of organizing white collar workers also concludes that women respond best to women organizers from their field.

47. Pat Armstrong, "Professionals, Unions or What? Learning from Nurses," in Briskin and McDermott, eds., *Women Challenging Unions: Feminism, Democracy, and Militancy,* 319.

48. Mary Bird, "A New Community: Today's Student Services Workers" (Unpublished paper presented at the CAUCUSS conference, Sherbrooke, Quebec, June 7-10, 1992).

49. Ontario Women's Directorate and CUPE Local 79, *Education at Work*. A Change Agent project (Toronto, June 1992).

50. The Beaudry Commission in Quebec (1982) recommended changing the law to allow bargaining units to represent employees from several employers, such as at shopping centres.

51. "Shell Canada to cut staff, $250-million profit gain eyed," *The Globe and Mail*, 21 August 1993, *Report on Business*, B1.

CHAPTER TWO

1. "After seven years of analysis of 10 major dailies we conclude that press coverage of labour is generally incomplete, often hostile and frequently biased" *Synthesis* (Toronto: CNSP Special Publications, 1980). See also John A. Hannigan, "Laboured Relations: Reporting Industrial Relations News in Canada" (Toronto: Centre for Industrial Relations and Department of Sociology, University of Toronto, no date, cites through 1985). Harrigan documents, among other things, that in the way the news is reported management makes "offers" and unions make "demands."

2. In 1992 the Ontario Community Newspaper Association and the Canadian Daily Newspaper Association placed ads in their newspapers strongly opposing the Ontario New Democratic Party government's proposed changes in the labour law.

3. Examples include, Brian Gable in *The Globe and Mail*, 5 June 1993; Andy in *The Toronto Star*, 4 June 1993; Mike Graston, *Windsor Star*, reprinted in *The Toronto Star*, 24 July 1993. Gable added two overfed women in overalls to his parade of fat men with lunch buckets in *The Globe and Mail's* Labour Day cartoon, 6 September 1993, 10.

4. Daniel Drache and Harry Glasbeek, *The Changing Workplace: Reshaping Canada's Industrial Relations System* (Toronto: James Lorimer & Company Limited, 1992), 135.

5. Nancy Zukewich Ghalam, *Women in the Workforce* (Ottawa: Labour Canada and Statistics Canada, March 1993).

6. Figures comparing 1990 union and non-union wages by sector from Statistics Canada, "Labour Market Activity Survey," No. 71-205, unpublished data.

7. Julie White, *Sisters and Solidarity: Women and Unions in Canada* (Toronto: Thompson Educational Publishing, Inc., 1993), 65, from unpublished data from the "Labour Force Activity Survey," Statistics Canada.

8. Statistics Canada, "Labour Market Activity Survey," 1990 Special Tabulations, unpublished data.

9. Shelly Gordon and Pramila Aggarwal, interview with author, Worker's Information and Action Centre, Toronto, Ontario, March 29, 1993.

10. White, *Sisters and Solidarity*, 64 and 65. White reports that while non-union women earn 70 per cent of men's wages, union women earn 84 per cent of the wages paid to men.

11. Conversations with representatives of the Canadian Union of Public Employees, the Ontario Federation of Labour, the Ontario Nurses' Association, and the Service Employees' International Union.

12. White and Drache and Glasbeek summarize Statistics Canada surveys proving this point.

13. Drache and Glasbeek, *The Changing Workplace*, 39.

14. Drache and Glasbeek, *The Changing Workplace*, 47.

15. Statistics Canada, *National Work Injuries Statistics Program: Work Injuries*, No. 72-208 (Ottawa: Ministry of Supply and Services, December 1991), 11.

16. Julie White, *Sisters and Solidarity*, chapter 4.

17. *Labour Relations Act*, s.1(1).

18. *Labour Relations Act*, s.74.

19. *Labour Relations Act*, s.49.1, s.43.1(1).

20. One year later, in *The Financial Post* under the headline "Battle still raging over Ontario labour law," Geoffrey Scotton wrote that the amendments "sparked one of the most acrimonious battles between government and business the province has ever seen," 14 August 1993, 7.

21. A Canadian Federation of Independent Business poster carried the message, "Bill 40 Destroys Democratic Rights."

22. David Surplis, Council of Ontario Construction Association in a brief to the government hearings on Bill 40, Toronto, Ontario, February 4, 1992.

23. See Leo Panitch and Donald Swartz, *The Assault on Trade Union Freedoms: From Wage Controls to Social Contract* (Toronto: Garamond Press, 1993).

24. Ontario Ministry of Labour, Office of Collective Bargaining Information, Collective Bargaining Review, 1992. In 1992 in Canada, 323 out of 351 bargaining units covering more than 500 employees settled their collective agreements without a strike or lockout. Information given over the

telephone, Labour Canada, Bureau of Labour Information, Major Collective Agreements By Stage of Settlement by Jurisdiction, 1992.

25. A February 1992 Vector-Labour Opinion Coalition poll concluded that "people have a grossly exaggerated sense of strike frequency (one-third think 40% of negotiations or more involve strikes.)" Noted in The National Vector Poll for the Ontario Federation of Labour (North York, Ontario: Vector Public Education Inc., June 1992).

26. *Labour Relations Act*, sections 14 to 48.

27. Richard B. Freeman and James L. Medoff, *What Do Unions Do?* (Basic Books: New York, 1984), 180.

28. Dale Belman, "The Quality of Labour Relations and Firm Performance," in Lawrence Mishel and Paula B. Voos, eds., *Unions and Economic Competitiveness* (Armonk, New York: M. E. Sharpe, Inc., 1992).

29. Maryellen R. Kelley and Bennett Harrison, "Unions, Technology and Labor-Management Cooperation," in Mishel and Voos, eds., *Unions and Economic Competitiveness*, 251: "Among branch plants of more complex organizations, unionized operations are significantly more efficient than...[plants that] have no unions."

30. Survey of 236 top executives in 95 U.S. corporations, "The awkward truth about productivity," *Harvard Business Review*, September/October 1982.

31. Freeman and Medoff, *What Do Unions Do?*, 165.

32. Statistics Canada, *Labour Market Activity Survey*, 1986. "56% of union members working full time had been in the same job for 5 or more years compared to 34% of nonunion members working full time."

33. Kelley and Harrison, "Unions, Technology and Labor-Management Cooperation," 251: "Plants with LMCs [labour-management committees] are estimated to be substantially less efficient than plants without such innovations....In dramatic contrast, plants that are unionized are more efficient."

34. Andrew Jackson, "Unions, Competitiveness, and Productivity: Towards a Labour Perspective," in *Queen's University Papers in Industrial Relations* (Kingston: December 1992),10.

35. Jeffrey H. Keefe, "Do Unions Hinder Technological Change?," in Michel and Voos, eds., *Unions and Economic Competitiveness*, 135-136.

36. Ministry of Economic Development and Trade. *Ontario Competitiveness Report* (Toronto, Ontario: June 1993), 2.

37. Two examples: *On the Waterfront*, starring Marlon Brando in battle with a corrupt New York dock workers' union boss and *F.I.S.T.*, where the star, Sylvester Stallone, links up with the Mob and goes on to lead a truckers' union.

38. Matt Sanger, "The Myth of Big Labour," in *The Facts* (Ottawa: Canadian Union of Public Employees, December 1992), 21. Sanger estimates that local unions have $550 million in assets.

CHAPTER THREE

1. Section 42(1).

2. Section 15.

3. Section 6(4).

4. Section 6(6).

5. Section 6(1).

6. Section 2(1)(b).

7. Section 1(1).

8. Section 1(3).

9. Section 2(b) and 2(2) of the *Agricultural Labour Relations Act*, Bill 91.

10. Section 6(1).

11. Sections 65 to 82.

12. Sections 91 to 92.

13. Sections 104 to 112.

14. Section 1(1).

15. Sections 5 to 8.

16. Section 13.

17. Section 6(2.1) to (2.5).

18. Section 8(4).

19. Section 92.2.

20. Section 11.1 (1) to (6).

21. *KMT Technical Services*, [1993] OLRB Rep. April 344, following *Northern Telecom Ltd. v. Communications Workers of Canada et al.* (1979), 98 D.L.R. (3d) 1 (S.C.C.).

CHAPTER FOUR

1. Section 1(3).

2. *Vere's Wire Industry Ltd.*, [1976] OLRB Rep. July at 651; and *Children's Aid Society of Metropolitan Toronto*, [1976] OLRB Rep. Nov. at 651.

3. Section 1(3.1)

4. Section 15 only gives unions the right to force employers to bargain.

5. Section 65.

6. Section 1(1).

7. Section 49.1

8. Section 6 of the *Human Rights Code*.

9. Section 15.

10. *Quetico Centre*, [1990] OLRB Rep. Nov. 149.

11. Section 1(3).

12. For a discussion of how to prove trade union status, see *Centre Tool and Mold Company Limited*, [1985] OLRB Rep. May 633; and *Opera Ghost Productions Inc.*, [1990] OLRB Rep. Mar. 325.

13. *The Constitution of the Canadian Labour Congress*, revised June 1992, Article IV, Section 3.

14. Section 5(4).

CHAPTER FIVE

1. Section 67.

2. Marilyn Spink, *Bring in the Part-Timers, Metro Labour Council Yearbook*,(Toronto: 1985), 15. During the debate in 1991-1992 over amendments to Ontario's labour law, employers vigorously and successfully opposed labour's proposal to give unions access to lists of employees.

3. Section 9.1(2).

4. Section 9.1(2).

5. Section 8(2).

6. Section 9(1)(2).

7. Section 8(1).

8. Section 91(5).

9. Section 81.2(1).

10. Section 81(1).

11. Section 48.

12. See Section 71; and *Tate Andale Canada Inc.*, [1993] OLRB Rep. April 383 at 388-390.

13. Jane Adams made many good suggestions for this section.

14. Beatrice J. Miller, *Unmasking the Labour Board*, Special Supplement on Labour Law, *Our Times*, May 1988, 4-6.

15. *Minnova Inc.*, [1991] OLRB Rep. May 644; and *Havlik Technologies Inc.*, [1992] OLRB Rep. April 468.

16. *Tate Andale Canada Inc.*, see note 12.

17. Beatrice J. Miller, *Unmasking the Labour Board.* In "The problem of Anti-Union Petitions," Miller notes, "In 1986, in situations where at least 55 per cent of the workers had signed cards at the time of application, and where a vote was held, the union lost 83 per cent of the time. The staggering failure rate of these votes reflects the pressures put upon workers during this process," 5.

CHAPTER SIX

1. John J. Lawler, *Unionization and Deunionization, Strategy, Tactics, and Outcomes* (Columbia, South Carolina: University of South Carolina Press, 1990), 215.

2. Martin Jay Levitt with Terry Conrow, *Confessions of a Union Buster* (New York: Crown Publishers, 1993), 5.

3. Margot Gibb-Clark's column, "Managing," *The Globe and Mail*, 4 January 1993, B-2.

4. Lawler, *Unionization and Deunionization*, 231.

5. Rules 86 to 93.

6. Frank Potter, *Unions Are Not Inevitable!* (Toronto: Brock Management Library, 1986.)

    Also, Ted Stringer, "Positive Employee Relations—Philosophy and Commitment: The Sine Qua Non of Corporate Survival" (Listed as a workshop of the Canadian Institute's conference — "Positive Employee Relations for the Union-Free Workplace/Becoming an Employer of Choice," Park Plaza Hotel, Toronto, Ontario, April 30 and May 1, 1992.)

7. The Canadian Institute, ad for a workshop at 1992 conference. See note 6.

8. Section 65.

9. Section 65.

10. Section 81(2).

11. Notes courtesy of the United Steelworkers of America, from materials distributed at a Personnel Association of Toronto Seminar in Toronto, Ontario, March 28 and 29, 1985.

12. See note 11.

13. This section is adapted from a pilot organizing workshop prepared by Lynn Spink for the Canadian Union of Public Employees in 1993. It was inspired by Daria Ivanochko and also by suggestions from Rick Arnold et al., in *Educating for a Change* (Toronto: Doris Marshall Institute For Education and Action, 1991).

CHAPTER SEVEN

1. Daniel Drache and Harry Glasbeek, *The Changing Workplace: Reshaping Canada's Industrial Relations System* (Toronto: James Lorimer & Company, 1992), 57.

2. Section 104(13) to (14.3).

3. Section 104(2).

4. Section 104(9) to (11).

5. Section 104(12).

6. Section 108(1) and Section 110.

7. Section 108(1).

8. Section 2.1.

9. *Preamble, Labour Relations Act.*

10. *810048 Ontario Limited c.o.b. Loeb Highland,* [1993] OLRB Rep. April 354.

11. Sections 92.2(2) and 92.1(1), Rules 86 to 93 and 99 to 108.

CHAPTER EIGHT

1. Section 1(1).

2. Section 6(1).

3. *Haley Industries Limited*, [1987] OLRB Rep. Mar. 373.

4. Section 6(1).

5. See section 6(1); LRA: *Hydro Electric Power Commission of Ontario*, [1973] OLRB Rep. Sept. 490.

6. *Kelsey-Hayes Canada Ltd.*, [1968] OLRB Rep. Jan. 1058.

7. *Homewood Health Centre*, [1992] OLRB Rep. Feb. 181.

8. *Hornco Plastics Inc. and Horn Plastics Ltd.*, [1993] OLRB Rep. May 411.

9. *Hospital for Sick Children*, [1985] OLRB Rep. Feb. 266; and *Hornco Plastics Inc. and Horn Plastics Ltd.*, see note 8.

10. *South Muskoka Memorial Hospital*, [1992] OLRB Rep. April 520.

11. *Hornco Plastics Inc.*, see note 8; and *Motor Coach Industries Limited*, [1992] OLRB June 744.

12. *Mississauga Hydro Electric Commission*, 1993 (Unreported, Board File #309-92-R), at 17-18.

13. *H. Paulin and Company Ltd.*, [1979] OLRB Rep. April 335.

14. *Board of Education for the City of Toronto*, [1970] OLRB Rep. July 430.

15. *Hornco Plastics Inc.* see note 8; and *South Muskoka Memorial Hospital*, see note 10.

16. *Hydro-Electric Commission*, see note 12.

17. *Hornco Plastics Inc.*, see note 8.

18. *Simcoe County Association for the Physically Disabled*, [1992] OLRB Rep. July 857.

19. Section 6(2.1).

20. Section 6(2.4).

21. Section 6(2.2).

22. *Wander Company of Canada Ltd.*, [1966] OLRB Rep. Aug. 341. However, the Labour Board does not apply the 24-hour rule inflexibly. Where the employees' hours of work fluctuated because of the nature of the employer's business, so that no one worked a full week, no one worked less than 20 hours, and no identifiable group of employees was hired to work full or part time, a single bargaining unit was allowed, as the workers shared common working conditions (*Paris Poultry Products Ltd.*, [1979] OLRB Rep. May 423); *Vaughan Public Libraries*, [1989] OLRB Rep. Dec. 1282.

23. *Price Club Westminster*, [1992] OLRB Rep. Oct. 1098.

24. *R.J.R. MacDonald Inc.*, [1992] OLRB Rep. Feb. 195.

25. *Mississauga Public Library Board*, [1987] OLRB Rep. April 554; and *Toronto General Hospital*, [1986] OLRB Rep. April 566.

26. *Board of Education for the Borough of Scarborough*, [1975] OLRB Rep. Sept. 657; *Victoria County Board of Education*, [1975] OLRB Rep. June 529; *Spramotor Ltd.*, [1976] OLRB Rep. May 215. An exception is found in industries such as canning and tobacco-picking, where seasonal employees are included if the application is made during the season and excluded if the application is made during the off-season, *Melnor Manufacturing Ltd.*, [1969] OLRB Rep. Mar. 1288; *Inter-City Bandag (Ontario) Limited*, [1980] Rep. Mar. 324.

27. *Tricil (Sarnia) Limited*, [1986] OLRB Rep Nov. 1604.

28. *Mississauga Hydro*, see note 12, at 34-37.

29. *Motor Coach Industries Limited*, [1992] OLRB Rep. June 744; and *H. Gray Ltd.* (1955), 1 CLLC 29, paragraph 18,011; *Vermilion Bay Co-operative Ltd.*, [1970] OLRB Rep. Dec. 920.

30. *Price Club Westminster*, see note 23.

31. Section 7(1).

32. Section 7(3).

33. *Mississauga Hydro*, see note 12, at 34-40.

34. *Mississauga Hydro*, see note 12, at 14.

35. *Mississauga Hydro*, see note 12, at 23-24 and 38.

36. Section 7.

37. *Olympia and York Developments Limited*, 1993 (Unreported, Board File #3249-92-R, 3250-92-R).

38. *Kingston Access Bus*, 1993 (Unreported, Board File #0254-93-R).

39. The exception to this is found in the construction industry where bargaining units are described in terms of much wider geographic regions predetermined by the Labour Board (see LRA, section 108(1),; and *Hornco Plastics*, see note 8.

40. *Wackenhut of Canada Limited*, [1993] OLRB Rep. April 393.

41. *Inglis Ltd.*, [1977] OLRB Rep. Mar. 128; *Humpty Dumpty Foods Ltd.*, [1977] OLRB Rep. Jul. 401.

42. *Hornco Plastics*, see note 8.

43. *Faber Castell Canada Limited*, [1986] OLRB Rep. April 449 cited in *Mobil Chemical Canada Ltd.*, [1987] OLRB Rep. Mar. 559 at 562.

44. *Mobil Chemical Canada Ltd.*, [1987] OLRB Rep. April 559 at 562.

45. *Canada Trustco Mortgage Company*, [1977] OLRB Rep. June 1977, 330; *Mobil Chemical Canada Ltd.*, see note 44; *Coca-Cola Ltd.* [1989] OLRB Rep. Jan. 1; *York Steel Construction Limited*, [1980] OLRB Rep. Feb. 293.

46. *Hornco Plastics*, see note 8.

47. *Children's Aid Society of Huron County*, [1971] OLRB Rep. Oct. 632.

48. *York University*, [1975] OLRB Rep. July 554.

49. *Jewish Vocational Services of Toronto*, [1977] OLRB Rep. Nov. 754.

50. The following cases review the Board's views on different fact situations where a union representing only RNA's has sought to get separate bargaining units: *South Muskoka Memorial Hospital*, see note 10; *Mississauga Hospital*, [1991] OLRB Rep. Dec. 1380; and *Strathroy Middlesex General Hospital*, [1992] OLRB Rep. Oct. 1103.

51. *Shelburne Residents*, [1991] OLRB Rep. Aug. 1005.

52. Section 6(4).

53. Sections 1(1) and 6(5).

54. Section 6(5).

55. Section 6(6).

56. *Keswick I.G.A. (H.W.Gluck c.o.b. as)*, [1987] OLRB Rep. Nov. 1395.

57. *Strathroy Middlesex General Hospital*, see note 50.

58. *University of Guelph*, [1975] OLRB Rep. Apr. 327; *Villacentres Management Ltd.*, [1979] OLRB Rep. Apr. 359; *Dollo Bros. Food Market Limited*, [1986] OLRB Rep. Jan. 82.

59. Section 6(3); *The Municipality of Metropolitan Toronto*, [1987] OLRB Rep. Feb. 278.

60. Section 6(3).

61. *Falconbridge Nickel Mines Ltd.*, [1966] OLRB Rep. Sept. 379.

62. G.W. Reed, *White Collar Bargaining Units under the OntarioLabour Relations Act* (Kingston: Queen's University Industrial Relations Centre, 1969).

63. Sections 119 to 155.

64. Section 1(3).

65. *Ford Motor Company of Canada Limited,* [1993] OLRB Rep. Jan. 1 at paragraph 18.

66. *McIntyre Porcupine Mines Ltd.,* [1975] OLRB Rep. April 261; *Board of Education of Peterborough County,* [1990] OLRB Rep. 940; *Transit Windsor,* [1991] OLRB Rep. 565.

67. *Ford Motor Company of Canada,* see note 65; *Transit Windsor,* [1991] OLRB Rep. 565; *Wraymar Construction and Rental Sales Ltd.,* [1989] OLRB Rep. 682; *Corporation of City of Thunder Bay,* [1981] OLRB Rep. 1121.

68. *Falconbridge Nickel Mines Ltd.,* see note 61; *McIntyre Porcupine Mines Ltd.,* see note 66; *Ajax and Pickering General Hospital,* [1970] OLRB Rep. Feb. 1283; *Belvedere Heights Home for the Aged,* [1978] OLRB Rep. Oct. 890; *Canadian Red Cross Society (Toronto Blood Service Centre),* [1991] OLRB Rep. Feb. 163.

69. *Ford Motor Company,* see note 65, at paragraph 18.

70. *Ford Motor Company of Canada,* see note 65.

71. *Inglis Ltd.,* [1976] OLRB Rep. June 270; *Champion Road Machinery Ltd.,* [1978] OLRB Rep. Feb. 174.

72. *Ford Motor Company,* see note 65, at paragraph 18.

73. *Champion Road Machinery Ltd.,* [1978] OLRB Rep. Feb. 174.

74. *Inglis Ltd.,* see note 41.

75. *Ford Motor Company of Canada Limited,* see note 65; which followed *The Corporation of the City of Thunder Bay,* [1981] OLRB Rep. Aug. 1121.

76. *Falconbridge Nickel Mines Ltd.,* see note 68; *Canadian Union of Public Employees, Local 434,* 1991, (Unreported, Board File # 0604-90-M); *Toledo Scale Division of Reliance Electric Ltd.,* [1974] OLRB Rep. June 406; *Nashua Canada Ltd.,* [1970] OLRB Rep. Dec. 921; *Family Services of Hamilton-Wentworth Inc.,* [1980] OLRB Rep Feb. 204.

77. *York University,* [1975] OLRB Rep. Dec. 945.

78. *Metropolitan Toronto Separate School Board,* [1974] OLRB Rep. April 220.

79. *York University,* see note 77; *Family Services of Hamilton-Wentworth Inc.,* see note 76.

80. *Wellesley Hospital,* [1981] OLRB Rep. Dec. 1843.

81. *Board of Education for the City of North York,* [1982] OLRB Rep. 918.

82. Here are some usual descriptions of different bargaining units.

    Plant Units

    All employees of the respondent company in the municipality of "X" save and except the foreperson, persons above the rank of foreperson, and office and sales staff.

    Office Units

    All office, clerical and technical employees of the respondent company in the municipality of "X," save and except office managers and persons above that rank.

    Where other units are represented by another union or by your union.

    All employees of the respondent company in the municipality of "X," save and except the foreperson, persons above the rank of foreperson, office and sales staff, and any employees for whom a union held bargaining rights as of [insert the date of your application here].

CHAPTER NINE

1. Sections 1(3.1), and 5 to 8.

2. Section 1(3.1); and *Woodstock Roofing and Sheet Metal*, [1993] OLRB Rep. May 91.

3. *Woodstock Roofing*, see note 2.

4. Sections 14, 16(3), and 81.2(1).

5. Section 61.

6. Section 61(4).

7. Section 47(4)(b).

8. Section 5(3).

9. Section 61.

10. Sections 65 and 49.

11. *Cedarvale Woodworking Limited*, [1990] OLRB Rep. Aug. 836 at 839; *York County Quality Food Ltd.*, [1984] OLRB Rep. Sept. 1340.

12. *Humpty Dumpty Foods Ltd.*, [1977] OLRB Rep. July 401; *Kennedy Lodge Inc.*, [1984] OLRB Rep. July 931. *Metropolitan Life Insurance Company*, [1989] OLRB Rep. Feb. 175.

13. Section 1(4).

14. *K Mart Canada Limited,* [1983] OLRB Rep. May 649; *Nichirin Inc.,* [1991] OLRB Rep. Jan. 78; and *Theatrecorp Ltd.,* [1992] OLRB Rep. Mar. 388.

15. Section 1(4); and *Theatrecorp Ltd.,* see note 14, at 396.

16. *Lawrence Construction,* [1991] OLRB Rep. Oct. 160; *Theatrecorp Ltd.,* see note 14; *Metropolitan Toronto Condominium Corporation #380,* [1992] OLRB Rep. Dec. 1145; *Ontario Legal Aid Plan,* [1989] OLRB Rep. Aug. 862.

17. *Industrial Mine Installations Ltd.,* [1971] OLRB Rep. Nov. 712; *Industrial Mine Installations Ltd.,* [1972] OLRB Rep. Dec. 1029; and *Metropolitan Toronto Condominium Corporation #380,* see note 16.

18. Section 1(5).

19. *Metropolitan Toronto Condominium Corporation #800,* [1992] OLRB Rep. Dec. 1145.

20. *Gallant Painting,* [1991] OLRB Rep. Sept. 1051; *Booth Fisheries,* [1991] OLRB Rep. Aug. 947; *Paperboard Industries Corporation,* [1992] OLRB Rep. Aug. 946.

21. *Accomodex Franchise Management Inc.,* [1993] OLRB Rep. April 281.

22. *Accomodex Franchise Management Inc.,* see note 21, at 291 to 301.

CHAPTER TEN

1. Section 8(1).

2. *Amarcord Carpenters Ltd.,* [1989] OLRB Rep. June 531; *Chimo Inns,* [1992] OLRB Rep. July 786; and *Circlet Food Inc.,* [1993] OLRB Rep. May 406.

3. Section 105(2)(i).

4. See Practice Note 7.

5. *Mohawk Services,* 1993 (Unreported, Board File #3068-92-G); and *Cara Operations Limited,* [1992] OLRB Rep. Feb. 131.

6. Available free of charge from the Labour Board.

7. Rules 43 through 51 deal specifically with applications for certification.

8. Rule 7.

9. Rule 8; *Hemlo Goldmines,* [1993] OLRB Rep. May 471.

10. Rule 43. The Board will accept the Form A-4 up until the hearing, unless the responding party can show that it would be prejudiced. *Syndicated*

Capital Properties Inc. operating as Travelodge North Bay, 1993 (Unreported, Board File #3665-92-K).

11. Section 8(4).

12. Section 8(5); and Rule 47.

13. *Moore Corporation Limited*, [1992] OLRB Rep. Mar. 614 at 635.

14. *Moore Corporation Limited*, see note 13.

15. *Pietrangelo Masonry*, [1981] OLRB Rep. Feb. 218. In the event where a declaration was not filed by mistake by the application filing date, the Board has allowed it to be filed if there was no prejudice or advantage. *Syndicated Capital Properties Inc.*, 1993 (Unreported, Board File #3665-92-K).

16. *Travelodge North Bay*, see note 10.

17. In a case where the original cards were lost through no fault of the union, the Board accepted photocopies. *Cara Operations Limited*, [1992] OLRB Rep. Feb. 131.

18. Rule 44.

19. Rule 28.

20. Rule 32.

21. Rule 46.

22. Carleton Board of Education, [1993] OLRB Rep. Feb. 102.

23. Rule 13.

24. *Delaney v. USWA v. Gallup Canada*, 1993 (Unreported Board File #1596 93-R).

25. Rule 33.

26. See *Malvern Drywall Systems Ltd.*, 1993 (Unreported, Board File #2957-92-R), where the Board made a related employer declaration under section 1(4) when no one appeared for the employer and it found that there were sufficient facts contained in the union's application.

27. Rule 45.

28. *Airline Limousine*, [1988] OLRB Rep. Mar. 225.

29. Sections 9.1(1) and 8(3).

30. Section 8(2).

31. Section 9.

CHAPTER ELEVEN

1. *Domtar Inc.*, [1992] OLRB Rep. Nov. 1184.

2. Section 8(4) to (7).

3. Section 8(6); and *Hemlo Gold Mines*, [1993] OLRB Rep. May 471; see also section 8(4) and (3); and *Riverside Fabricating Limited*, [1992] OLRB Rep. Aug. 958.

4. Rule 47 and Section 8(5).

5. Section 8(7)(b); see also Rule 50.

6. *Cara Operations Limited*, [1992] OLRB Rep. Feb. 131.

7. See Section 8(6) and *Hemlo Gold Mines*, see note 3; see also section 8(4) and (3); and *Riverside Fabricating Limited*, see note 3.

8. *Mac-Wood Machine Ltd.*, [1975] OLRB Rep. Nov. 842; *Summit Food Distributors Inc.*, [1991] OLRB Rep. June 780; see also Rule 50; and *Thermogenics Inc.*, [1992] OLRB Rep. May 224.

9. *Radio Shack*, [1978] OLRB Rep. Nov. 643; *Havlik Technologies Inc.*, [1992] OLRB Rep. April 468.

10. *Sentry Department Stores Ltd.*, [1968] OLRB Rep. Nov. 851; and *Custom Foam Speciality Limited*, [1986] OLRB Rep. Dec. 1680.

11. *Elks Inc.*, [1985] OLRB Rep. Feb. 244.

12. *Peacock Lumber Ltd.*, [1979] OLRB Rep. May 423; *Terminal Hotel*, [1979] OLRB Rep. June 580; *Blue Bell Canada Incorporated*, [1990] OLRB Rep. Feb. 121.

13. *Radio Shack*, [1978] OLRB Rep. Nov. 643.

14. *Muirhead Instruments*, [1966] OLRB Rep. Dec. 670; *Valley Bottling of Canada Ltd.*, [1978] OLRB Rep. Aug. 784; *Mayloft Steakhouse Limited*, [1987] OLRB Rep. May 717; *Havlik Technologies Inc.*, see note 9.

15. *Murley Corporation*, [1992] OLRB Rep. May 582; *Camaro Enterprises Limited*, [1992] OLRB Rep. 901; and Thermogenics Inc., see note 8.

16. *Camaro Enterprises Limited*, see note 15.

17. *New Ontario Dynamics Ltd.*, [1975] OLRB Rep. Nov. 845; and *Novocol Pharmaceutical of Canada Inc.*, [1991] OLRB Rep. Feb. 228; *Thermogenics Inc.*, see note 8.

18. *New Ontario Dynamics Ltd.*, see note 17; and *Action Electrical Ltd.*, [1989] OLRB Rep. Feb. 79.

19. *Morgan Adhesives of Canada Ltd.*, [1975] OLRB Rep. Nov. 813; *N.J. Spivak Ltd.*, [1976] OLRB Rep. April 158; *Genwood Industries Ltd.*, [1976] OLRB Rep. Aug. 417; *Dad's Cookies Ltd.*, [1976] OLRB Rep. Sept. 545; *Conference Cup Co. Ltd.*, [1986] OLRB Rep. Jan. 72; *Tate Andale Canada Inc.*, [1993] OLRB Rep. April 383.

20. *Julian Roofing (Ontario) Limited*, [1985] OLRB Rep. Jan. 84.

21. *Thermogenics Inc.*, see note 8.

22. *Tate Andale Canada Inc.*, see note 19.

23. *Selinger Woods Ltd.*, [1979] OLRB Rep. May 434.

24. *Fram Canada Inc.*, [1989] OLRB Rep. Feb. 133.

25. *Accurcast Die Casting Ltd.*, [1978] OLRB Rep. July 585.

26. *Carleton Board of Education*, [1993] OLRB Rep. Feb. 102.

27. *Neo Industries Ltd.*, [1976] OLRB Rep. Mar. 88; *Essex Health Association*, [1967] OLRB Rep. Feb. 885; *ESB Canada Limited*, [1979] OLRB Rep. Dec. 1156; and *Domtar Inc.*, [1992] OLRB Rep. Nov. 1184.

CHAPTER TWELVE

1. Ontario Labour Relations Board Notice to Community dated December 1, 1992.

2. *Moore Corporation Ltd.*, [1992] OLRB Rep. Mar. 614 at 615.

3. *Cor Jesu Re-education Centre of Timmins Inc.*, [1992] OLRB Rep. Mar. 298.

4. *Fort Erie Duty-Free Shoppe Inc.*, [1991] OLRB Rep. Nov. 1268; and *Cor Jesu Re-Education Centre of Timmins Inc.*, see note 3.

5. *Moore Corporation Limited*, see note 2; and *Grant Paving and Materials Limited*, [1993] OLRB Rep. June 512.

6. *Transit Windsor (Re: ATU Local 616)*, [1990] OLRB Rep. Jan. 94.

7. *Caterpillar of Canada Ltd.*, [1987] OLRB Rep. Jan. 27.

8. Section 82(1).

9. See *Statutory Powers Procedure Act*, Statutes of Ontario, 1971, Vol.2, Chapter 4, Sections 12 and 13.

10. Section 111.

11. Section 113.

12. *Delaney v. USWA v. Gallup Canada*, 1993 (Unreported, Board decision File

#1596-93-R).

13. Rules 11, 12, 16, 17 to 22, and 25.

14. *Morrison Meat Packers Ltd.*, [1993] OLRB Rep. Mar. 226.

15. *Morrison's Meat Packers Ltd.*, see note 14.

16. *Network North*, 1993 (Unreported, Board File #3132-92-R).

17. Section 8(4).

18. Rules 43 to 51, and 15.

19. *Camaro Enterprises Limited*, [1992] OLRB Rep. April 423 at 425.

20. Sections 104 to 105.

CHAPTER THIRTEEN

1. Section 9.2.

2. Section 11.1(2) and (5).

3. Section 65.

4. Section 67.

5. Section 71.

6. Section 82(1).

7. Section 81(2).

8. Section 92.2.

9. Section 92.2(6).

10. *The Brick Warehouse Corporation*, [1992] OLRB Rep Oct. 1118.

11. *Royal Ottawa Health Care Groups/Services De Santé Royal Ottawa*, [1992] OLRB Rep. Nov. 1222.

12. *Aurora Resthaven Extended Care and Convalescent Centre*, [1986] OLRB Rep. 1031; and *J. Sousa Contractor Ltd.*, [1988] OLRB Rep. 1027.

13. *Jacmorr Manufacturing Ltd.*, [1986] OLRB Rep. Dec. 1709.

14. *DeVilbiss (Canada) Ltd.*, [1975] OLRB Rep. Sept. 678; *Delhi Metal Products Ltd.*, [1974] OLRB Rep. July 450.

15. *DeVilbiss (Canada) Ltd.*, see note 14; *Delhi Metal Products Ltd.*, see note 14; *Mike's Painting and Decorating Ltd.*, [1991] OLRB Rep. Jan. 67.

16. *Repla Limited*, [1990] OLRB Rep. Dec. 1319.

17. *Havlik Technologies Inc.*, [1992] OLRB Rep. April 468; and *Thermogenics Inc.*, [1992] OLRB Rep. May 224.

18. *Ronal Canada Inc.*, [1989] OLRB Rep. Jan. 60; *Havlik Technologies Inc.*, see note 17; and *Barton Feeders Inc.*, [1993] OLRB Rep. Feb. 89.

19. *Beaver Lumber*, [1992] OLRB Rep. May 553.

20. *Call-A-Cab Limited*, [1991] OLRB Rep. April 440.

21. *Thermogenics Inc.*, see note 17.

22. *G. Tamblyn Ltd.*, [1975] OLRB Rep. Feb. 80.

23. *Thermogenics Inc.*, see note 17.

24. *Custom Converters Printers Ltd.*, [1976] OLRB Rep. July 357.

25. *DeVilbiss (Canada) Ltd.*, see note 14.

26. *Sudbury Youth Services Inc.*, [1990] OLRB Rep. Dec. 1339.

27. *DeVilbiss (Canada) Ltd.*, see note 14.

28. *Call-A-Cab Limited*, see note 20.

29. *Corporation of the City of London*, [1976] OLRB Rep. Jan. 990.

30. *Delhi Metal Products Ltd.*, see note 14.

31. *Devilbiss (Canada) Ltd.*, see note 14; and *Delhi Metal Products Ltd.*, see note 14.

32. *Wm. J. Davidson Electric Inc.*, [1992] OLRB Rep. Jan. 101.

33. *Barrie Examiner*, [1975] OLRB Rep. Oct. 745.

34. *Barrie Examiner*, see note 33.

35. *Repla Limited*, see note 15.

36. Section 9.2; *Mike's Painting and Decorating Ltd.*, see note 16.

37. Section 92.1; *810048 Ontario Limited c.o.b. as Loeb Highland*, [1993] OLRB Rep. April 354.

38. Section 92.2.

39. Section 9.2.

40. *Royal Homes Limited*, [1992] OLRB Rep. Feb 199.

41. Rule 16.

42. *Amorim Enterprises Ltd.*, [1992] OLRB Rep. Feb. 123; and *John Craven*, [1991] OLRB Rep. Aug. 969.

43. Rule 20; *U.A.W.V. Morrison's Meat Packers Ltd.*, [1993] OLRB Rep. Mar. 226.

44. Rule 25.

45. Rule 22.

46. Rule 27.

47. *Morrison Meat Packers Ltd.*, see note 43.

48. *810048 Ontario Limited c.o.b. as Loeb Highland*, see note 37.

49. *810048 Ontario Limited c.o.b. as Loeb Highland*, see note 37.

50. *810048 Ontario Limited c.o.b. as Loeb Highland*, see note 37; and *Morrison Meat Packers Ltd.*, see note 43.

51. Section 91(5).

52. *Sudbury Youth Services Inc.*, see note 29; *Toronto Star Newspapers Limited*, [1991] OLRB Rep. Mar. 415; and *Havlik Technologies Inc.*, see note 17.

53. *Call-a-Cab Limited*, see note 20; *Thermogenics Inc.*, see note 17; and *Kautex of Canada Inc.* [1992] OLRB Rep. Nov. 1197.

54. Section 91(4).

55. *810048 Ontario Limited c.o.b. as Loeb Highland*, see note 37; *Radio Shack*, [1979] OLRB Rep. Dec. 1220.

56. *810048 Ontario Limited c.o.b. Loeb Highland*, see note 37.

57. *810048 Ontario Limited c.o.b Loeb Highland*, see note 37.

58. *810048 Ontario Limited c.o.b. Loeb Highland*, see note 37.

59. *Academy of Medicine*, [1977] OLRB Rep. Dec. 783 and [1978] April 375.

60. *Radio Shack*, see note 55.

61. *Jacmorr Manufacturing Ltd.*, see note 13.

62. *Barton Feeders Inc.*, see note 18.

63. *Jacmorr Manufacturing Ltd.*, see note 13.

64. *Jacmorr Manufacturing*, see note 13; and *Peter Gorman and Sons (Wholesale) Ltd.*, [1992] OLRB Rep. Nov. 1209.

65. Section 102.

66. Section 71.

67. Section 69.

68. *Lindsay, Balford; Re: C.A.W., Local 1451; Re: Budd Canada Inc.*, [1989] OLRB Rep. Mar. 264.

69. *Robert Robinson*, [1986] OLRB Rep. 1151; *Don Roe*, [1986] OLRB Rep. 1429.

CHAPTER FOURTEEN

1. Section 105(2); and Rule 36.

2. Practice Note 4.

3. *Gromy's Country Oven Bakery Ltd.*, [1972] OLRB Rep. May 511.

4. Practice Note 4.

5. The employee may also be asked questions that raise the issue of whether or not he or she is believable. *Maple Engineering and Construction Canada Ltd.*, [1990] OLRB Rep. Nov. 1142.

6. *Moore Corporation Limited*, [1991] OLRB Rep. May 663.

7. Rule 37.

8. Rule 38; *Dacon Construction Ltd.*, [1969] OLRB Rep. Oct. 912.

9. *Thomas Construction (Galt) Ltd.*, [1973] OLRB Rep. Aug. 437.

CHAPTER FIFTEEN

1. Section 9.1(2).

2. Section 8(2).

3. Section 9.1(2).

4. Section 9.

5. *A.B.S. Masonry*, [1992] OLRB Rep. May 535.

6. Section 9(3); and *The Board of Education for the City of Toronto*, [1983] OLRB Rep. July 1229.

7. *London District Crippled Children's Treatment Centre*, [1980] OLRB Rep. April 461.

8. Practice Note 9.

9. *City Plumbing (Kitchener) Limited*, [1987] OLRB Rep. June 810.

10. *Flo-Con Canada Inc.*, [1989] OLRB Rep. June 594.

11. *Peacock Lumber Ltd.*, [1992] OLRB Rep. Oct. 1093.

12. *Vaunclair Meats Ltd.*, [1982] OLRB Rep. March 508.

13. *Cobi Foods Inc.*, [1987] OLRB Rep. June 815.

14. *KBM Forestry Consultants Inc.*, [1987] OLRB Rep. July 1007.

15. *GSW Inc.*, [1990] OLRB Rep. May 535; *Cobi Foods Inc.*, [1987] OLRB Rep. June 815.

16. *Irwin Toy Ltd.*, [1983] OLRB Rep. July 1064.

17. *ABS Masonry*, [1992] OLRB Rep. May 535 at 536; and *Northfield Metal Products Ltd.*, [1989] OLRB Rep. Jan. 57.

18. *Polytech Coatings Ltd.*, [1992] OLRB Rep. Mar. 362.

19. Section 105(5); and *Polytech Coatings Limited*, [1992] OLRB Rep. Mar. 372.

20. *Polytech Coatings Limited*, see note 18 at 373.

21. *Rygiel Home*, [1983] OLRB Rep. July 1064.

22. *Moore Corporation Ltd.*, [1992] OLRB Rep. May 614.

23. *AluminArt Products Limited*, [1991] OLRB Rep. July 797.

24. *J.R. Menard Ltd.*, [1972] OLRB Rep. Oct. 915.

25. *Polytech Coatings Limited*, see note 18 at 375.

26. *ABS Masonry*, see note 17 at 536.

27. Rule 40.

28. *Alexandria Sash and Door Co. Limited*, [1993] OLRB Rep. April 303.

29. *Daheim Nursing Home Ltd.*, [1980] OLRB Rep. Nov. 1639.

30. *AluminArt Products Ltd.*, see note 23.

31. Rule 41.

CHAPTER SIXTEEN

1. Sections 14 and 15. Our thinking for this chapter was guided by Steven David and the Canadian Union of Public Employees' document, "The Collective Bargaining Process," and also by "Madeleine Parent on Negotiations," a transcript of Madeleine Parent's discussion with FOCAS, a new union of social service workers, in September 1975.

2. Section 60(1).

3. Section 10(13) of the *Hospital Labour Disputes Arbitration Act*.

4. Section 15.

5. Section 1(1).

6. Parts of Ontario's 1993 Social Contract Act sanctions standards that are less than some required by the *Employment Standards Act*. You should never agree to a provision in your collective agreement that is less than the law requires.

7. Sections 43.1(1) and 81.2.

8. Section 43.1(2).

9. Section 42(1).

10. Section 43.

11. Section 45(1).

12. Section 44.1.

13. Section 44.1(3).

14. Section 44(1).

15. Sections 16 to 41.1 and 74.

16. Section 41(1.2).

17. Section 41(3), (4) and (5).

18. Section 41.(1.4) and (1.5).

19. Section 41(18).

20. Sections 41(1) and (1.2).

21. Section 41(1.3).

22. Section 41(2).

23. *MacMillan Bloedel Building Material Limited*, [1990] OLRB Rep. Jan. 58.

24. *Grant Forrest Products Corporation*, [1991] OLRB Rep. July 848.

25. Section 41(3.1).

26. Section 41(4) and (5).

27. Section 41(13.1).

28. Section 41(13.2). The Labour Board may order exceptions to the seniority rule to permit the start-up of operations.

29. Section 41(15). During this time employees can't apply to decertify the union, and a raiding union can't apply for a certificate to represent the employees. Section 41 (23-24).

APPENDIX A

1. Section 1(1).

2. *Alpha Wood Mouldings Company*, [1992] OLRB Rep. Aug. 891 at 896.

3. *Diamond Taxi Cab Association (Toronto) Limited*, [1992] OLRB Rep. Nov. 1143.

4. *Supreme Carpentry Inc.*, [1989] OLRB Rep. Nov. 1181.

5. *Alpha Wood Mouldings Company*, see note 2 at 891.

APPENDIX C

1. Section 49.

2. Section 5(4).

3. Section 5(2).

4. Section 62(3).

5. In order to show that there is a collective agreement in place that will bar a certification application, there must be evidence to show clearly that an agreement was reached between the parties and sufficient documentation of that agreement to show its precise terms. In the absence of this, there will be no bar to an application by another union. See *Muller's Meats Limited*, [1992] OLRB Rep. Aug. 942.

6. Section 105(2)(i).

7. *Thomas Fuller Construction Co.*, [1964] OLRB Rep. May 108; and *NCR Canada Ltd.*, [1974] OLRB Rep. Dec. 847.

8. *Bestview Holdings Ltd.*, [1974] OLRB Rep. Feb. 112.

9. *Steinberg's Ltd.*, [1972] OLRB Rep. Jan. 116.

10. Section 105(5) and (6).

APPENDIX F

1. *810048 Ontario Limited c.o.b Loeb Highland*, [1993] OLRB Rep. April 354; citing *DI-AL Construction Limited*, [1983] OLRB Rep. Mar. 356.

2. *810048 Ontario Limited c.o.b Loeb Highland*, see note 1.

3. *810048 Ontario Limited c.o.b Loeb Highland*, see note 1 at 354 to 357.

4.   *810048 Ontario Limited c.o.b Loeb Highland,* see note 1.

5.   *810048 Ontario Limited c.o.b Loeb Highland,* see note 1.

6.   *810048 Ontario Limited c.o.b Loeb Highland,* see note 1.

7.   *810048 Ontario Limited c.o.b Loeb Highland,* see note 1.

8.   *Reynolds-Lemmerz Industries,* [1993] OLRB Rep. Mar. 242.

9.   *810048 Ontario Limited c.o.b Loeb Highland,* see note 1.

10. *Reynolds-Lemmerz Industries,* see note 8 at 245.

11. *Morrison Meat Packers Ltd.,* [1993] OLRB Rep. Mar. 226.

12. *Morrison Meat Packers Ltd.,* see note 11.

13. *Morrison Meat Packers Ltd.,* see note 11.

◆

DEFINITIONS OF LABOUR TERMS (ONTARIO)

ACCESSIBILITY	making a workplace and its opportunities and benefits equally available to all workers, for example, installing ramps for employees who cannot walk up steps
ADJUDICATORS	person or group of persons who make the decision at the Labour Board or at arbitration
AFFIRMATIVE ACTION/ EMPLOYMENT EQUITY	a way to make sure past discrimination against a group, such as women, is removed
1993 AMENDMENTS	the changes to Ontario's Labour Relations Act as a result of Bill 40 — An Act to Amend the Labour Relations Act
APPLICATION FILING DATE	the date an application for certification is delivered to the Labour Board or sent by registered mail
ARBITRATION	process of having a dispute under a collective agreement decided by an independent person or persons
ARBITRATION BOARD	outside, independent people who hear and make decisions on grievances that an employer and union cannot resolve

ARTICLE	a section of a collective agreement
AUTOMATIC CERTIFICATION	when the Board gives a group of employees union status without a workplace vote
BAD FAITH	a kind of bargaining that the Labour Board considers improper
BARGAINING AGENT	a union which has been legally certified or voluntarily recognized to represent a group of employees
BARGAINING UNIT	a group of employees who bargain together for a collective agreement; a single workplace may have several bargaining units
BENEFITS	items that employees receive in addition to wages, such as dental plans, safety boots, educational leave
BOOK OFF	when the union arranges for a member to be away from work on union business, or attend educational programs, etc., either with pay (from the employer or the union), or without pay
CAUCUS	an informal, private grouping of people who meet to advance their common interests; during contract bargaining union representatives may withdraw from face to face negotiations to "caucus" in order to decide how to respond to the employer
CERTIFICATION	the process of having the Labour Board recognize a union as the employees' representative in a workplace
CLAUSE	numbered paragraph in a collective agreement

CLOSED SHOP	when a union contract requires that all employees must become union members before being hired, and new employees must be hired through the union (common in the construction industry)
COLLECTIVE AGREEMENT	legal, written contract between an employer and a union representing a group of employees; while the agreement is in force there can be no strike or lockout
COMMUNITY OF INTEREST	sharing similar work-related issues or concerns
CONCILIATION	process where by a government officer assists a union and an employer to reach a settlement of a collective agreement
CONDUCT MONEY	cash that is given with a summons to a witness to compensate the person for the expenses of attending a hearing
CONSOLIDATION	when two or more related bargaining units of an employer are combined into a single bargaining group
COUNT	the degree of support a union has, expressed as a percentage of the number of employees in the proposed bargaining unit; also, the process of deciding whether a union has enough support for automatic certification or must have a vote
CRAFT WORKERS	groups of employees recognized by the Labour Board who practice certain skills, such as carpenters or bricklayers
CREDIBILITY	how believable a witness is

CROSS EXAMINATION | questions you ask the opposition's witnesses in order to dispute or lessen the impact of their evidence; these questions can be very direct

DIRECT EXAMINATION | see examination in chief

EXAMINATION IN CHIEF | questions you ask your own witnesses in order to get information to prove your case; these questions are usually short, simple and open-ended

EXAMINEE | someone whom a labour relations officer questions

EXPEDITED HEARING | a hearing that the Labour Board takes on very quickly because it is important and urgent

FINAL OFFER | the last proposals for a contract that the employer and the union are willing to make during negotiations

FIRST CONTRACT ARBITRATION | if a union and an employer are bargaining for the first time and cannot reach an agreement, either one can ask the Labour Board or labour minister to order that an arbitration board decide on their collective agreement

FIRST HAND EVIDENCE | information that a person knows because he or she personally saw or heard it

FREEZE | once an application for certification is filed, the working conditions must stay the same for a period of time, unless the union agrees to a change

GOOD CARDS | properly signed cards that can be counted by the Labour Board

GRIEVANCE

a complaint an employee or union makes when the employer does not follow the collective agreement

HEARING

a process whereby the Labour Board listens to all sides and then makes a decision

HEARSAY

evidence given by a witness who has no personal knowledge about the matter, but is only repeating what someone else said about the matter

INCUMBENT UNION

a union that already legally represents employees in a workplace

INTERIM RELIEF

when the Labour Board makes a temporary order to go into effect until it makes a final decision

INTERVENOR

a union or individual who wants to have a say in a hearing involving an employer and another union

JOB EVALUATION

process of finding out what the pay for a job will be by looking at skill, effort, responsibility and working conditions

JURISDICTION

the range of issues a Labour Board can make decisions about; for example the Labour Board cannot grant a divorce

JURISDICTIONAL ISSUES

issues concerning which union has the right to have its members do a particular type of work

JUST CAUSE

legal, proper reasons for disciplining or firing an employee

LABOUR BOARD

expert body set up to determine when a union can legally represent a group of employees

LABOUR RELATIONS OFFICER (LRO)	a person from the Labour Board who tries to help the union and the employer solve a problem, or, who holds an inquiry to find out facts
LAY-OFF	when an employer temporarily or permanently no longer employs a worker or a group of workers; may also include a temporary or permanent reduction of hours of work
LEAVE OF ABSENCE	when someone is away from work for a period of time but will be returning and is still an employee
LIST	the names of all the employees at a workplace who are eligible to be members of a new bargaining unit
LOCAL UNION	the basic unit of union organization; a local union can represent several bargaining units
LOCKOUT	an employer can refuse to let employees work, that is "lock them out," but only under the same conditions and following the same steps as a union must take before going on strike (see "strike")
MANAGEMENT-TAINTED OR DOMINATED PETITION	a petition where the employer has unfairly influenced people to sign it
MATERIAL FACT	a very important fact that is necessary to support the legal position that a person or union is taking in a legal dispute
NO-BOARD REPORT	a report from a government official to the minister of labour, recommending that the minister not appoint a conciliation board to try to settle a contract dispute between a union and an

	employer; 14 days after this report a union may strike and an employer may impose a lockout
OBJECTORS	employees who tell the Labour Board they do not want a union
ONUS OF PROOF	in a hearing, the party that has the onus of proof has the obligation to prove all of the facts that are necessary to win the case
ORGANIZING DRIVE/ CAMPAIGN	the process of getting support from a group of employees (by having each one sign a membership card) proving that they want a union to be their legal representative
PAY EQUITY/EQUAL PAY	a process to make sure women get paid the same as men in comparable work
PETITION	list of signatures from employees who declare they do not want a union
PRO-ACTIVE	taking a step without being asked to
PROBATION	the period of time during which an employer is judging a new employee, and deciding whether or not to continue to employ the person
RAIDING	when one union tries to convince members of another union to change unions
RAND FORMULA	a clause in a collective agreement saying that the employer will deduct an amount equal to union dues from all members of the bargaining unit, whether or not they are members of the union

RATIFICATION VOTE	when bargaining unit members vote on a proposed collective agreement
REAFFIRMATION	when an employee declares in writing, after already signing a union card, that he or she supports the union
REEXAMINATION	questions you ask after the other side cross-examines; these questions are limited to ones that clarify or explain matters raised in cross-examination
REMEDY	a Labour Board order to fix a situation, such as giving a fired union organizer her job back
SCOPE OF BARGAINING UNIT	the range of jobs that legally belong in a bargaining unit
SENIORITY	a term that describes an employee's status in relation to other employees, for deciding the order of lay-off, recall, vacations, and so on; may be based on how long an employee has worked for the employer, or on other measures
SEVERANCE	the pay the employer must give employees whom it terminates or permanently lays off
SEXUAL HARASSMENT	any unwelcome comments or gestures or unfavourable working conditions because of a person's sex
SPLIT SHIFT	having to come to work for two periods of less than eight hours in one twenty-four hour period
STATEMENTS OF DESIRE	a statement by employees that they do not want a union — same as petition

STEWARD	person whom co-workers choose to represent them
STRIKE	union members can strike — refuse to work — only when a collective agreement is not in effect and only after following a series of legal steps controlled by government officials
SUMMONS	legal document issued by the Labour Board or by an arbitration board that orders the witness named in it to go to the hearing to give evidence and bring any required evidence
SWEETHEART OR COMPANY UNION	a union which is not independent of the employer
REPRESENTATIONS	the opportunity any affected employee has to make their wishes known during a hearing of the Board
RETURNING OFFICER	someone who is appointed to monitor and count the votes during a representation vote
TERMINAL DATE	date set by the Labour Board by when responses and documents must be filed
TESTIFY	when a witness answers questions in front of the Labour Board
TIMELINESS	a term referring to whether an application was made or an action took place within the strict time limits contained in the law or a collective agreement
TRANSCRIPT	typed version of what was said at a hearing
UNION OR MANAGEMENT PRESENTER	the person who will make the arguments for either side during a hearing

UNION SHOP	where a union negotiates a collective agreement that says every employee must join the union
UNLAWFUL LOCKOUT	when the employer has not followed the rules for strikes and lockouts and improperly prevents employees from working
VOLUNTARY RECOGNITION	where the employer agrees in writing to recognize a union to represent the employees, and the union then does not have to apply to the Labour Board for certification
WAIVER PROGRAM OR PROCESS	Board procedure using a Labour Relations Officer or Waiver Officer to try to get everyone to agree on issues so there is no need for an oral hearing
WEIGHT	the amount of importance the Labour Board gives to evidence in a hearing

◆

LABOUR ORGANIZATIONS

Listed here are Ontario labour organizations — consult your yellow pages for the unions in your province.

ALLIED PRINTING TRADES COUNCIL OF TORONTO
202-15 Gervais Drive,
Don Mills, Ontario
M3C 1Y8   (416) 444-0499

ALUMINUM, BRICK AND GLASSWORKERS INTERNATIONAL UNION
2-406 North Service Road East
Oakville, Ontario
L6H 5R2   (416) 842-9710

AMALGAMATED CLOTHING AND TEXTILE WORKERS UNION
700-15 Gervais Drive
Don Mills, Ontario
M3C 1Y8   (416) 441-1806

AMALGAMATED TRANSIT UNION
606-15 Gervais Drive
Don Mills, Ontario
M3C 1Y8   (416) 445-6204

ASSOCIATION OF ALLIED HEALTH PROFESSIONALS
305-234 Eglington Avenue East
Toronto, Ontario
M4P 1K5   (416) 484-9685

BRICKLAYERS, MASONS INDEPENDENT UNION OF CANADA
1876 St. Clair Avenue West
Toronto, Ontario
M6N 1J8   (416) 656-7380

CANADIAN AUTO WORKERS
205 Placer Court
Willowdale, Ontario
M2H 3H9   (416) 497-4110

CANADIAN AUTO WORKERS (formerly United Electrical, Radio and
Machine Workers of Canada)
10 Codeco Court
Don Mills, Ontario
M3A 1A2   (416)447-5196

CANADIAN UNION OF EDUCATIONAL WORKERS
304-385 Yonge Street
Toronto, Ontario
M5B 1S1   (416) 979-7393

CANADIAN UNION OF POSTAL WORKERS
601-121 Richmond Street West
Toronto, Ontario
M5H 2K1   (416) 366-6174

CANADIAN UNION OF PUBLIC EMPLOYEES
21 Florence Street
Ottawa, Ontario
K2P 0W6   (613) 237-1590

CANADIAN UNION OF PUBLIC EMPLOYEES
Airline Division
600-180 Atwell Drive,
Islington, Ontario
M9W 6A9   (416)798-3399

CANADIAN BROTHERHOOD OF RAILWAY, TRANSPORT
AND GENERAL WORKERS
403-15 Gervais Drive,
Don Mills, Ontario
M3C 1Y8   (416) 441-1212

CANADIAN LABOUR CONGRESS
2841 Riverside Drive
Ottawa, Ontario
K1V 8X7   (613)521-3400

COMMUNICATIONS, ENERGY AND PAPERWORKERS
UNION OF CANADA
200-701 Evans Avenue,
Etobicoke, Ontario
M9C 1A3   (416)622-2740

COMMUNICATIONS, ENERGY AND PAPERWORKERS UNION OF
CANADA (formerly Energy and Chemical Workers Union)
500-150 Consumers Road,
Willowdale, Ontario
M2J 1P9   (416)496-1536

COMMUNICATIONS WORKERS OF AMERICA
288 Dalhousie Street, Suite B
Ottawa, Ontario
K1N 7E6   (613)234-9159

FEDERATION OF WOMEN TEACHERS' ASSOCIATIONS OF ONTARIO
1260 Bay Street, 3rd Floor
Toronto, Ontario
M5R 2B8   (416) 964-1232

GRAPHIC COMMUNICATIONS
International Union
600-1110 Finch Avenue West,
Downsview, Ontario
M3J 2T2   (416)661-9761

HOTEL EMPLOYEES RESTAURANT EMPLOYEES UNION
Canadian Regional Office
1140 de Maisonneuve Blvd
Montreal, Quebec
H3A 1M8   (514) 844-4167

INTERNATIONAL ASSOCIATION OF BRIDGE,
STRUCTURAL AND ORNAMENTAL IRON WORKERS
501-284 King Steet West
Toronto, Ontario
M5V 1J1   (416) 593-7155

INTERNATIONAL ASSOCIATION OF MACHINISTS
AND AEROSPACE WORKERS
291 Eglinton Avenue East
Toronto, Ontario
M4P 1L3   (416) 661-9761

INTERNATIONAL BROTHERHOOD OF ELECTRICAL WORKERS
401- 45 Sheppard Avenue East
Willowdale, Ontario
M2N 5Y1   (416) 226-5155

INTERNATIONAL BROTHERHOOD OF TEAMSTERS
1194 Matheson Boulevard
Mississauga, Ontario
L4W 1Y2   (416) 629-4144

INTERNATIONAL LADIES' GARMENT WORKERS' UNION
33 Cecil Street
Toronto, Ontario
M5T 1N1   (416) 977-1384

LABOURERS' INTERNATIONAL UNION OF NORTH AMERICA
102-180 Atwell Drive,
Rexdale, Ontario
M9W 6A9   (416) 675-9166

NATIONAL UNION OF PUBLIC AND GENERAL EMPLOYEES
204 - 2841 Riverside Drive
Ottawa, Ontario
K1V 8N4   (613) 526-1663

NEWSPAPER GUILD — Canadian Regional Office
103-30 Concourse Gate
Nepean, Ontario
K2E 7V7   (613) 727 0990

OFFICE AND PROFESSIONAL EMPLOYEES INTERNATIONAL UNION
25 Trent Avenue, 2nd Floor
Toronto, Ontario
M4C 5C6   (416)691-7388

ONTARIO ENGLISH CATHOLIC TEACHERS FEDERATION
65 St. Clair Avenue, East
Toronto, Ontario
M4T 2Y8   (416)925-2493

ONTARIO LIQUOR BOARD EMPLOYEES UNION
737 Kipling Avenue
Toronto, Ontario
M8Z 5G6   (416)252-3080

ONTARIO NURSES' ASSOCIATION
600-85 Grenville Street
Toronto, Ontario
M5S 3A2   (416) 964-8833

ONTARIO PUBLIC SCHOOL TEACHERS' FEDERATION
1260 Bay Street
Toronto, Ontario
M5R 2B7   (416) 928-1128

ONTARIO PUBLIC SERVICE EMPLOYEES UNION
100 Lesmill Road
North York, Ontario
M3B 3P8   (416) 443-8888

ONTARIO SECONDARY SCHOOL TEACHERS' FEDERATION
60 Mobile Drive
Toronto, Ontario
M4A 2P3   (416) 751-8300

PROVINCIAL BUILDING AND CONSTRUCTION
TRADES COUNCIL OF ONTARIO
604-15 Gervais Drive,
Don Mills, Ontario
M3C 1Y8   (416)449-4830

PUBLIC SERVICE ALLIANCE OF CANADA
233 Gilmour Street
Ottawa, Ontario
K2P 0P1   (613) 560-4200

RETAIL, WHOLESALE AND DEPARTMENT STORE UNION
200-5045 Orbitor Drive
Mississauga, Ontario
L4W 4Y4   (416) 441-1414

SERVICE EMPLOYEES INTERNATIONAL UNION
1 Credit Union Drive
Toronto, Ontario
M4A 2S6   (416) 752-4770

TORONTO-CENTRAL ONTARIO BUILDING
AND CONSTRUCTION TRADES COUNCIL
801-15 Gervais Drive,
Don Mills, Ontario
M3C 1Y8   (416)449-5115

TRANSPORTATION-COMMUNICATIONS UNION
300-15 Gervais Drive,
Don Mills, Ontario
M3C 1Y8   (416)441-1083

UNITED BROTHERHOOD OF CARPENTERS AND
JOINERS OF AMERICA
807- 5799 Yonge Street
Willowdale, Ontario
M2M 3V3   (416) 225-8885

UNITED FOOD AND COMMERCIAL WORKERS
INTERNATIONAL UNION
300- 61 International Boulevard
Rexdale, Ontario
M9W 6K4   (416) 675-1104

UNITED STEELWORKERS OF AMERICA
234 Eglinton Avenue East
7th Floor
Toronto, Ontario
M4P 1K5   (416) 487-1571

UNITED RUBBER, CORK, LINOLEUM AND
PLASTIC WORKERS OF AMERICA
202-61 International Boulevard,
Rexdale, Ontario
M9W 6K4   (416)674-2011

◆

SELECTED BIBLIOGRAPHY

BOOKS

The Answer is Organize! Instructor Manual. Ottawa: Canadian Labour Congress Educational Services, November 1987.

Argue, Robert, Charlene Gannage, and D.W. Livingstone, eds. *Working People and Hard Times: Canadian Perspectives.* Toronto: Garamond Press, 1987.

Armstrong, Pat. *Labour Pains: Women's Work in Crisis.* Toronto: The Women's Press, 1984.

Armstrong, Pat, and Hugh Armstrong. *The Double Ghetto: Canadian Women and Their Segregated Workplace,* 3rd ed. Toronto: McClelland & Stewart, 1994.

Armstrong, Pat, Jacqueline Choiniere, and Elaine Day. *Vital Signs: Nursing in Transition.* York University: Garamond Press, 1993.

Arnold, Rick, Bev Burke, Carl James, D'Arcy Martin, and Barb Thomas. *Educating for a Change.* Toronto: Doris Marshall Institute for Education and Action, 1991.

Briskin, Linda, and Patricia McDermott, eds. *Women Challenging Unions: Feminism, Democracy, and Militancy.* Toronto: University of Toronto Press, 1993.

Connelly, M. Patricia, and Pat Armstrong, eds. *Feminism in Action: Studies in Political Economy.* Toronto: Canadian Scholars' Press, 1992.

Cornish, Mary, and Laurell Ritchie. *Getting Organized: Building a Union.* Toronto: The Women's Press, 1980.

Diamond, Virginia R. *Organizing Guide for Local Unions.* New Jersey: George Meany Center for Labor Studies, 1992.

Drache, Daniel, ed. *Getting on Track: Social Democratic Strategies for Ontario.* Ottawa: Canadian Centre for Policy Alternatives and McGill-Queen's University Press, 1992.

Drache, Daniel, and Harry Glasbeek. *The Changing Workplace: Reshaping Canada's Industrial Relations System.* Toronto: James Lorimer & Co., 1992.

Field, Lloyd M. *Unions Are Not Inevitable!* Toronto: Brock Management Library Ltd., 1986.

Freeman, Richard B., and James L. Medoff. *What do Unions Do?* New York: Basic Books, Inc., 1984.

Kahn, Si. *Organizing: A Guide for Grassroots Leaders.* New York: McGraw Hill, 1982.

La Botz, Dan. *A Troublemaker's Handbook: How to Fight Back Where You Work — And Win.* Detroit: A Labor Notes Book, 1991.

Lawler, John J. *Unionization and Deunionization: Strategy, Tactics, and Outcomes.* Columbia, South Carolina: University of South Carolina Press, 1990.

Levitt, Martin Jay, with Terry Conrow. *Confessions of a Union Buster.* New York: Crown Publishers, 1993.

Mishel, Lawrence, and Paula B. Voos, eds. *Unions and Economic Competitiveness.* Armonk, New York: M.E. Sharpe Inc., 1992.

Panitch, Leo, and Donald Swartz. *The Assault on Trade Union Freedoms: From Wage Controls to Social Contract.* Toronto: Garamond Press, 1993.

Penney, Jennifer. *Hard Earned Wages: Women Fighting for Better Work.* Toronto: The Women's Press, 1983.

Reiter, Esther. *Making Fast Food: From the Frying Pan into the Fryer.* Montreal and Kingston: McGill-Queen's University Press, 1991.

Roberts, Wayne. *Where Angels Fear to Tread: Eileen Tallman and the Labour Movement.* Hamilton, Ontario: McMaster University Labour Studies, July 1981.

Sangster, Joan. *Dreams of Equality: Women on the Canadian Left, 1920-1950.* Toronto: McClelland & Stewart, 1989.

White, Julie. *Women and Part-time Work*. Ottawa: The Canadian Advisory Council on the Status of Women, 1983.

———. *Sisters and Solidarity: Women and Unions in Canada*. Toronto: Thompson Educational Publishing, Inc., 1993.

REPORTS

Anderson, John. *Total Quality Management: Should Unions Buy Into TQM?* Don Mills, Ontario: Technology Adjustment Research Programme, Ontario Federation of Labour, 1993.

Canada. Ministry of Labour. Commission of Inquiry into Part-time Work. *Part-time Work in Canada*. Ottawa: Ministry of Supply and Services, 1983.

Edelson, Miriam. *Challenging Unions: Feminist Process and Democracy in the Labour Movement*. Ottawa: Canadian Research Institute for the Advancement of Women, 1987.

"Empowering Workers in a Global Economy: A Labour Agenda for the 1990s." Paper presented at the United Steelworkers of America conference, Toronto, Ontario, October 1991.

Ghalam, Nancy Zukewich. *Women in the Workplace*. 2nd ed. Ottawa: Labour Canada and Statistics Canada, March 1993.

"Hard Times, New Times: Fighting for our Future CAW/TCA Canada." Paper presented at the CAW/TCA National Collective Bargaining and Political Action Convention, Toronto, Ontario, May 4 - May 7, 1993.

Johnson, Theresa. *Go Home ... And Stay There? A PSAC Response to Telework in the Federal Public Service*. Ottawa: Public Service Alliance of Canada, August 1993.

Machine Bites Dog: A Study in Progress of Technology and Work in the Newspaper Industry in Ontario. Toronto: Southern Ontario Newspaper Guild, 1993.

Meeting the Needs of Vulnerable Workers: Proposals for Improved Employment Legislation and Access to Collective Bargaining for Domestic Workers and Industrial Homeworkers. Toronto: Ontario District Council of the International Ladies' Garment Workers' Union and INTERCEDE, February 1993.

The Myth of the 'New Economy' — 'Positive Restructuring' in Manufacturing. Ottawa: Canadian Labour Congress, October 1993.

Ontario Labour Relations Board. *Annual Reports 1990-91, 1991-92.* Toronto, 1992.

Statistics Canada. National Work Injuries Statistics Program: Work Injuries. No. 72-208. Ottawa: Ministry of Supply and Services, December, 1991.

REVIEWS, MAGAZINES, PAPERS

"An Organizing Model of Unionism." Labour Research Review, Vol. 10, no.1 (Spring 1991).

Bird, Pat. *Just Managing.* Toronto: forthcoming book on the history of clerical work in Canada.

Canadian Union of Public Employees. "Big Time Lobbying." *The Facts,* Vol.13, no.3 (December 1992).

Fudge, Judy. "Labour Law's Little Sister: The *Employment Standards Act* and the Feminization of Labour." Ottawa: Canadian Centre for Policy Alternatives, 1991.

Gindin, Sam. "Putting the Con Back in the Economy." *This Magazine,* May 1992.

Hoerr, John. "What Should Unions Do?" *Harvard Business Review,* May-June 1991.

Jackson, Andrew. "Unions, Competitiveness, and Productivity: Towards a Labour Perspective." *Queen's University Papers in Industrial Relations.* Kingston, Ontario: Queen's University, Department of Industrial Relations, 1992.

Miller, Beatrice J. "Unmasking the Labour Board," Special Supplement on Labour Law, *Our Times,* May 1988.

O'Grady, John. "Assigning Economic Power in the Labour Market: Collective Bargaining and Wage Determination Structure." Paper presented at a conference on broader-based bargaining, York University, Toronto, Ontario, 1992.

Ontario Federation of Labour. "OLRA Workshop." Toronto, 1991.

Ritchie, Laurell. "Women Workers and Labour Organizations." Toronto: Institute on Women and Work, City of Toronto, 1987.

GENERAL TEXTS

Adams, G.W. *Canadian Labour Law.* Toronto: Canada Law Book, 1985. An excellent reference text.

Canadian Labour Law Terms. Don Mills: CCH Canadian 1984. A 105-page pamphlet providing brief definitions of labour law terms.

Carrothers, A.W.R., E.E. Palmer, and W.B. Rayner. *Collective Bargaining Law in Canada,* 2nd ed. Toronto: Butterworths 1986. A discussion of collective bargaining legislation and its historical development.

Dorsey, J. *Canada Labour Relations Board: Federal Law and Practice.* Toronto: Carswell 1983. An excellent text on the *Canada Labour Code.*

Foisy, C.H., D.E. Lavery, and L. Martineau, *Canada Labour Relations Board: Policies and Procedures.* Toronto: Butterworths 1986. A valuable treatment of the law under the *Canada Labour Code.*

Government of Ontario. *The Labour Relations Act: Revised Statutes of Ontario, 1990, Chapter c.L.2., as amended.* Toronto.

Government of Ontario. *The Labour Relations Act: Rules of Procedure, Regulations and Practice Notes.* Toronto, 1993.

McGrady, Leo. *A Guide to Organizing Unions.* Toronto and Vancouver: Butterworths Canada Ltd., 1989.

Ontario Ministry of Labour. *A Guide to the Ontario Labour Relations Act.* Toronto.

Randazzo, Daniel P. *The Annotated Ontario Labour Relations Act.* Toronto: Carswell, 1992.

Sack, J. and C.M. Mitchell. *Ontario Labour Relations Board Law and Practice.* Toronto: Butterworths, 1985.

ONTARIO LABOUR BOARD AND COURT DECISIONS

Ontario Labour Relations Board Reports. Toronto: Ontario Labour Relations Board. Contains the text and summaries of important Board decisions.

Canadian Labour Relations Boards Reports. Toronto: Butterworths. This series consists of a number of hard bound texts published annually, as well as monthly soft cover reports and summaries of most of the important decisions issued by the various provincial labour relations boards and the Canada Board.

Canadian Labour Law Reporter. Don Mills, Ontario: CCH Canadian. The Reporter includes bound volumes containing most major court decisions and Labour Relations Board decisions on labour law issues. It also provides the relevant legislation from all Canadian labour law jurisdictions. The set is kept up to date in three looseleaf binders.

◆

OTHER BOOKS FROM SECOND STORY PRESS